Microsoft®

EXCEL VISUAL BASIC® FOR APPLICATIONS

Step by Step

Version 5 for Windows™

REED JACOBSON

***Microsoft*Press®**

PUBLISHED BY
Microsoft Press
A Division of Microsoft Corporation
One Microsoft Way
Redmond, Washington 98052-6399

Library of Congress Cataloging-in-Publication Data
Jacobson, Reed.
    Microsoft Excel Visual Basic for Applications step by step / Reed
Jacobson.
      p.   cm.
    Includes index.
    ISBN 1-55615-589-1
    1. Microsoft Visual BASIC.   2. Microsoft Excel (Computer file)
    1. Title.
    QA76.73.B3J34 1994
    005.369--dc20   93-38174
                                                    CIP

Printed and bound in the United States of America.

    5 6 7 8 9 MLML 9 8 7 6 5

Distributed to the book trade in Canada by Macmillan of Canada, a division of Canada Publishing Corporation.

A CIP catalogue record for this book is available from the British Library.

Microsoft Press books are available through booksellers and distributors worldwide. For further information about international editions, contact your local Microsoft Corporation office. Or contact Microsoft Press International directly at fax (206) 936-7329.

Paradox is a registered trademark of Ansa Software, a Borland company. Macintosh is a registered trademark of Apple Computer, Inc. dBASE is a registered trademark of Borland International, Inc. 1–2–3 and Lotus are registered trademarks of Lotus Development Corporation. Microsoft, Microsoft Access, Microsoft Press, MS-DOS, and Visual Basic are registered trademarks and PivotTable, TipWizard, Windows, and Windows NT are trademarks of Microsoft Corporation. Paintbrush is a trademark of ZSoft Corporation.

For Jacobson GeniusWorks
Author: Reed Jacobson
Graphics Editor: Brian Jacobson
Technical Editor: Carl Cutter

For Microsoft Press
Acquisitions Editor: Geri Younggren
Project Editor: Laura Sackerman

Reed Jacobson

Reed Jacobson owns Jacobson GeniusWorks, a company that specializes in creative training, consulting, and custom development services for Excel and other Microsoft Office products. Jacobson GeniusWorks is one of the original partner companies in the Microsoft Excel Consulting Relations Program.

Reed received a BA in Japanese and Linguistics and an MBA from Brigham Young University, and a graduate fellowship in Linguistics from Cornell University. He worked as a Software Application Specialist for Hewlett-Packard for ten years.

Reed is the author of *Excel Trade Secrets for Windows*. He has given presentations on Excel at Tech•Ed and other Microsoft conferences and seminars, he has created training video tapes for Microsoft Excel, and he publishes the newsletter *HotTips for Microsoft Excel*.

Reed Jacobson
Jacobson GeniusWorks
P. O. Box 3632
Arlington, WA 98223
(206) 652-9454

WE'VE CHOSEN THIS SPECIAL LAY-FLAT BINDING

to make it easier for you to work through the step-by-step lessons while you're at your computer.

With little effort, you can make this book lie flat when you open it to any page. Simply press down on the inside (where the paper meets the binding) of any left-hand page, and the book will stay open to that page. You can open the book this way every time. The lay-flat binding will not weaken or crack over time.

It's tough, flexible, sturdy—and designed to last.

Contents

Part 3 Exploring Objects

Part 4 Exploring Visual Basic

About This Book

Microsoft Excel is a powerful tool for analyzing and presenting information. One of the strengths of Excel has always been its macro language. Since it first appeared, Excel has always had the most extensive and flexible macro language of any spreadsheet program. The macro language in Excel 5 is even better.

Excel's macro language is no longer a specialized language that works only with Excel. Excel's macro language is now the Microsoft Visual Basic Programming System, Applications Edition.

Visual Basic for Applications is very similar to the stand-alone Visual Basic programming language. It will also soon be the macro language for all of Microsoft's major application products. Visual Basic for Applications is in many ways much simpler and easier to use—and at the same time more flexible and powerful—than Excel's earlier macro language.

When you start writing macros in Excel, you really need to learn two different tools. First, you need to learn how to work with Visual Basic. Everything you learn about Visual Basic will be true not only for Microsoft Excel, but also for other Microsoft applications as they begin to incorporate Visual Basic. Second, you need to learn how to control Excel. The more you know about Excel as a spreadsheet, the more effective you can be at developing macros that control Excel. While this book focuses on Visual Basic as Excel's macro language, much of what you learn will help you to be more effective using the spreadsheet as well.

Finding the Best Starting Point for You

Learning everything you need to know about Visual Basic and also about how Excel works with Visual Basic can seem overwhelming. That's why you need this book. This book starts with simple, practical tasks and then takes you *step by step* on to advanced concepts and powerful applications.

The book is divided into five parts. Parts 1 and 2 teach practical skills without explaining underlying theoretical concepts. Parts 3 and 4 teach theoretical concepts, but in a very hands-on, experiential way. Part 5 puts the concepts to work to build a complete application.

Start by reading "Getting Ready," the next section in this book. Then find where you fit in the following table to determine where to start in the main body of the book.

If you are	Follow these steps
Experienced with Excel but new to macros	Start with the lessons in Part 1, "Automating Everyday Tasks." These lessons teach you how to work with Excel's macro recorder to produce effective results, without unnecessary conceptual explanations.
Experienced with Excel macros but new to Visual Basic	Skim the lessons in Parts 1 and 2, and then start working through the lessons in Part 3, "Exploring Objects," and Part 4, "Exploring Visual Basic." The lessons in Parts 3 and 4 teach the new concepts you will need for working with Excel objects using Visual Basic. They provide a solid foundation for the advanced practical skills presented in Part 5.
Experienced with Visual Basic but new to Excel	Skim Parts 1 and 2, work through the lessons in Part 3, skim the lessons in Part 4, and then work through the lessons in Part 5, "Building an Application." The lessons in Part 5 teach how to put Excel macros to work building solutions to serious business problems and assume an understanding of the concepts from Parts 3 and 4.

Using This Book as a Classroom Aid

If you're an instructor, you can use *Microsoft Excel Visual Basic for Applications Step by Step* for teaching Microsoft Excel macros to beginning macro writers and for teaching specific concepts and techniques to experienced macro writers. You may want to select certain lessons that meet your students' needs and incorporate your own demonstrations into the lessons.

If you plan to teach the entire contents of this book, you should probably set aside four or five full days of classroom time to allow for discussion, questions, and any customized practice you may create.

Conventions Used in This Book

Before you start any of the lessons, you should understand the terms and conventions used in this book.

Typographic conventions

Characters for you to type appear in **bold**.

Important terms and the titles of books appear in *italic*.

Names of keys appear in SMALL CAPITAL LETTERS.

Samples of code appear in a monospaced font:

```
Sub MyFirstMacro()
```

Procedural conventions

Numbered lists (1, 2, 3, and so on) indicate steps for you to follow.

Triangular bullets (▶) indicate single tasks for you to do.

Selected check box

Cleared check box

The word *choose* means to execute a command from a menu. For example, "From the File menu, choose the Save As command."

The word *select* means to highlight an item. For example, "Select range A1:E5" or "Select Microsoft Excel Workbook from the File Type list."

With check boxes, *select the check box* means to put an X in the check box and *clear the check box* means to remove the X from the check box.

Other features of this book

Bold button

You can perform many operations by clicking a button in a toolbar. When you can click a toolbar button, a picture of the button appears in the left margin of the book, as the Bold button does here.

Text in the left margin provides tips, keyboard alternatives, and cross references to related topics.

Cross-References to the Microsoft Excel Documentation

References to the documentation that comes with Excel 5 appear at the end of each lesson.

Printed references

- *Microsoft Excel User's Guide*
  This manual provides a detailed description of the features of Excel when used as an interactive spreadsheet.

- *Microsoft Excel Visual Basic User's Guide*
  This manual discusses Visual Basic for Applications as it applies to Microsoft Excel.

- *Microsoft Query User's Guide*
  This manual describes in detail how to use Microsoft Query to browse data sources, whether from Excel or as a standalone program.

On-line references

- *Microsoft Help Reference*
  This is the help file you first go to when you choose the Contents command from the Help menu. This help file gives detailed information about all aspects of the worksheet, including detailed information on each worksheet function.

- *Visual Basic Reference*
  If you choose Programming With Visual Basic from the main Microsoft Help Reference contents, you get this help file. The Visual Basic Reference help file contains reference information and examples on both Visual Basic for Applications and how Microsoft Excel objects work with Visual Basic for Applications.

- *Examples and Demos*
  If you choose Examples and Demos from the Help menu, you get a large selection of example worksheet files and demonstrations that show you how to use Excel interactively as a spreadsheet.

Comparing the Old and New Macro Languages

Excel 5 can run both Excel 4 and Visual Basic for Applications macros. In fact, Excel 5 includes a version of the Excel 4 macro language that has been enhanced to work with all the new features of Excel 5. Future versions of Excel will run Excel 4 macros, but the new features of Excel 6 and later versions may not be accessible.

If you have developed macros using the Excel 4 macro language, you may wonder about the differences between Visual Basic and Excel 4 macros.

- Excel 4 macro sheets are essentially worksheets. All Excel 4 macro commands are functions entered in individual cells. Visual Basic modules are not worksheets, even though they are kept in an Excel 5 workbook.

- A single Excel 4 command must be entered into a single cell; you cannot split a long command into multiple lines. Visual Basic statements may be split into multiple lines.

- Visual Basic has true variables that can be restricted to certain data types and restricted to the current procedure or module. Excel 4 macros use ordinary Excel names as variables.

- Visual Basic code is compiled; an Excel 4 macro is interpreted when you run the macro. This makes Visual Basic much faster at executing loops and other traditional programming tasks. Excel 4 macros may, however, be faster when interacting heavily with Excel objects.

- Text strings in Excel are limited to 255 characters. This limit applies to both worksheets and Excel 4 macros. Visual Basic strings are not limited to 255 characters, except when transferring the text string to Excel.

- The Excel 4 macro language is used only by Microsoft Excel. Visual Basic belongs to the tradition of Basic languages, and Visual Basic for Applications will soon be the language used to automate all major Microsoft applications.

- Because Visual Basic for Applications will be shared by all Microsoft applications, any improvements made to Visual Basic will be immediately available to all applications. For example, if the code editor becomes easier to use in Microsoft Project, it will also be easier to use in Microsoft Excel.

- Excel 4 macros can use all Excel worksheet functions and operators, and they can manipulate Excel arrays in the same ways that Excel worksheets can. Visual Basic macros can use Excel worksheet functions but not Excel operators, and Visual Basic operators do not work with arrays.

- Excel 4 macros can refer directly to Excel named references and constants. Visual Basic macros require extra steps to access Excel named references and constants.

In brief, Visual Basic for Applications has many advantages relative to the older Excel 4 macro language, but it is still a new product. In future versions of Excel the benefits of Visual Basic for Applications will be even more significant. If you already know how to work with Excel 4 macros, you may want to continue to use Excel 4 macros for some tasks. If you do not already know Excel 4 macros, you will probably want to focus your attention on learning Visual Basic for Applications.

Comparing Versions of Visual Basic

The Visual Basic Programming System is available both as a separate product (Visual Basic 3) and as the Applications Edition that is integrated with applications such as Microsoft Excel. If you are familiar with Visual Basic, you may wonder about the differences between Visual Basic 3 and Visual Basic for Applications.

- Visual Basic 3 is available only for Microsoft Windows and MS-DOS. Visual Basic for Applications was written to be portable to other platforms, such as the Macintosh and Windows NT.

- Visual Basic for Applications has several new syntax features that are not available in Visual Basic 3. For example, it has a line continuation character, the With statement, and the ability to discard unneeded values returned by functions.

- Visual Basic for Applications also has some new data types. For example, it has a strong Variant data type, transparent huge arrays, and a new data type for dates.

- Visual Basic for Applications is tightly integrated with each host application. For example, it comes with an Object Browser that can help you find Visual Basic functions as well as Excel objects. Also, in Microsoft Excel, Visual Basic modules are stored directly in workbooks.

- Procedures written with Visual Basic 3 must be compiled into a separate executable file. To control Excel from a Visual Basic 3 application you must run both Excel and the application. Procedures written with Visual Basic for Applications can be run as part of the Excel application, without a separate executable file.

- With Visual Basic for Applications, you can create effective dialog boxes, but they are not as powerful as forms in Visual Basic 3.

- Visual Basic 3 allows you to attach code to any of several events for each control on a form; Visual Basic for Applications currently supports only one event per control.

- Visual Basic 3 can integrate custom controls that you can purchase or write; Visual Basic for Applications can use only the standard controls that come with the product.

- Visual Basic 3 has some editing features that are not yet available in Visual Basic for Applications. For example, in Visual Basic 3 you can edit a module while stepping through the code, but in Visual Basic for Applications you must halt the procedure in order to modify the code.

In summary, if you are developing an application to control Excel, in most cases you should use Visual Basic for Applications, which is closely integrated with Excel. However, if you must use custom controls or other features available only in Visual Basic 3, you can use Visual Basic 3 and still manipulate Excel objects using the concepts you will learn in this book.

Getting Ready

While completing the lessons in this book, you'll use the sample files on the accompanying disk to get hands-on practice with macros in Microsoft Excel. Install the sample files on your computer's hard disk, review the list of files, and then start learning Visual Basic!

Installing the Step by Step Practice Files

Included with this book is a disk named "Practice Files for Microsoft Excel Visual Basic for Applications Step by Step." Some of the files on the disk contain sample data that you will use as you go through the lessons in this book. Other files are the finished result of the projects in the book.

Install the sample files

1 Start Windows and activate the Main group in the Program Manager.

2 Start the File Manager by double clicking its icon.

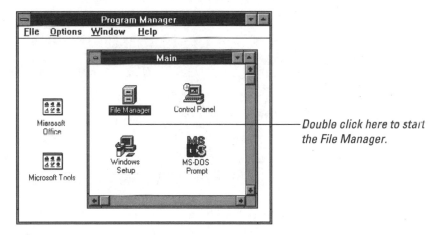

Double click here to start the File Manager.

3 In the File Manager, click the icon for the A drive.

Note If you are installing the practice files from a different drive, substitute that drive letter for *A*.

4   Click the EXCELVBA directory to select it.

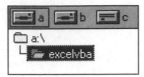

5   From the File menu, choose Copy.

6   In the To box, type **C:**, and click OK.

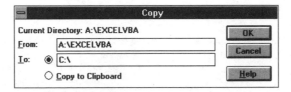

Note If you prefer to install the sample files to a different location, type that location in the To box.

---

7   To see the sample files, click the icon for the C drive, and then click the EXCELVBA directory.

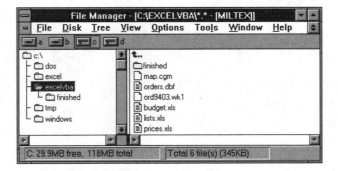

The EXCELVBA directory contains all the files you will use as you go through the lessons in this book. The FINISHED subdirectory contains completed copies of the files you create in the lessons.

Using the Sample Files

As you work through the lessons using the sample files, be sure to follow the instructions for saving the sample files and giving them new names. Renaming the sample files allows you to make changes, experiment, and observe results without affecting the original files. Keeping the sample files intact allows you to reuse the original file later if you want to repeat a lesson or try a new experiment.

In these lessons, you are the bookkeeper and financial analyst for the screen printing division of Miller Textiles. Your division designs, prints, and sells artistic transfers for T-shirts. Throughout these lessons, you will use macros to simplify tasks you do for the company.

Description of the sample files

These are the files you will use as you automate tasks during the lessons.

Filename	Description	Used in
BUDGET.XLS	The annual budgeting worksheet for the division.	Lesson 1
ORDERS.DBF	The Miller Textiles order history database. This file contains the monthly orders for different shirt designs.	Lessons 2, 3, 5, 12, 13, and 14
ORD9403.WK1	A Lotus 1-2-3 worksheet containing the most recent month's order information.	Lesson 2
LISTS.XLS	The lists of categories, states, price groups, and distribution channels that appear in the order history database.	Lesson 13
MAP.CGM	A map of the region in which Miller Textiles does business.	Lesson 5

In addition, the FINISHED subdirectory contains the workbooks for each lesson as they will look at the end of the lesson.

1 Automating Everyday Tasks

Make a Macro Do Simple Tasks

Have you ever lived with a squeaky door? Every time you open it, you're annoyed. "Oh, I really should put a drop of oil on that hinge." But you're in the middle of something, and the oil can is in the garage, and you'll do it as soon as you go back downstairs, but by the time you get downstairs you've forgotten about the hinge. Until next time. Grrr. If only that oil can were *where* you needed it, *when* you needed it.

Creating a convenience macro in Microsoft Excel is like putting oil on a squeaky door hinge. "Yes, I really should make a little macro to add that underline." Except that in Excel, the oil can isn't in the garage. It's called a *macro recorder* and it's part of Excel, ready when you are. All you have to do is use it. In this lesson, you'll learn how to use Excel's macro recorder to get those handy little macros written, quickly and easily, even if you're in the middle of something else.

You will learn how to:

- Record and run a macro.
- Make a macro always available.
- Understand and edit simple recorded macros.
- Run a macro by using a shortcut key or a toolbar button.

Estimated lesson time: 40 minutes

Start the lesson

▶   Start Excel, change to the directory that contains the practice files from the disk, and open the file BUDGET.XLS. Save a copy of the file as LESSON1A.XLS.

The Macro Recorder

In some spreadsheet programs, macros are collections of keystrokes. For every key you press, you enter that keystroke into the macro. Keystroke macros can be easy to interpret because of the one-to-one correspondence between what you do on the keyboard and what you see in the macro. It doesn't take very long, however, before keystroke macros become hopelessly illegible and inflexible.

Excel's macro language—Visual Basic for Applications—is a real programming language. You will probably never find the limits of what you can do with Visual Basic. The trade off for this power is that the language can be a little bit hard to understand right at first.

The macro recorder can help you get started creating macros and learning Visual Basic. You don't need to know anything at all about the language to turn on the recorder, work for a while, turn off the recorder, and then play back the resulting macro. But recording one long, extended macro rarely produces the results you want.

The best approach to learning Visual Basic is to use the macro recorder for simple tasks—you can get immediately usable results—and gradually learn more about the language, preferably with a good coach along the way.

That's precisely the approach this book takes. The lessons in Parts 1 and 2 of this book center around the macro recorder. Virtually everything you do in these lessons will consist of either recording a macro or making minor modifications to a recorded macro. The macro recorder is a great way to begin creating macros in Excel, and you can automate many tasks using nothing more than the techniques in these first few lessons. By the end of these lessons, you will be surprised at how much you can accomplish with the macro recorder. You will become comfortable with Visual Basic and Excel objects by performing real-world tasks, without worry about technical concepts. You will learn to look at a clock and tell the time, without worrying about how the clock works internally.

Eventually, however, you will want the greater power that comes from understanding the concepts behind how Visual Basic and Excel work together. In Parts 3 and 4 you will take apart the clock and see what makes it work. Then in Part 5, you will build a complete new clock. You will deal once again with real-world problems, but depending less on the macro recorder and more on correct concepts.

The Best Macro Is No Macro

Before you create a macro to automate a task. always find out if Excel provides a built-in solution ready for you to use.

*New Workbook
button*

For example, when you click the New Workbook button in Excel, you get a workbook that has 16 blank worksheets. Maybe you never use 16 worksheets. Maybe you really never use more than 4, and having those extra worksheets is really annoying. You could record a macro to delete the extra 12 worksheets. But don't. Change Excel's default instead.

Change the default number of worksheets

1   From the Tools menu, choose the Options command and the General tab.

2   In the Sheets In New Workbook box, type **4**, and click OK.

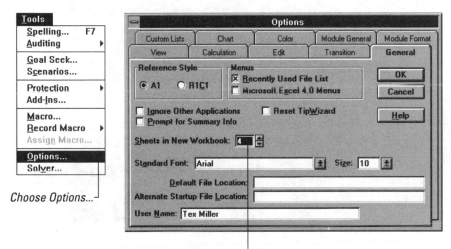

Choose Options...

...and change this setting to 4.

Now if you click the New Workbook button, your new workbook will have only 4 sheets, and you didn't need a macro at all.

Which is not to say anything against macros. Macros are good, useful, and important. I want you to write lots and lots of macros. I want you to convince all your friends, coworkers, relatives, and casual aquaintances you pass on street corners to write lots and lots of macros (and, naturally, to buy lots and lots of copies of this book).

Watch the TipWizard

You may wonder how you can find out all of Excel's built-in conveniences. Sometimes it seems Excel has an endless stream of tricks that are impossible to learn. Even when you read or hear about new tips, those tips may not relate to tasks you are currently doing. The TipWizard can help you learn the shortcuts that are most likely to help with the tasks you do.

TipWizard button

Excel watches every action you take. When you take an action that may have a more convenient alternative, the TipWizard lightbulb turns yellow. When you click the button, you see one or more tips related directly to the tasks you are doing—and none of these tips requires any macros.

Creating a Simple Macro

Excel has a large collection of convenience tools readily available as shortcut keys and as buttons in toolbars. Sometimes the built-in convenience tool doesn't work quite the way you want. Enhancing a built-in tool is a good first macro to create.

Format currency with no decimal places

On the Formatting toolbar, Excel has a button that formats the current selection as currency: the Currency Style button.

1   In the LESSON1A.XLS workbook, click the Budget94 tab and select cells D3:F4.

Currency Style button

2   Click the Currency Style button.

The selected cells are reformatted as currency.

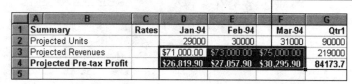

Click the Currency Style button to reformat the selection as currency.

The currency format Excel applies when you click the Currency button has two decimal places. Sometimes you want to display currency with two decimal places—perhaps in your checkbook. But other times you don't want two decimal places—perhaps your budget doesn't warrant that kind of precision. You may want to create a macro to format the currency without them.

Record a macro to format currency

1   Select cells D9:F10 on the Budget94 worksheet.

2   From the Tools menu, choose the Record Macro, Record New Macro command.

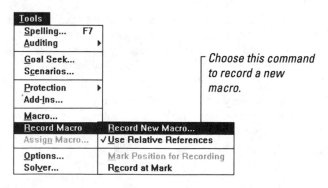

Choose this command to record a new macro.

3 Type **FormatCurrency** as the name of the macro, and click OK.

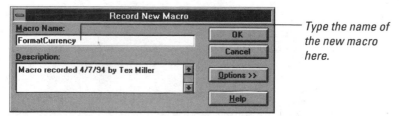

Type the name of
the new macro
here.

The word *Recording* appears in the status bar, and a Stop Recording toolbar appears. You are recording.

4 From the Format menu, choose the Cells command, and select the Number tab. Select Currency from the Category list, select the first currency format from the Format Codes list, and click OK.

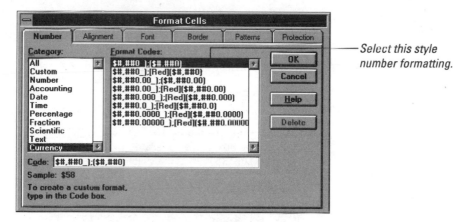

Select this style
number formatting.

The selected cells are formatted as currency without decimal places.

Stop Macro button

5 Click the Stop Macro button (or from the Tools menu, choose the Record Macro, Stop Recording command) to stop the recorder.

That's it. You recorded a macro to format the selection with the currency format you want. Now you probably want to try out the macro to see how it works.

Run the macro

1 Select cells D11:F12 on the Budget94 worksheet.

2 From the Tools menu, choose Macro.

3   Select the FormatCurrency macro name in the list, and click Run.

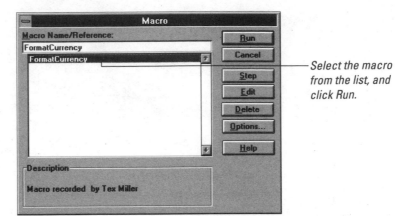

Select the macro from the list, and click Run.

Your macro gives the selected cells your customized currency format. Running the macro from the Macro dialog box is not very much of a shortcut, though.

Assign a shortcut key to the macro

1   From the Tools menu, choose Macro.

2   Select the FormatCurrency macro from the list, and click Options.

The Macro Options dialog box is like an extended version of the Record New Macro dialog box you saw before. In the Macro Options dialog box you can change certain attributes of a macro, including the shortcut key assignment.

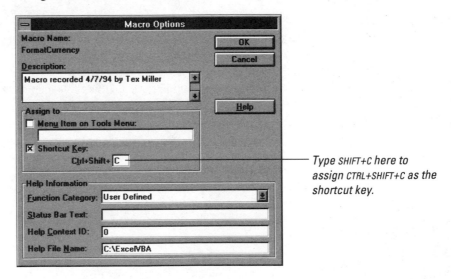

Type SHIFT+C here to assign CTRL+SHIFT+C as the shortcut key.

3   You want to assign CTRL+SHIFT+C as the shortcut key. Select the box to the right of the Shortcut Key label, hold down the SHIFT key, and type **C**. Excel changes the prefix next to the box from CTRL+ to CTRL+SHIFT+ when you use a capital letter.

4   Choose OK to return to the Macro dialog box and then Close to get back to the worksheet.

5   Select cells D16:F16, and press CTRL+SHIFT+C to run the macro.

Now you have successfully recorded, run, and modified a macro. All without seeing anything of the macro itself. Aren't you burning with curiosity to see just what exactly you have created?

Look at the macro

When you created the LESSON1A.XLS workbook, it had a single worksheet tab at the bottom of the workbook, Budget94. Now there is a second tab, labeled *Module1*.

▶   Click the Module1 tab.

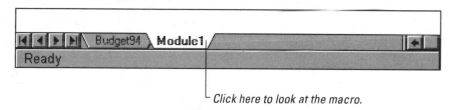

Click here to look at the macro.

A sheet with no worksheet gridlines appears. Your macro is on the Module1 sheet. Here's what it looks like:

```
'
' FormatCurrency Macro
' Macro recorded 4/7/94 by Tex Miller
'
'
Sub FormatCurrency()
    Selection.NumberFormat = "$#,##0_);($#,##0)"
End Sub
```

The five lines that start with apostrophes at the beginning of the macro are *comments*. The recorder puts in the comments partly to remind you to add comments as you write macros. You can add to them, change them, or delete them as you wish without changing how the macros run. Anything in any line that follows an apostrophe is a comment. On a color monitor, comments are green to help you distinguish them from statements that do something.

The macro is written in Visual Basic and follows standard Visual Basic rules. The macro itself begins with the word *Sub*, followed by the name of the macro. The word *Sub* is used because a macro is typically hidden, out of sight, like a *sub*marine. Or perhaps it stands for *sub*machine gun because macros make everything so fast. Or perhaps it stands for *Sub*routine for reasons you will learn at the end of Lesson 2. The last line of a macro always consists of the words *End Sub*.

The *Selection.NumberFormat* statement does the real work. It is the *body* of the macro. The word *Selection* stands for the "current selection." The word *NumberFormat* refers to one of the settings—or *properties*— of the selection. Read the statement like this: "Let '$#,##0' be the number format of the selection."

Note Some people wonder why the word *NumberFormat* comes after the word *Selection* if you read *Selection.NumberFormat* as "number format of the selection." In an Excel worksheet, you do not use the English language convention of stating the action first and then the objects after. ("Copy these cells. Put the copy in those cells.") Instead, on an Excel worksheet you select the object first and then do the action after. ("These cells—copy. Those cells—paste.") Selecting the object first in the worksheet makes carrying out multiple actions more efficient.

Macro statements in Visual Basic work backwards the same as actions in an Excel worksheet. In a macro statement, you tell what you're going to work on, and then you do something to it.

Make your macro always available

Your new shortcut key will format cells on any worksheet in the whole workbook. In fact, as long as LESSON1A.XLS is open, you can use that shortcut on any worksheet in *any* workbook. When you close the LESSON1A.XLS workbook, the shortcut key turns off. When you open the workbook, the shortcut key turns back on.

On the one hand, you should be happy that you can use your FormatCurrency macro on any worksheet as long as it's part of an open workbook. On the other hand, you may not want to keep the LESSON1A.XLS workbook open all the time just so you can use this macro. Delete this macro and make a different version that will be always available.

1 Activate Module1 by clicking its tab.

2 From the Edit menu, choose Delete Sheet and click OK when asked for confirmation.

3 Select cells D17:F17.

4 From the Tools menu, choose the Record Macro, Record New Macro command.

5 Type FormatCurrency as the name of the macro, and click Options.

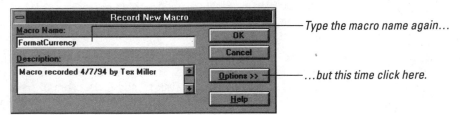

Type the macro name again...

...but this time click here.

6   At the bottom of the Record New Macro dialog box, in the group labeled Store In, change the selected option from the default This Workbook to Personal Macro Workbook.

When you click the Options button, the Record New Macro dialog box changes to an extended version that looks very much like the Macro Options dialog box you used to change the shortcut key assignment. While you're here, you might as well fix the description and the shortcut key.

7   In the Description box, replace the default description with **Assign modified currency format to the current selection**, and change the shortcut key to CTRL+SHIFT+C.

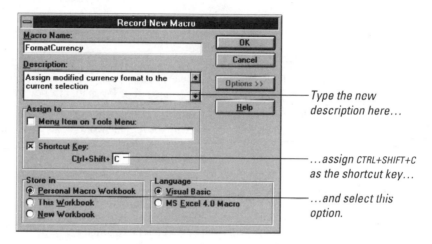

Type the new description here...

...assign CTRL+SHIFT+C as the shortcut key...

...and select this option.

8   Click OK to start recording.

9   Choose the Cells command from the Format menu, choose the first currency format, and click OK.

10   Click the Stop Macro button to quit recording.

Stop Macro button

11   Select cells D18:F18 and press CTRL+SHIFT+C to try out the re-recorded macro. (If Excel complains that it cannot find the original FormatCurrency macro, just click OK and press CTRL+SHIFT+C again.)

The macro works, but notice that the workbook does not have a Module1 tab at the bottom. It doesn't have any new tabs at all. Where is the macro now? Well, remember that the option in the dialog box did use the words *Personal Macro*. Maybe this new macro is just shy about personal matters.

Look at the personal macro workbook

1   Click the Window menu.

Notice the Unhide command. The Unhide command is usually disabled, but now it is black.

2   Choose the Unhide command.

The Unhide dialog box lists all hidden windows.

The Unhide dialog box reveals to you the hiding place of the personal macro workbook. It is named PERSONAL.XLS.

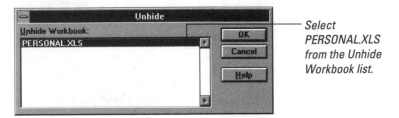

Select PERSONAL.XLS from the Unhide Workbook list.

3   Click OK.

The PERSONAL.XLS workbook appears. It has only one sheet, labeled Module1, and that module sheet contains your FormatCurrency macro.

The personal macro workbook is just like any other workbook. It typically contains only macro sheets, but you can put regular worksheets into it if you want. When you save the personal macro workbook, Excel saves it into the startup directory. Excel opens all files in the startup directory (except template files) when you start Excel, so the personal macro workbook is always available.

Note The PERSONAL.XLS personal macro workbook in Excel 5 is equivalent to the GLOBAL.XLM global macro file in Excel 4. As did the Excel 4 global macro file, the personal macro workbook provides you with a place to record macros that are not attached to one particular project.

Arrange the workbook windows

Before you record any more macros, change your screen so that you can watch the macros grow as you record them. That way, you don't have to be patient and wait until you've finished recording to see how a macro is progressing. Put the LESSON1A.XLS workbook, where you will carry out the actions, above the PERSONAL.XLS workbook, where the macro will be growing.

1   From the Window menu, choose LESSON1A.XLS so that the budget worksheet's window is active.

2   From the Window menu, choose the Arrange command, select the Horizontal option, and click OK.

Excel arranges the window with the budget worksheet above the window with the macro.

	LESSON1.XLS						
	A	**B**	**C**	**D**	**E**	**F**	**G**	**H**
1	**Summary**		Rates	Jan-94	Feb-94	Mar-94	Qtr1	Apr-94
2	Projected Units			29000	30000	31000	90000	32000
3	Projected Revenues			$71,000.00	$73,000.00	$75,000.00	219000	77000
4	**Projected Pre-tax Profit**			$26,819.90	$27,057.90	$30,295.90	84173.7	35033.9
5								
6	**Variable Costs**							

Budget94

PERSONAL.XLS

```
' FormatCurrency Macro
' Assign modified currency format to the current selection.
'
' Keyboard Shortcut: Ctrl+C
'
```

Module1

Now when you turn on the recorder and perform actions in the window on top, you can watch what the recorder is doing in the window on the bottom.

Changing Multiple Properties at Once

The FormatCurrency macro changes a single attribute of the current selection—the number format. In Excel macros, the word for an attribute or setting is *property*. NumberFormat is a property of a cell. Sometimes when you record an action, the macro changes multiple properties at the same time.

Center text vertically with a command

Align Center button

Excel has a toolbar button that centers text horizontally in a cell: the Align Center button. But if the row height is taller than the text, you may want to center the text vertically in the cell as well as horizontally. Excel does not have a toolbar button that will center both horizontally and vertically, but you can record a macro that will. Start by carrying out the actions interatively, using menu commands.

1   Drag the bottom border of the row header for row 1 down until the row is about twice as high as before.

	A	**B**	**C**	**D**	**E**	**F**
1	Summary		Rates	Jan-94	Feb-94	Mar-94
2	Projected Units			29000	30000	31000
3	Projected Revenues			$71,000.00	$73,000.00	$75,000.00

Drag here to increase row height.

2   Select cell C1.

The text is in the bottom left corner of the cell.

3   From the Format menu, choose Cells and select the Alignment tab.

The Alignment tab has several option groups: a Horizontal alignment group, a Vertical alignment group, an Orientation group, and a check box off by itself for Wrap Text.

4   Select Center as the Horizontal option and Center as the Vertical option, and click OK to center the text in the cell.

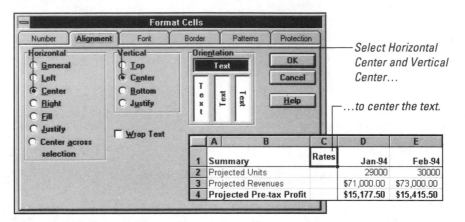

Select Horizontal Center and Vertical Center...

...to center the text.

Record a macro to center text

1   Select cell D1, and from the Tools menu, choose Record Macro, Record New Macro.

2   In the Record New Macro dialog box, type **CenterText** as the macro name and **Center text both horizontally and vertically** as the description, and click Options.

3   Change the shortcut key to CTRL+SHIFT+C.

The macro is already set to record to the personal macro workbook. Excel remembers the setting for where to store the macro until you change it, even after you exit and restart Excel.

4   Click OK.

Excel displays a warning. CTRL+SHIFT+C is the same shortcut key you used for FormatCurrency. Excel displays this warning only if you try to replace a shortcut key used by another macro. You don't get a warning if you replace a built-in shortcut key.

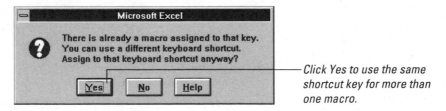

Click Yes to use the same shortcut key for more than one macro.

5 Click Yes. You would rather use CTRL+SHIFT+C for center than for currency.

Note When two macros have the same shortcut key, the macro that comes first in the Macro dialog box is the one that runs when you press the shortcut key.

Immediately, the recorder puts the comment lines and the Sub and End Sub lines into the macro.

```
                            PERSONAL.XLS
' CenterText Macro
' Center text both horizontally and vertically
'
' Keyboard Shortcut: Ctrl+C
'
Sub CenterText()
End Sub

|◄|◄|►|►|  Module1
```

6 From the Format menu, choose Cells. In the Format Cells dialog box select the two Center options and click OK.

The recorder puts several lines into the macro all at once.

In the comments, the macro recorder puts Ctrl+C for the CTRL+SHIFT+C *shortcut key and Ctrl+c for the* CTRL+C *shortcut key.*

7 Click the Stop Macro button and look at the macro code.

```
'
' CenterText Macro
' Center text both horizontally and vertically
'
' Keyboard Shortcut: Ctrl+C
'
Sub CenterText()
    With Selection
        .HorizontalAlignment = xlCenter
        .VerticalAlignment = xlCenter
        .WrapText = False
        .Orientation = xlHorizontal
    End With
End Sub
```

The macro shows four different property settings for the cell alignment. These relate directly to the groups of options you saw in the dialog box: Horizontal, Vertical, Wrap Text, and Orientation.

Each of the property settings affects an attribute of the current selection just as the Style property setting did in the FormatCurrency macro. In the FormatCurrency macro, the property name was attached directly to the word *Selection* with a period, to show that the property affected the cells in the current selection. In this macro, each of the property names just hangs there.

The pair of statements *With Selection* and *End With* means that every time there is a period with nothing in front of it, pretend that the word *Selection* is there. The With structure makes the code easier to read because you can tell instantly that all the properties relate to the current selection. The With structure also makes the macro run faster because the macro has to figure out only once what the current selection is.

You could change the CenterText macro to the following code and it would produce exactly the same result.

```
Sub CenterText()
    Selection.HorizontalAlignment = xlCenter
    Selection.VerticalAlignment = xlCenter
    Selection.WrapText = False
    Selection.Orientation = xlHorizontal
End Sub
```

When you use the With statement, you can read the code as "With the current selection, let the horizontal alignment be centered and the vertical alignment be centered, and the text wrapping be false…." When you don't use the With statement, you read the code as "Let the horizontal alignment of the selection be centered. Let the vertical alignment of the selection be centered…."

Eliminate unnecessary lines from the macro

In many dialog boxes, the macro recorder records all the possible settings, even though you change only one or two of them. You can make your macro easier to understand if you eliminate unnecessary settings.

In this macro, you need to change only the HorizontalAlignment and VerticalAlignment properties. You can delete the other lines from the macro.

1   On the sheet with the macro, click immediately to the left of the words *End With*.

2   Drag straight up until the mouse pointer is on the line containing the words *WrapText*.

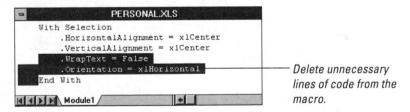

Delete unnecessary lines of code from the macro.

3   Press DELETE.

The macro is finished and ready to go. Now test it to find out whether it works.

Test the macro

1   Select cells E1:G1.

2   Press CTRL+SHIFT+C.

The macro centers the text in all the selected cells.

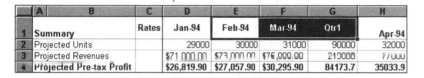

	A	B	C	D	E	F	G	H
1	Summary		Rates	Jan-94	Feb-94	Mar-94	Qtr1	Apr-94
2	Projected Units			29000	30000	31000	90000	32000
3	Projected Revenues			$71,000.00	$73,000.00	$76,000.00	219000	77000
4	Projected Pre-tax Profit			$26,819.90	$27,057.90	$30,295.90	84173.7	35033.9

Now you have not only recorded a macro, you have also deleted parts of it and it still works. Next you'll record a macro and make *additions* to it.

Editing a Recorded Macro

In Excel 5, each workbook has tabs at the bottom to show the worksheets in the workbook. The sheet tabs share the same row of the screen as the horizontal scroll bar. If you need to do a lot of horizontal scrolling, you may want to temporarily remove the sheet tabs. First remove the tabs interactively with menu commands, and then record a macro to make the change.

Remove sheet tabs with a command

1   Click in the worksheet window to activate it.

2   From the Tools menu, choose the Options command and select the View tab.

3   Clear the Sheet Tabs check box at the bottom of the Window Options group.

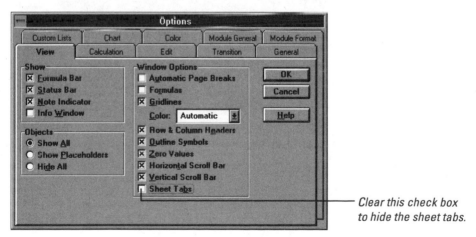

Clear this check box to hide the sheet tabs.

4 Click OK.

The sheet tabs are gone from the bottom of the window, so the scrollbar can take the whole width of the window.

5 Repeat the above steps, and turn the sheet tabs back on.

Sheet tabs are a setting—or a *property*—of the window. You can select the Sheet Tabs check box so that the property is True and the window displays the tabs, or you can clear the check box so that the property is False and the window does not display the tabs. Next change the Sheet Tabs property with a macro.

Remove sheet tabs with a macro

1 From the Tools menu, choose the Record Macro, Record New Macro command.

2 Type **RemoveTabs** as the name of the macro, and click Options.

3 Set the shortcut key to CTRL+SHIFT+T, and click OK.

The recorder puts the shell of the macro (the comments and the Sub and End Sub lines) into the module sheet.

4 From the Tools menu, choose Options, clear the check box labeled Sheet Tabs, and click OK.

The tabs disappear at the bottom of the window.

Stop Macro button

5 Click the Stop Macro button and look at the resulting code.

```
'
' RemoveTabs Macro
' Macro recorded 4/7/94 by Tex Miller
'
' Keyboard Shortcut: Ctrl+T
'
Sub RemoveTabs()
    ActiveWindow.DisplayWorkbookTabs = False
End Sub
```

This macro is very similar to the FormatCurrency macro. You can read it as "Let 'False' be the display workbook tabs property of the active window." This time you're not changing a property of the selection, but rather a property of the active window. The *thing* that you change the property of is called an *object*. This time the object is not a cell, but a window.

Test the macro

1 Activate the worksheet window, bring up the Options dialog box, select the Sheet Tabs check box, and click OK to make the sheet tabs appear.

2 Press CTRL+SHIFT+T to make the tabs disappear.

Which is easier, turning the sheet tabs on with the dialog box, or turning them off with the macro?

Toggle the window setting with a macro

You could record a second macro to turn the sheet tabs on, but somehow, letting a single macro *toggle* the setting seems more natural. Just change the macro to switch the property to the opposite of it's current value.

1 Activate the personal macro workbook window.

2 Select the words *ActiveWindow.DisplayWorkbookTabs,* and press CTRL+C to copy them to the clipboard.

```
Sub RemoveTabs()
    ActiveWindow.DisplayWorkbookTabs = False
End Sub
```
Module1

3 Double click the word *False* later in the same line, and press CTRL+V to paste the words you copied.

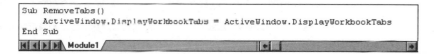

```
Sub RemoveTabs()
    ActiveWindow.DisplayWorkbookTabs = ActiveWindow.DisplayWorkbookTabs
End Sub
```
Module1

Putting the property on the right side of the equal sign retrieves the current value for the property. But so far, all you've done is made the macro set the property to the same thing that it was before. Not particularly useful.

4 Click just after the equal sign. Press the SPACEBAR, and then type **Not**. You should have a space on both sides of the word *Not*.

This is what the macro should look like now:

```
Sub RemoveTabs()
    ActiveWindow.DisplayWorkbookTabs = Not ActiveWindow.DisplayWorkbookTabs
End Sub
```
Module1

5 Click back on the LESSON1A.XLS workbook window, and press CTRL+SHIFT+T several times.

The macro reads the old value of the property, changes it to the opposite with the keyword *Not*, and assigns the newly inverted value back to the property.

Simplify the macro

The macro is only one line long, but that one line is rather long and a little hard to read. The DisplayWorkbookTabs property on the right applies to the same ActiveWindow object as the DisplayWorkbookTabs property on the left. Didn't Visual Basic have a *With* keyword that could eliminate the need to keep repeating the name of an object?

1 Put the cursor right before the word *ActiveWindow* at the beginning of the line.

2 Type **With** and a space.

3 Move the cursor to just before the period and press ENTER to move the rest of the statement to the next line.

4 Press TAB to indent the new line.

5 Double click the second occurrence of *ActiveWindow,* and press DELETE, leaving only the period and the property behind.

6 Move the cursor to the end of the line, and press ENTER to create a new line.

7 Press BACKSPACE to align the insertion point with the beginning of the *With ActiveWindow* statement, and type **End With**.

The final macro should look like this:

```
Sub RemoveTabs()
    With ActiveWindow
        .DisplayWorkbookTabs = Not .DisplayWorkbookTabs
    End With
End Sub
```
Module1

8 Activate the worksheet window and press CTRL+SHIFT+T a few times to test the revised macro.

The new version of the macro is not remarkably different than the earlier one, but you may find it a little easier to see that both sides of the assignment relate to the same ActiveWindow object. Besides, you made some significant changes to the recorded macro and learned a lot about how the With statement works.

This is a pretty nice macro, but now the name is wrong. This macro does not remove tabs anymore; it toggles the tab setting. You need to change the name of the macro from RemoveTabs to something that better matches its new functionality.

Rename the macro

1 Select the part of the macro name that says *Remove* and replace it with **Toggle**.

```
Sub ToggleTabs()
    With ActiveWindow
        .DisplayWorkbookTabs = Not .DisplayWorkbookTabs
    End With
End Sub
```
Module1

2 From the Tools menu, choose the Macro command. The list reflects the new name of the macro.

3 Select ToggleTabs from the list, and click Run. The macro still works.

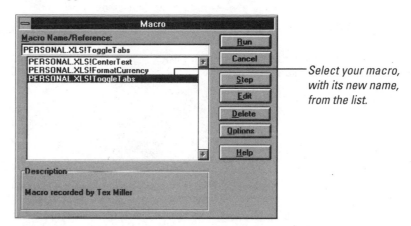

Select your macro, with its new name, from the list.

4 Delete (or fix) the comment line that told the old name of the macro. Comments do not automatically adjust when you rename the macro.

Aside from updating any comments, all you have to do to rename a macro is to change the name in the line beginning with *Sub*.

Recording Actions in a Macro

You should see a pattern to creating a simple convenience macro: Try out an action interactively. Once you know how to do the task, turn on the recorder. Do the task with the recorder on. Turn off the recorder.

So far, all the macros you have recorded have assigned a new setting to one or more properties of an object. Some actions that you can record do not assign settings to properties. For example, copying and pasting cells do not change properties; they carry out tasks. Let's see what a macro looks like when you record simple actions.

Suppose you want to freeze the formulas in the first quarter of the budget worksheet to their current values. First change the formulas in January to values using menu commands, and then create a macro that can change any formulas to values.

Convert formulas to values interactively

1 Click the heading of column D to select the entire January column.

You can also press CTRL+C to copy the current selection.

2 From the Edit menu, choose the Copy command.

Copying the current selection to the clipboard is an action. The copy action does not display a dialog box.

3   Don't change the selection. From the Edit menu, choose the Paste Special command. The Paste Special dialog box appears.

4   Select the Values option from the Paste group, and click OK.

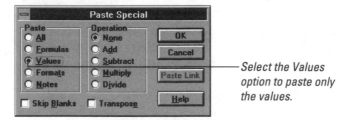

Select the Values option to paste only the values.

Excel pastes the values from the cells over the top of the existing cells, eliminating any formulas that may have been in them. The marquee is still visible around the cells. You could paste them again somewhere else if you wanted.

Pasting the value of the cells is an action just like copying cells, but the paste values action displays a dialog box.

5   Press ESC to get out of copy mode and clear the marquee.

As you carry out the copy and paste actions with the menus, notice that the Copy command does not bring up a dialog box. You see a marquee around the cells and a message in the status bar, but you don't need to tell Excel how to do the copying. The Paste Special command, on the other hand, does require additional information from you in order to carry out it's job, so it displays a dialog box. Some actions in Excel need you to give additional information about how to carry out the action, and some don't.

Convert formulas to values with a macro

Watch how the macro recorder handles actions that display a dialog box, compared to how it handles actions that don't.

1   Select column E, the February column.

2   From the Tools menu, choose the Record Macro, Record New Macro command.

3   Type **ConvertToValues** as the name of the macro, and click Options.

4   Set the shortcut key to CTRL+SHIFT+V, and click OK.

5   From the Edit menu, choose the Copy command.

6   From the Edit menu, choose the Paste Special command, select the Values option, and click OK.

7   Press ESC to get rid of the copy marquee.

8   Click the Stop Macro button.

Stop Macro button

The recorded macro appears in the lower window.

```
' ConvertToValues Macro
' Macro recorded 4/7/94 by Tex Miller
'
' Keyboard Shortcut: Ctrl+V
'
Sub ConvertToValues()
    Selection.Copy
    Selection.PasteSpecial Paste:=xlValues, Operation:=xlNone, _
        SkipBlanks:=False, Transpose:=False
    Application.CutCopyMode = False
End Sub
```
Module1

The basic structure of this macro is the same as the other macros you have seen in this lesson. The last line, for example, sets the CutCopyMode property of the application in much the same way that the ToggleTabs macro changed the DisplaySheetTabs property of the active window. The two lines that begin with *Selection*, however, are something new.

The words *Selection.Copy* look similar to the words *Selection.NumberFormat* from the very first macro. In that first macro, NumberFormat was a property of the selection and you were assigning a new value to the NumberFormat property. Copy, however, is not a property. You don't assign anything to Copy; you just do it. Actions where you don't assign a setting to a property—that is, actions like Copy—are called *methods*.

When you execute the Copy command interactively, Excel does not ask you for any extra information. In the same way, when you execute the Copy method in a macro, you don't give any extra information to the command.

The word *PasteSpecial* is also a method in Excel. PasteSpecial is not a property that you assign a value to. The Paste Special command on the Edit menu does display a dialog box, but the dialog box does not show you properties to change; it just asks *how* to carry out the paste special action. When you execute the PasteSpecial method in a macro, you give the extra information to the method. The extra pieces of information you give to a method are called *arguments*.

Using a method with an object is like giving some instructions to your nine-year-old son. With some instructions—like "Come eat"—you don't have to give any extra information. With other instructions—like "Go to the store for me"—you have to tell what to buy (milk), how to get there (on your bike), and when to come home (immediately). Giving these extra pieces of information to your son is like giving arguments to an Excel method. (You call them *arguments* because whenever you tell your son how to do something, you end up with an instant argument.)

The four arguments you give to PasteSpecial correspond exactly to the four option groups in the Paste Special dialog box. Each argument consists of a name for the argument (for example, Paste) joined to the argument value (for example, xlValues) by a colon and an equal sign (:=).

When you assign a new value to a property, you separate the value from the property with an equal sign, as in the statement:

```
ActiveWindow.DisplayWorkbookTabs = False
```

You read this statement as "Let 'False' be the display workbook tabs property of the active window."

When you use a named argument with a method, you separate the argument value from the argument name with a colon and an equal sign and you separate the argument from the name of the method with a space. When you have more than one argument, separate them from each other with commas, as in this statement:

```
Selection.PasteSpecial Paste:=xlValues, Operation:=xlNone
```

Arguments look a lot like properties, but arguments always come after a method name. Properties are attributes of an object. Arguments are special instructions to an action.

Make a long statement more readable

When one of the statements in a macro gets to be longer than about 70 characters, the macro recorder puts a space and an underscore (_) after a convenient word and continues the statement on the next line. The underscore tells the macro that it should treat the second line as part of the same statement. You can break long statements into as many lines as you want, as long as you always break the line where there is already a space.

► Make the PasteSpecial statement with it's many arguments more readable. Put each argument on a separate line, using a space and an underscore character at the end of each line except the last.

```
Sub ConvertToValues()
    Selection.Copy
    Selection.PasteSpecial _
        Paste:=xlValues, _
        Operation:=xlNone, _
        SkipBlanks:=False, _
        Transpose:=False
    Application.CutCopyMode = False
End Sub
```

In Part 3 you will learn more about objects.

Most of the macros in this chapter have changed object properties. This macro executes object methods. Properties and methods look very similar: Both are separated from the object by periods. You assign new values to properties. You just do methods, sometimes giving the method arguments along the way.

Adding a Macro to a Toolbar

Keyboard shortcuts and toolbar buttons both make running macros more convenient. Keyboard shortcuts can be faster—if you remember them—but toolbar buttons can be easier to remember and use. When you recorded the ConvertToValues macro, you created a shortcut key for it, but CTRL+SHIFT+V may be too hard to remember. You can create an easy-to-remember toolbar button for your macro.

Customize the toolbar

To add a custom button to a toolbar, you need to *customize* the toolbar. Appropriately enough, Excel has a Customize dialog box that allows you to work with toolbars.

1   Activate the budget worksheet. From the View menu, choose Toolbars.

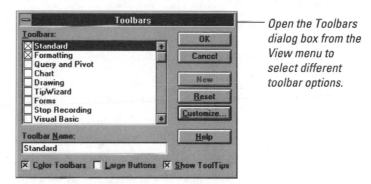

Open the Toolbars dialog box from the View menu to select different toolbar options.

2   Click the Customize button. While the Customize dialog box is displayed, you can click toolbar buttons without running them.

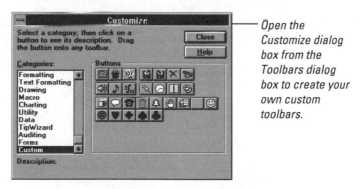

Open the Customize dialog box from the Toolbars dialog box to create your own custom toolbars.

To make room for your new button, remove the Sort Descending button.

Sort Descending button

3 Click the Sort Descending button and drag it off the toolbar.

4 In the Customize dialog box, scroll down the Categories list to the bottom and select the Custom category.

5 From the collection of buttons, click the one with the happy face and drag it up to the place where the Sort Descending tool was.

6 As soon as you drag the new custom tool up to the toolbar, Excel prompts you for a macro to assign to the tool. Select ConvertToValues from the list, and click OK.

7 Click the Close button to close the Customize dialog box.

8 Click the heading for column F in the worksheet and then click the new happy tool to convert the formulas to values.

Add status line text to your macro

One of the purposes of putting a custom button on a toolbar is to make the macro easy to remember and use. Most toolbar button pictures are a little hard to interpret, and a happy face does not immediately suggest converting to values. Excel's built-in toolbar buttons display a comment in the status line. When you move the mouse cursor over a toolbar button, the status line tells you what the button does. You assign a status line messsage in much the same way that you assign a shortcut key.

1 From the Tools menu, choose the Macro command.

2 From the list of macros, select ConvertToValues, and click Options.

3 Towards the bottom of the dialog box is a text box labeled Status Bar Text. Type **Convert formulas to values** in that box, and click OK.

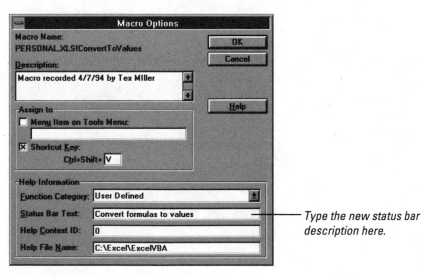

Type the new status bar description here.

4 Close the Macro Options dialog box.

5 Move the mouse cursor over the happy face button, and look at the status bar.

Change the picture on the toolbar button

Adding a status bar message helps you interpret what the toolbar button does, but the happy face still doesn't seem to have anything to do with converting formulas to values. You need to change the picture on the button.

Paste Values button

1   From the View menu, choose Toolbars, and then click Customize.

2   Select Edit from the Category list, and click the Paste Values button.

The Paste Values button performs the same action as your ConvertToValues macro, except that it does not copy the selection first. The picture on the Paste Values button will serve as a good starting point for creating your picture though.

3   Choose the Copy Button Image command from the Edit menu, then click on the happy face button and choose Paste Button Image from the Edit menu.

4   Use the right mouse button to click the new Paste Values button. Then choose the Edit Button Image command.

The Button Editor dialog box appears, displaying an enlarged version of your button.

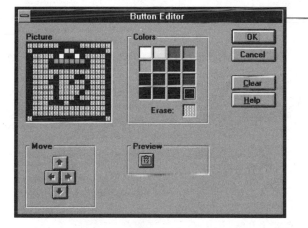

Create your own custom toolbar buttons with the Button Editor.

Click the blue color in the palette, and then click the dots of the black border of the clipboard to change them to blue. This difference will remind you that this is the enhanced Paste Values button.

5   Click OK to return the revised image to your button, and click the Close button to remove the Customize dialog box.

Note   When Excel closes, it saves any changes you made to the toolbars in the file EXCEL5.XLB that is stored in your Windows directory. To reset all toolbars back to their default values, delete the file EXCEL5.XLB.

Exit Microsoft Excel

You don't need to save changes to the LESSON1A.XLS workbook, but you may want to save the macros you created in PERSONAL.XLS into a different file.

1   Activate the LESSON1A.XLS workbook, and choose Close from the File menu. Click No when asked for permission to save changes.

2   Save the personal macro workbook as LESSON1B.XLS in the directory containing the sample files for this book, and then close the workbook.

3   From the File menu, choose Exit to close Excel. (If you saved the personal macro workbook during the course of the lesson, use File Manager to delete the file PERSONAL.XLS from the XLSTART directory where Excel is installed.)

Lesson Summary

To	Do this
Turn on the recorder	From the Tools menu, choose the Macro, Record New Macro command.
Turn off the recorder	Click the Stop Macro button.
Run a macro	From the Tools menu, choose the Macro, Run command, select the macro, and click Run.
Add a shortcut key	In the Macro dialog box, click the Options button and enter the shortcut key.
Attach a macro to a toolbar button	Click a toolbar with the right mouse button, choose Customize, and drag a button from the Custom category to a toolbar.
Edit a tool face	Display the toolbar's Customize dialog box, click the button you want to edit with the right mouse button, and choose Edit Tool Image.

For more information on	See
Recording macros	Chapter 1, "Automating Repeated Tasks," in the *Microsoft Excel Visual Basic User's Guide*.

Preview of the Next Lesson

In the next lesson you will learn how to combine multiple small macros to automate whole tasks. You will also learn more about how to find and fix problems when your macros don't work quite the way you want.

Make a Macro Do Complex Tasks

Rube Goldberg was famous for intricate, involved contraptions where a ball drops into a bucket and the weight of the bucket lifts a lever that releases a spring that wakes up a cat, and so forth. Rube Goldberg contraptions are fun to look at. Milton Bradley has been successful for years with the Mousetrap game based on a Rube Goldberg concept. Boston's Logan International Airport has two massive, perpetually working Rube Goldberg contraptions in the lobby that entertain irritated travelers for hours.

Entertainment is one thing. Getting your job done is another. Sometimes the list of steps you have to go through to get out a monthly report can seem like a Rube Goldberg contraption. First you import the monthly order file and add some new columns to it. Then you sort it and print it and sort it a different way and print it again. Then you paste it onto the end of the cumulative order history file, and so forth. Each step has to be completed just right before the next one is started, and you start making sure you don't schedule your vacation during the wrong time of the month because you would never want to have to explain to someone else how to get it all done right. Right?

One good use for macros is putting together all the steps for a Rube Goldberg monthly report. This lesson will help you learn how to do it.

You will learn how to:

- Break a complex task into manageable pieces.

- Watch a macro run one statement at a time.

- Enter values into the macro while it is running.

- Record movements relative to the active cell.

- Create a macro that runs other macros.

Estimated lesson time: 45 minutes

Start the lesson

▶ Start Microsoft Excel, and change to the directory that contains the practice files for this book. Open the PRICES.XLS workbook, and save a copy of the workbook as LESSON2.XLS.

Divide and Conquer

The secret to creating a macro capable of handling a long, intricate task is to break the task into small pieces, create a macro for each separate piece, and then glue the pieces together. If you just turn on the recorder, carry out four hundred steps, and cross your fingers and hope for the best, you have about a one in four hundred chance of having your macro work properly.

As the bookkeeper at Miller Textiles' Screen Printing division, you have an elaborate month-end task you would like to automate so that you can go on vacation next month. Each month, you get a summary report of orders for the previous month from the order processing system.

```
                     Miller Textiles
              Order Summary for March 1994

   State     Channel    Category      Price  Qty    Dollars
   ========  ==========  =============  ======  ======  =========
   WA        Retail      Kids          Mid        9      40.50
                                       Low      143     434.06
                         Art           High      17      93.50
                                       Mid       23     103.50
                         Sports        High      26     143.00
                                       Mid        6      27.00
                                       Low        4      14.00
                         Seattle       High      13      71.50
                                       Mid        7      31.50
                                       Low       25      87.50
                         Dinosaurs     Mid       22      99.00
```

The report shows the units and net dollars for each state, channel, price, and category combination. The order processing system can export the report in Lotus 1-2-3 format. You need to manipulate the file, produce some reports (complete with charts), and then add the new month's orders to a cumulative order history database.

This lesson will show you how to record the individual subtasks that make up a large, complex task and then combine the small macros into one comprehensive macro. Along the way, you may learn some useful techniques for completing everyday tasks as well.

Getting Ready to Record

The orders for the most recent month, March 1994, are in the Lotus 1-2-3 worksheet ORD9403.WK1. You will open that 1-2-3 worksheet and copy it into the LESSON2.XLS workbook before you start manipulating the orders.

Copy the order summary report to the active workbook

1   From the File menu, choose Open, select Lotus 1-2-3 Files from the List Files Of Type list, select ORD9403.WK1 from the File Name list, and click OK.

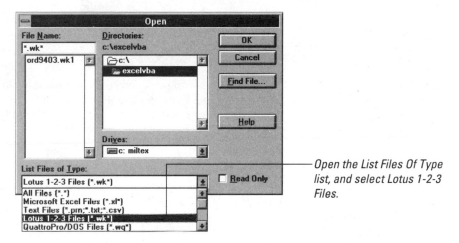

Open the List Files Of Type list, and select Lotus 1-2-3 Files.

The ORD9403.WK1 workbook appears, with a single worksheet tab labeled ORD9403.

2   Double click the ORD9403 tab, type **Orders** as a new name for the worksheet, and click OK.

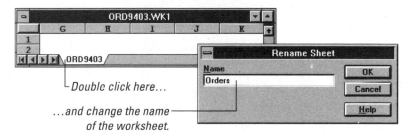

Double click here...

...and change the name of the worksheet.

3   Drag the bottom left corner of the ORD9403.WK1 workbook window up and to the right a couple of inches so that you can see the worksheet tabs for the LESSON2.XLS workbook below.

4   Drag the Orders tab in the ORD9403.WK1 workbook over to the LESSON2.XLS workbook, just to the right of the Prices tab.

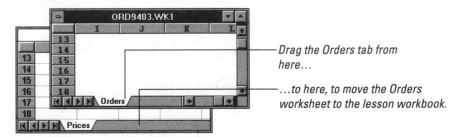

Drag the Orders tab from here...

...to here, to move the Orders worksheet to the lesson workbook.

5   The ORD9403.WK1 workbook disappears completely. After you drag the last sheet out of a workbook, the workbook ceases to exist in the computer's memory, even if it is a workbook that contained a 1-2-3 worksheet. The original copy of the file on your hard disk, however, remains intact.

6   From the Format menu, choose the Style command.

The current style is Normal_Orders. This is a new style Excel created when you dragged the 1-2-3 worksheet into the LESSON2.XLS workbook. This style simulates the format of a 1-2-3 worksheet.

7   Click the Delete button, and then click Close.

This converts the worksheet to look like an Excel worksheet. The worksheet still doesn't have gridlines (because 1-2-3 worksheets don't have gridlines), but you don't need gridlines anyway, so don't worry about it.

8   You need an extra copy of the Orders worksheet so that you can practice writing the macros and still get back to the original worksheet when necessary.

9   Hold down the CTRL key and drag the Orders tab to the right until a plus sign (+) appears in the middle of the tab.

13			Low	22	77.00
14		Humorous	Mid	143	554.32
15			Low	13	45.50
16		Environme	Mid	35	157.50
17			Low	40	140.00

Prices \ Orders

Hold down CTRL and drag from here...

...to here to duplicate the worksheet.

An identical copy of Orders, labeled Orders (2), appears.

Now practice the steps you will take to build the macros using Orders (2), and whenever you need to start over from the beginning, recopy the original Orders worksheet.

Task One: Filling in Missing Labels

When the order processing system produces a summary report, it enters a label in a column only the first time that label appears. Leaving out duplicate labels is one way to make a report easier for a human being to read, but for the computer to sort and summarize the data properly, you need to fill in the missing labels.

	A	B	C	D	E	F
1	State	Channel	Category	Price	Qty	Dollars
2	WA	Retail	Kids	Mid	9	40.50
3				Low	143	434.06
4			Art	High	17	93.50
5				Mid	23	103.50
6			Sports	High	26	143.00

Fill the blank cells with the missing labels.

First fill in the labels using worksheet tools. Get Excel to do as much of the work as possible before starting the macro.

Select only the blank cells

Look at the places where you want to fill in missing labels. What value do you want in each of the empty cells? You want each empty cell to contain the value from the first nonempty cell above it. In fact, if you selected each empty cell in turn and put into it a formula pointing at the cell immediately above it, you would have the result you want. The range of empty cells is an irregular shape, however, which makes the prospect of filling all the cells with a formula daunting. Fortunately, Excel has a built-in tool for selecting an irregular range of blank cells.

1   Select cell A1.

You can also press F5 to open the Go To dialog box.

2   From the Edit menu, choose the Go To command.

The Go To dialog box appears.

3   In the Go To dialog box, click the Special button.

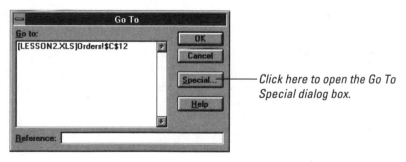

Click here to open the Go To Special dialog box.

You can also select the current region by holding down the CTRL key and pressing the star key on the numeric keypad.

4   In the Go To Special dialog box, select the Current Region option and click OK.

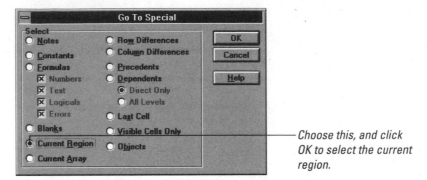

Choose this, and click OK to select the current region.

Excel selects the current region—the rectangle of cells including the active cell, that is surrounded by blank cells or worksheet borders.

5   From the Edit menu, choose the Go To command, and click the Special button again.

6   In the Go To Special dialog box, select the Blanks option and click OK.

Excel selects only the blank cells from the selection. These are the cells that need new values.

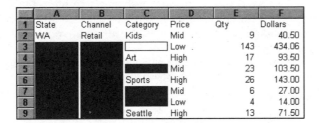

	A	B	C	D	E	F
1	State	Channel	Category	Price	Qty	Dollars
2	WA	Retail	Kids	Mid	9	40.50
3				Low	143	434.06
4			Art	High	17	93.50
5				Mid	23	103.50
6			Sports	High	26	143.00
7				Mid	6	27.00
8				Low	4	14.00
9			Seattle	High	13	71.50

You might have expected that you would need to write a macro to search through the block of cells to find all the blank cells that needed a new value, but Excel's built-in Go To Special feature can save you—and your macro—a lot of work.

Fill the selection with values

1   With the blank cells selected and C3 as the active cell, type = and press UP ARROW to point at cell C2.

The cell reference C2—when found in cell C3—actually means "one cell above me in the same column."

2   Hold down the CTRL key and press ENTER to fill the formula into all the currently selected cells.

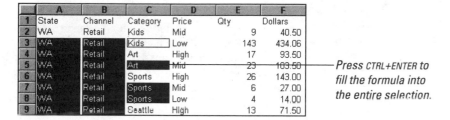

Press CTRL+ENTER to fill the formula into the entire selection.

With more than one cell selected, if you type a formula and press ENTER, the formula goes into the one active cell. If you type a formula and press CTRL+ENTER, the formula goes into all the cells of the selection.

Each cell with the new formula contains the address of the cell above it.

3   Select cell A1 and press CTRL+STAR (CTRL+SHIFT+8) to select the current region.

4   Choose Copy from the Edit menu, choose Paste Special from the Edit menu and select the Values option, and click OK. Then press ESC to get out of copy mode.

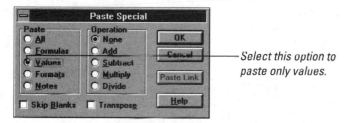

Select this option to paste only values.

Now the block of cells contains all the missing label cells—as values so they won't change if you happen to re-sort the summary data. Get back the original sheet and follow the same steps, but with the macro recorder turned on.

Get back the original sheet

1   Use the right mouse button to click the Orders (2) tab, choose Delete, and confirm that you want to delete the worksheet.

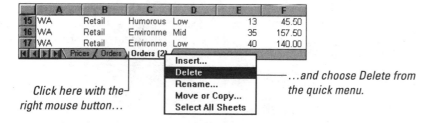

Click here with the right mouse button...

...and choose Delete from the quick menu.

2   Hold down the CTRL key and drag the Orders tab to the right to create a new copy.

Activate the Visual Basic toolbar

Before you start creating the macro, take one simple step that will make your work with macros much easier.

In Lesson 1, each time you wanted to record a macro, you had to go to the Tools menu, choose the Record Macro command, and then choose the Record New Macro subcommand. Each time you wanted to run a macro, you had to either set a keyboard shortcut or go to the Tools menu, choose the Macro command, and then select the macro to run. Excel has a special toolbar filled with buttons that are useful when working with macros.

The Visual Basic toolbar typically appears whenever you activate a module sheet. But some of the buttons in the Visual Basic toolbar are useful when you are on a worksheet and want to record or run a macro.

1   Click the right mouse button anywhere on a toolbar.

A menu showing most of the available toolbars appears.

2   Choose Visual Basic from the list.

The Visual Basic toolbar appears. You can change the location and shape of this toolbar the same as any other Excel toolbars.

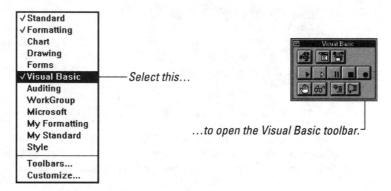

Select this...

...to open the Visual Basic toolbar.

Now when you are ready to record a macro, all you have to do is click the red circle. When you are ready to run a macro, click the green triangle.

Note   The Visual Basic toolbar is typically *context sensitive*. It appears when you activate a module sheet and disappears when you activate any other sheet. If you display the Visual Basic toolbar when it would not normally appear, it becomes permanently visible. To restore the toolbar to its original context sensitive state, turn it off when a worksheet is active.

Record Macro button

Stop Macro button

Record filling the missing values

1   On the Visual Basic toolbar, click the Record Macro button, type **FillLabels** as the name for the macro, and then click Options.

2   In the extended dialog box, select This Workbook as the Store In option, and then click OK.

3   Select cell A1, and press CTRL+STAR.

4   Press F5, click the Special button, select the Blanks option, and click OK.

5   Type =, press the UP ARROW key, and press CTRL+ENTER.

6   Select cell A1 and press CTRL+STAR.

7   From the Edit menu, choose Copy.

8   From the Edit menu, choose Paste Special, select the Values option, and click OK.

9   Click the Stop Macro button in the Visual Basic toolbar.

You've finished creating the FillLabels macro. Look at it first, and then try it out.

Look at the FillLabels macro

▶   Click the new Module1 tab next to the Orders (2) tab.

The window switches to display the Module1 sheet, which contains your new macro.

```
'
' FillLabels Macro
' Macro recorded 4/7/94 by Tex Miller
'
'
Sub FillLabels()
    Range("A1").Select
    Selection.CurrentRegion.Select
    Selection.SpecialCells(xlBlanks).Select
    Selection.FormulaR1C1 = "=R[-1]C"
    Range("A1").Select
    Selection.CurrentRegion.Select
    Selection.Copy
    Selection.PasteSpecial Paste:=xlValues, Operation:=xlNone, _
        SkipBlanks:=False, Transpose:=False
End Sub
```

The macro recorder puts comment lines before the macro. You can always add, change, or delete comment lines without affecting the way a macro works. The macro begins with *Sub* and ends with *End Sub*, and in between are the statements that correspond to the tasks you performed.

Read the statement

```
Range("A1").Select
```

as "Select range A1." It doesn't matter how you got to cell A1—whether you clicked the cell directly, pressed CTRL+HOME, or pressed various arrow key combinations—the macro recorder always records just the result of the selection process.

Read the statement

```
Selection.CurrentRegion.Select
```

as "Select the current region of the original selection." Always read the macro statements from right to left. Once you get past the first verb, each time you see a period, read it as *of*.

Read the statement

```
Selection.SpecialCells(xlBlanks).Select
```

as "Select the blank special cells of the original selection," and read the statement

```
Selection.FormulaR1C1 = "=R[-1]C"
```

For more information about R1C1 notation, see "References Make Formulas More Powerful" in the Microsoft Excel User's Guide.

as "Let '=R[-1]C' be the formula of the entire selection." When you entered the formula, the formula you saw was =C2, not =R[-1]C. But the formula =C2 really means "get the value from the cell just above me," and the formula must change with each cell that it goes into. The formula =R[-1]C also means "get the value from the cell just above me," but the formula doesn't have to change from cell to cell.

You could change this statement to *Selection.Formula = "=C2"* and the macro would work exactly the same—provided that the order file when you run the macro is identical to the order file you used when you recorded the macro, and the active cell happens to be cell C3 when the macro runs. If the command to select blanks produces a different active cell, the revised macro will fail. The macro recorder uses the R1C1 form of the formula so that your macro will always work correctly.

When you use CTRL+ENTER to fill all the cells of the selection with a formula, the macro has the word *Selection* in front of the word *Formula*. When you just use ENTER to put the formula into a single cell, the macro has the word *ActiveCell* in front of the word *Formula*, as you will see when you add a column of dates later in this lesson.

The remaining statements of the macro convert the formulas to values, the same as you did in Lesson 1.

Run the macro

Now it is time to run the macro.

1   Use the right mouse button to click the Orders (2) tab, choose the Delete command, and confirm that you want to delete the worksheet.

2   Hold down the CTRL key and drag a copy of the Orders tab to the right of the original tab.

Run Macro button

3   With the Orders (2) worksheet active, click the Run Macro button.

4   Select FillLabels from the list of macros—it may be the only macro in the list—and click Run.

The macro runs, filling the missing labels in the columns.

Append to the macro

Notice that the status bar still says "Select destination and press ENTER or choose Paste" and that the selection still has the copy marquee glittering around it. This means that Excel is still in copy mode. You can press ESC now to turn off copy mode, but you want to append a step to the macro to turn it off each time you run the macro.

1   From the Tools menu, choose Record Macro, Record at Mark.

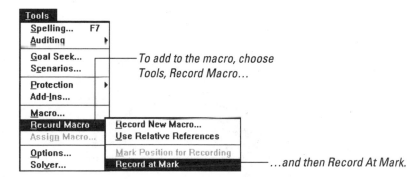

Excel does not prompt you for a macro name. It just starts recording new statements.

2   Press ESC.

3   Select cell A1.

4   Click the Stop Macro button.

5   Click the Module1 tab to see the newly improved macro.

Stop Macro button

The macro has two new statements at the bottom:

```
Application.CutCopyMode = False
Range("A1").Select
```

These new statements turn off copy mode and select cell A1, just as you would expect.

Watch the macro work

When you ran the macro before, it probably completed its tasks so fast that you were unable to see individual steps. Sometimes—especially when a macro is *not* working quite right—you may want to watch the macro work in slow motion.

1   Delete the Orders (2) worksheet, and make a new copy of Orders.

2   With the new Orders (2) worksheet selected, click the Run Macro button.

3   Select FillLabels, and this time, click the Step button.

The Debug window appears, with your macro at the bottom.

4   Drag the left border of the Debug window about halfway across the screen so that you can see the worksheet behind it. You can also drag the gray horizontal line in the middle of the Debug window up so that you can see more of your macro.

The first statement of the macro has a box around it. The box shows the *next* statement that the macro is ready to run.

5   Click the Step Into button in the Visual Basic toolbar.

Step Into button

The first statement of the macro runs, and the box moves down to surround the next statement.

6   Click the Step Into button over and over through your whole macro.

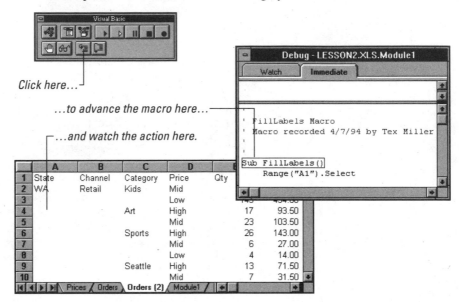

Stepping through a macro can be an effective way to see what is working and what is not working.

That concludes the macro for the first subtask of your month-end processing. Now you can start a new macro to carry out the next subtask.

Task Two: Adding a Column of Dates

The order summary report you are working with does not include the date in each row, since it includes numbers for only the most recent month. Before you can append these new records to the order history database, you will need to add the current month to each record. You will insert a new column A and then put *Mar-94* into each row of the summary.

While developing and testing the macro, you will add the new date column several times. You don't need to create another copy of the Orders worksheet, however, because you can easily delete the date column whenever you want.

Do the task with commands

First carry out the necessary steps without recording them, to get clear in your mind what you have to do before turning on the recorder.

1   Make sure cell A1 of the Orders (2) worksheet is selected. From the Insert menu, choose the Columns command.

Excel inserts a new column A, shifting the other columns over to the right.

2   Type **Date** into cell A1, and press ENTER.

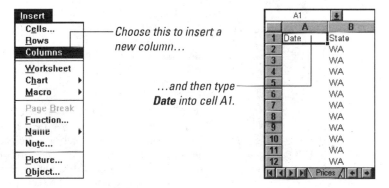

3   Drag from cell A2 down through the last row that has values in it—cell A179.

Note   Rather than using the mouse to drag through the range you want, you can use the list of states as a help. Select cell B2, the first state name in the list. Holding down the SHIFT key, press END, press DOWN ARROW, and press LEFT ARROW. Press CTRL+PERIOD three times to change the active cell to cell A2. Finally, hold down the SHIFT key and press LEFT ARROW. When you record a macro, it doesn't matter whether you drag with the mouse or use SHIFT with direction keys. Excel records only the final selection.

---

4   Type **Mar94,** and press CTRL+ENTER.

Excel fills all the rows with the date.

Record the macro

1   With cell A1 selected, choose Delete from the Edit menu, select the Entire Column option, and click OK.

2   Click the Record Macro button, type **AddDates** as the macro name, and click OK.

3   Click cell A1. (Even if it was already selected, click it again for the sake of the recorder.)

Record Macro button

4   From the Insert menu, choose Columns.

5   Enter **Date** into cell A1, select the range A2:A179, type **Mar94**, and press CTRL+ENTER.

6   Select cell A1.

7   Click the Stop Macro button.

8   Click the tab for Module1 and scroll to the bottom of the sheet to see the macro.

Stop Macro button

```
'
' AddDates Macro
' Macro recorded 4/7/94 by Tex Miller
'
Sub AddDates()
    Range("A1").Select
    Selection.EntireColumn.Insert
    ActiveCell.FormulaR1C1 = "Date"
    Range("A2:A179").Select
    Selection.FormulaR1C1 = "Mar94"
    Range("A1").Select
End Sub
```

This macro is pretty straightforward. Notice that the statement that enters the word *Date* changes the formula of the active cell, whereas the statement that enters the actual date changes the formula of the entire selection. The recorder always records the formula of a cell using the suffix R1C1, just in case the formula might have references that point to a relative cell, like the one in the FillLabels macro. In this case, since you're assigning constants to the cells, you could change *FormulaR1C1* to just *Formula* without making any difference at all to the macro.

Prompt for the date

Your recorded macro should work just fine if you always run it using the same month's data file. But the next time you actually use this macro, you will be working with April's orders, not March's orders. One possible solution would be to modify the macro each month to change the month to the current month. Somehow that doesn't seem like the right thing to do. You need to change the macro so that it *asks* you for the date when you run it.

Excel accepts many date formats. It interprets Mar94, Mar-94, Mar 94, and 3/94 all as March 1994.

1 Select the text "*Mar94*" in the macro. Be sure to include the quotation marks in the selection.

2 Press DELETE to get rid of the constant date.

3 Type **InputBox("Enter the date in MMM-YY format")** where the old date used to be.

The word *InputBox* is a Visual Basic function (keyword) that displays an input box when the macro runs. You tell the InputBox function what prompt string to use in the input box.

4 Click the Orders (2) tab, and delete column A.

5 Click the Run Macro button, select AddDates, and click Run.

The macro prompts you for the date and then inserts the date into the appropriate cells in column A.

Run Macro button

Enter the Date in MMM-YY format

OK

Cancel

Mar 94

— *Type the date into your newly created input box.*

The InputBox function is a useful tool for making a macro work in slightly changing circumstances.

Note The Add Dates macro stores the specific cell addresses for adding the new values. The macro will work correctly as long as the new file each month has the same number of rows as the report file used to record this original macro. In Lesson 8 you will learn a way to make this macro work even if the size of the input file changes.

This completes your second subtask. If you want, you can delete the Orders (2) worksheet, copy the Orders worksheet to create a new Orders (2) worksheet, and run both the FillLabels and the AddDates macros to make sure they work together.

Now you're ready to add calculated columns to the order summary.

Task Three: Adding Calculated Columns

On the Orders (2) worksheet, after you run the FillLabels and AddDates macros, your current month order summary shows only the actual net dollars for each group of orders. If you want to compare the undiscounted value of the orders to the discounted value, you need to add the list price to each row. At Miller Textiles, you have only three price grades for the shirt designs: Low, Mid, and High. You do, however, have different prices for wholesale and retail. After you look up the list price for each row in the order summary file, you will calculate the gross dollars for the orders by multiplying the units by the list price. Finally, you will convert all the formulas to values in preparation for appending the orders to the permanent order history database.

Create the lookup formula

The cells in column H need a formula that will look up the list price for the current Price and Channel combination. You use Excel's built-in functions to find the list price. On the Price worksheet is a range named PriceList that has the price grades down the left column, the channels listed across the top, and the list prices in body of the table.

	A	B	C
1		Retail	Wholesale
2	High	5.50	2.75
3	Mid	4.50	2.25
4	Low	3.50	1.75
5			

First enter the formula without using the recorder, then repeat the process, recording the actions in a macro.

1   Type **List** into cell H1 on the Orders (2) worksheet, and press ENTER.

2   Type the formula **=VLOOKUP(E2,PriceList,IF(C2="Retail",2,3))** into cell H2, and press ENTER.

The value 4.5 appears in the cell. This formula looks up the word *Mid* (the value in cell E2) in the first column of the range named PriceList on the Prices worksheet. Then it returns the value from column number 2 in the list, since the value of cell C2 is *Retail*. The retail price for a mid-price shirt design is $4.50.

This is a complicated formula for calculating the list price, but when you finish creating your macro, you won't have to enter the formula by hand any more.

3   Type **Gross** into cell I1, and press ENTER.

4   Type the formula **=F2*H2** into cell I2, and press ENTER.

5   Drag with the mouse to select cells H2:I179.

6   From the Edit menu, choose Fill, Down.

Record a macro to add calculated columns

Now you're ready to record adding the new calculated columns in a macro.

Record Macro button

1   Drag from the H column label through the I column label to select the two columns, and press DELETE.

2   Click the Record Macro button, type **AddColumns** as the macro name, and then click OK.

3   Select cell H1 and enter **List**.

4   Select cell I1 and enter **Gross**.

5   Select cell H2 and enter **=VLOOKUP(E2,PriceList,IF(C2="Retail",2,3))**.

6   Select cell I2 and enter **=F2*H2**.

7   Select cells H2:I179 and choose the Fill, Down command from the Edit menu.

8   Click the Stop Macro button.

9   Click the Module1 tab, and scroll to the bottom to see the macro.

Stop Macro button

```
'
' AddColumns Macro
' Macro recorded 4/7/94 by Tex Miller
'
'
Sub AddColumns()
    Range("H1").Select
    ActiveCell.FormulaR1C1 = "List"
    Range("I1").Select
    ActiveCell.FormulaR1C1 = "Gross"
    Range("H2").Select
    ActiveCell.FormulaR1C1 = _
        "=VLOOKUP(RC[-3],PriceList,IF(RC[ 5]-""Retail"",2,3),FALSE)"
    Range("I2").Select
    ActiveCell.FormulaR1C1 = "=RC[-3]*RC[-1]"
    Range("H2:I179").Select
    Selection.FillDown
End Sub
```

Once again, you read each statement of the macro from right to left: "Select range H1. Let 'List' be the formula of the active cell. Select range I1. Let 'Gross' be the formula of the active cell. Select range H2. Let the big, long VLOOKUP function be the formula of the active cell." (Notice that the recorder splits long statements by putting a space and an underscore where it breaks the statement to a new line. Notice also that the recorder uses R1C1 notation for the references in the formula so that your macro will work more reliably.) "Select range I2. Let this string be the formula of the active cell. Select range H2:I179. Fill down the selection."

You may not have been able to write all that from scratch without the recorder, but then, you didn't need to. As long as you can read and understand the macro that the recorder created, you can make minor adjustments to it as needed.

Test the AddColumns macro

Run Macro button

1   Activate the Orders (2) worksheet, select columns H and I, and press DELETE.

2   Click the Run Macro button, select AddColumns, and click Run.

Just think, the VLOOKUP formula is in all those cells, and you didn't have to type a formula even once.

Convert the formulas to values

The VLOOKUP formulas are still formulas. You won't want to append these new order records to the order history database with formulas in them, so make the macro turn the formulas into values.

1   Make sure the range H2:I179 is still selected.

2   From the Tools menu, choose Record Macro, Record At Mark.

3   From the Edit menu, choose Copy.

4   From the Edit menu, choose Paste Special, select Values, and click OK.

5   Press ESC.

Stop Macro button

6   Click the Stop Macro button.

You can probably guess what the three new statements added to the macro look like. If you want, you can clear columns H and I and test the macro again.

Task Four: Adjusting the Columns

Ultimately, you're going to want to append the new month's orders to the cumulative order history database. You need to make sure that the columns in the new month's orders match up properly with the columns in the order history database.

Open the order history database

In Lessons 6 and 13 you will learn how to interact with database files without opening them into Excel.

The order history database is in a dBase database file format, but you can still open it into an Excel workbook that you can manipulate directly.

1   From the File menu, choose Open.

2   Select dBase Files from the List Files Of Type list.

3   Select ORDERS.DBF from the File Name list, and click OK.

Compare the columns

1   Look at the column headings in the history database.

They are Date, State, Channel, Price, Category, Units, Net, List, and Gross.

	A	B	C	D	E	F	G	H	I
					ORDERS.DBF				
1	DATE	STATE	CHANNEL	PRICE	CATEGORY	UNITS	NET	LIST	GROSS
2	3/1/91	WA	Wholesale	High	Seattle	40	110.00	2.75	110.00
3	3/1/91	WA	Wholesale	High	Art	25	68.75	2.75	68.75

2   Press CTRL+TAB to activate the LESSON2.XLS window, and look at the column headings on the Orders (2) worksheet.

They are Date, State, Channel, Category, Price, Qty, Dollars, List, and Gross.

	A	B	C	D	E	F	G	H	I
							LESSON2.XLS		
1	Date	State	Channel	Category	Price	Qty	Dollars	List	Gross
2	Mar-94	WA	Retail	Kids	Mid	9	40.50	4.5	40.5
3	Mar-94	WA	Retail	Kids	Low	143	434.06	3.5	500.5

As you might have expected, the columns don't quite match up. The Category and Price columns in the new file are reversed, and the labels for the Units and Net columns are different. You need to swap the order of the Category and Price columns and change the titles of the Qty and Dollars columns to match the official list.

Create a macro to fix the columns

Usually, you should try out the steps for a macro first before you turn on the recorder. The steps in this subtask, however, should be simple enough to try recording directly. Just make an extra copy of the Orders (2) worksheet before turning on the recorder so that you can start over easily.

1   Hold down the CTRL key and drag the Orders (2) tab to the right.

A new copy of the worksheet, labeled Orders (3), appears.

Record Macro button

2   Click the Record Macro button, type **FixColumns** for the name, and click OK.

3   Click the E heading at the top of the Price column, and from the Edit menu, choose the Cut command.

Click here to select the entire column, and then cut the column.

	C	D	E	F	G
1	Channel	Category	Price	Qty	Dollars
2	Retail	Kids	Mid	9	40.50
3	Retail	Kids	Low	143	434.06
4	Retail	Art	High	17	93.50

4   Click the D heading at the top of the Category column, and from the Insert menu, choose the Cut Cells command.

Click here, and insert the Price column.

	C	D	E	F	G
1	Channel	Category	Price	Qty	Dollars
2	Retail	Kids	Mid	9	40.50
3	Retail	Kids	Low	143	434.06
4	Retail	Art	High	17	93.50

5   Select cell F1 (the cell containing the word *Qty*), type **Units**, and press ENTER.

6   Select cell G1 (the cell containing the word *Dollars*), type **Net,** and press ENTER.

7   Click the Stop Macro button.

Stop Macro button

8   Click the tab for Module1, and scroll to the bottom of the sheet to see the macro.

This is what your macro should look like:

```
'
' FixColumns Macro
' Macro recorded 4/7/94 by Tex Miller
'
Sub FixColumns()
    Columns("E:E").Select
    Selection.Cut
    Columns("D:D").Select
    Selection.Insert Shift:=xlToRight
    Range("F1").Select
    ActiveCell.FormulaR1C1 = "Units"
    Range("G1").Select
    ActiveCell.FormulaR1C1 = "Net"
    Range("G2").Select
End Sub
```

Once you get the hang of reading right to left, the macro isn't that hard to follow: "Select column E. Cut the selection. Select column D. Shifting cells to the right, insert the selection. Select range F1. Let 'Units' be the formula of the active cell. Select range G1. Let 'Net' be the formula of the active cell. Select range G2."

Test the FixColumns macro

Even with simple macros, you should always try out the macro to make sure it works. One of the advantages of breaking a large task into small subtasks is that you can easily test each separate piece. Then when you assemble all the pieces, you increase significantly the probability that the whole process will work properly.

1   Delete the Orders (3) worksheet, and make a new copy of Orders (2).

Run Macro button

2   With the new Orders (3) worksheet selected, click the Run Macro button in the Visual Basic toolbar.

3   Select FixColumns from the list of macro names, and click Run. (Or, click Step, and then click the Step Into button repeatedly to watch the macro run.)

Now you have created macros that take care of all the steps necessary for converting the order summary report. You are ready to append the current month's orders to the cumulative order history database.

Task Five: Appending the Orders

Since the Orders (3) worksheet now has an identical column layout to the order history database, you can just copy the worksheet and append it to the first blank row below the database. Of course, you don't want to include the column headings in the copy. As usual, you should go through the steps first without the macro recorder turned on so that you will reduce the probability of recording mistakes.

You will want to include opening the database itself as part of the macro, but now it is already open, so you can skip that step in the practice run.

Select the first blank row below the database

CTRL+TAB moves the top window to the bottom of the stack. CTRL+SHIFT+TAB moves the bottom window to the top of the stack.

1   Press CTRL+SHIFT+TAB to go back to the window with the database.

2   Select cell A1 and press CTRL+STAR to select the entire database. Notice that the word *Database* appears in the Reference area. When you open a dBase file into Excel, the entire database range has the name *Database*.

3   Select cell A1 and press END and then DOWN ARROW to go to the last row of the database.

4   Press DOWN ARROW to select the first cell below the database (cell A3301).

Select this cell, and then reactivate the LESSON2.XLS window.

5   Press CTRL+TAB to go back to the LESSON2.XLS window.

Even though you have left the database window, when you reactivate that window, the same cell will be the active cell.

Copy the current month's orders to the database

1   Select cell A2.

2   While holding down the SHIFT key, press END, then DOWN ARROW, then END, and then RIGHT ARROW to select the entire database.

3   Press CTRL+C to copy the selection.

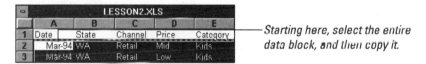

Starting here, select the entire data block, and then copy it.

4   Press CTRL+SHIFT+TAB to go back to the database window.

5   Press CTRL+V to paste the copied rows.

Return to the cell below the database, and paste the current month's orders.

6   Press ESC to remove the copy message from the status bar.

Now the current month's orders are appended to the database. You can close and save the file, but first you must include the new records in the range named *Database*.

Define the new Database range

As previously mentioned, when you open a dBase file into Excel, the range containing the actual database records is automatically named *Database*. When you save the updated ORDERS.DBF file as a dBase file, only the values within the range named Database will be saved. Any other cell values in the file will be discarded. In order to have the new rows saved with the file, you must enlarge the Database range name to include them.

1   With at least one cell in the database selected, press CTRL+STAR to select all the records in the current region.

2   From the Insert menu, choose the Names, Define command.

3   Do *not* select the name Database from the list of names. If you do, the range name will keep its current definition.

4   Type **Database** in the Name box, and click OK.

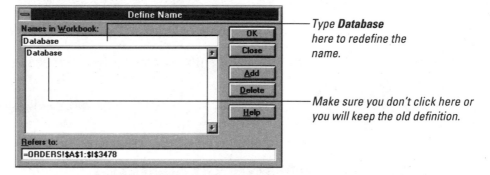

*Type **Database** here to redefine the name.*

Make sure you don't click here or you will keep the old definition.

5   Now the entire database—including the new rows—is included in the Database range name and will be saved with the file.

For now, you don't want to actually save the database with the new records back to the ORDERS.DBF file, because you will want to record and run the macro, so close the database without saving changes.

6   From the File menu, choose Close, and click the No button when asked to save changes.

Those are the steps for appending to and saving the order history database. Now you can record a macro to automate the process.

Create a macro to append to the database

Record Macro button

1   Click the Record Macro button, type **AppendDB** as the name for the macro, and click OK.

2   Open the ORDERS.DBF file. (Tip: it should be in the recently used file list on the File menu.)

3   Select the first blank row by pressing END, then DOWN ARROW, and then DOWN ARROW again.

4   Press CTRL+TAB to get back to the Orders (3) worksheet. The cells to append are probably already selected, but select them again for the sake of the recorder: Select cell A2. While holding down the SHIFT key, press END, then DOWN ARROW, then END, and then RIGHT ARROW.

5   Press CTRL+C to copy the cells, press CTRL+SHIFT+TAB to get back to the database window, press CTRL+V to paste the cells, and then press ESC to remove the copy message.

6   Press CTRL+STAR to select the entire database, and redefine the Database range name using the Name, Define command from the Insert menu.

7   Choose the Close command from the File menu and, again, click No when asked to save changes.

8   Click the Stop Macro button.

9   Click the Module1 tab and scroll to the bottom of the sheet to see the new macro.

Stop Macro button

```
'
' AppendDB Macro
' Macro recorded 4/7/94 by Tex Miller
'
'
Sub AppendDB()
    Workbooks.Open Filename:="C:\EXCELVBA\ORDERS.DBF"
    Selection.End(xlDown).Select
    Range("A3301").Select
    ActiveWindow.ActivateNext
    Range("A2:I179").Select
    Selection.Copy
    ActiveWindow.ActivatePrevious
    ActiveSheet.Paste
    Application.CutCopyMode = False
    Selection.CurrentRegion.Select
    ActiveWorkbook.Names.Add Name:="Database", RefersToR1C1:= _
        "=ORDERS!R1C1:R3478C9"
    ActiveWorkbook.Close
End Sub
```

This macro shows each of the tasks as you did them. If you read each statement from right to left, you should be able to get a general idea of what the macro does.

Step through the AppendDB macro

Now step through the macro to see it work, and then you will see some important changes you should make.

Run Macro button

Step Into button

You can also press F8 to step through a macro.

1   Activate the Orders (3) worksheet.

2   Click the Run Macro button, and select AppendDB from the list of macro names.

3   Click the Step button and resize the Debug window if necessary so that you can watch the macro work.

4   Click the Step Into button repeatedly to step through the macro. When the macro closes the database at the end and asks whether to save changes to the file, click the No button.

5   After the macro is finished, click the Module1 tab again to look at the macro.

The macro should work. You're running it under identical circumstances to those when you recorded it, with the same current month file and the same database file. Look closely at the macro and see some possible problem statements.

Generalize the macro

The first statement of the macro,

```
Workbooks.Open Filename:="C:\EXCELVBA\ORDERS.DBF"
```

contains the full pathname of the file. If you copied your files to a different location, this statement of the macro would fail. If you remove everything but the filename, Excel will open the file from the current directory, which is a much better idea.

▶   Delete everything but the actual filename, ORDERS.DBF, from the pathname in the macro. Be sure to leave the quotation marks.

The next two statements are supposed to select the first blank row below the database. The statement

```
Selection.End(xlDown).Select
```

will select the last row in the database, but the statement

```
Range("A3301").Select
```

will always select cell A3301. Since the database currently ends on row 3300, cell A3301 is the first blank cell this month. But after you append March's rows to the database, you will need a new first blank row. If you don't change this statement before next month when you import April's orders, you will simply replace March's orders with April's. The solution to this problem is a little tricky, so let's leave it until the next section.

The next several statements,

```
ActiveWindow.ActivateNext
Range("A2:I179").Select
Selection.Copy
ActiveWindow. ActivatePrevious
ActiveSheet.Paste
Application.CutCopyMode = False
Selection.CurrentRegion.Select
```

will copy and paste the new orders properly, provided that each new month's order summary file is the same size as the one you used when you recorded the macro. The problem with selecting the correct range if the size of the input file varies is the same problem you saw earlier in this lesson when you added computed columns. You'll have to wait until Lesson 8 to learn the solution.

The statement that defines the Database range name,

```
ActiveWorkbook.Names.Add Name:="Database", RefersToR1C1:= _
    "=ORDERS!R1C1:R3478C9"
```

is a potentially serious problem. This statement sets the name Database to the range that the database occupies at the end of this month. If you don't change this statement before next month, April's orders will be discarded from the database when you save it. The solution is to change the RefersTo value from the text string that the recorder used to the general term *Selection*, which, as you have seen, refers to the entire currently selected range.

▶ Replace the entire RefersToR1C1 text string ("=ORDERS!R1C1:R3478C9") with the word *Selection*. Since the new statement is shorter, you can delete the underline at the end of the first line and put the whole statement on one line.

Click here

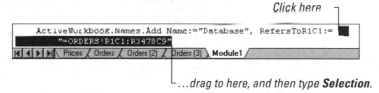

*…drag to here, and then type **Selection**.*

The new statement should look like this:

```
ActiveWorkbook.Names.Add Name:="Database", RefersToR1C1:= Selection
```

The statement that closes the database file,

```
ActiveWorkbook.Close
```

triggers a prompt that asks you if you want to save changes to the file, since you have made changes to it since you opened it. Being able to choose each time whether or not to actually save the database may occasionally be useful. In Lesson 6 you will learn how to close a changed file without triggering a prompt.

Recording a relative movement

Now it's time to solve the problem of finding the first blank row. Let's take a closer look at those first few statements in the macro. The macro recorder did not do a good job of selecting the blank row below the database. After you add more rows to the database, the statement

```
Selection.End(xlDown).Select
```

will select the bottom row, but then the statement

```
Range("A3301").Select
```

will always select the absolute cell A3301 anyway. The problem is simply that when you select a cell, the macro recorder does not know whether you want the absolute cell you selected or a cell relative to where you started. For example, when you select a cell in row 1 to change the label of a column title, you always want the same absolute cell, without regard to where you started. But when you select the first blank cell at the bottom of a database, you want the macro to select a cell relative to where you started.

The macro recorder cannot automatically know whether you want to record absolute cell addresses or relative movements, but you can tell the recorder which kind of selection you want. Use the recorder to replace the offending statement in the macro with one that will work.

1   With the Module1 window active, select the entire offending row and press DELETE.

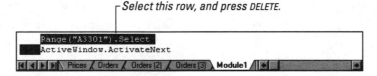

┌Select this row, and press DELETE.

2   Without moving the insertion point, from the Tools menu choose Record Macro, Mark Position For Recording.

This puts an invisible mark into the module. Now you can use the Record At Mark command and the macro will start inserting new commands at the mark.

Tip If you close and reopen a workbook, the macro recorder starts recording new macros on a new module sheet. If you want to record new macros on an existing module sheet, use the Mark Position For Recording command to mark the location for new macros to go. The next time you use the Record Macro button, the new macro will be recorded at the mark.

Since you want to record the action of moving down one cell, you can record the macro from any cell, anywhere.

3   Activate any worksheet, and select any single cell.

4   From the Tools menu, choose Record Macro, Record At Mark.

5   From the Tools menu, choose Record Macro, Use Relative References.

Choose this command to record relative movements.

This command changes the recorder to record all new cell selections *relative* to the original selection.

6   Press the DOWN ARROW key once to record a relative movement.

7   Click the Stop Macro button.

Stop Macro button

8   From the Tools menu, choose the Record Macro, Use Relative References command to clear the check mark from before the command.

This tells the macro recorder to record absolute cell addresses in the future.

9   Activate the macro window, and look at the change.

The new statement you recorded should look like this:

```
ActiveCell.Offset(1, 0).Range("A1").Select
```

This statement means "Select the cell below the active cell." It really does. At this point, you don't need to understand everything about how this statement works. Just trust the recorder. But you may wonder why the statement includes the words *Range("A1")* when it has nothing to do with cell A1. This statement calculates a new range shifted down one cell from the original active cell—the new range consists of only a single cell—and then the macro treats that new range as if it were the entire worksheet and selects cell A1 of that microworksheet! (You can delete *.Range("A1")* from the statement, and it will work exactly the same.)

If you want, you can run the macro again now. It will work exactly as it did before, but now it is ready for next month, when the database will have more records.

Assembling the Pieces

Now you have all the subtasks recorded for carrying out your complex monthly task. Each piece is prepared and tested. Now you get to put them all together. First create a clean copy of the Orders worksheet.

Prepare for the macro

1   Click the Orders (2) tab.

2   Hold down the CTRL key and click the Orders (3) tab.

3   From the Edit menu, choose the Delete Sheet command and confirm that you want to delete the sheets.

4   Hold down the CTRL key and drag the Orders tab to create a new Orders (2) worksheet.

Record running the macros

You may want to run the macros in turn before you create the macro that assembles them.

1   Click the Record Macro button, type **DoAll** as the name, and click OK.

2   Click the Run Macro button.

The Macro dialog box appears with all the macros you have recorded so far. You are ready now to run each of them in turn.

3   Select the first macro, FillLabels, and click Run.

Run Macro button

4   Click the Run Macro button, select the AddDates macro, click Run, and enter **Mar-94** in the input box.

5   Click the Run Macro button, select the AddColumns macro, and click Run.

6   Click the Run Macro button, select the FixColumns macro, and click Run.

7   Click the Run Macro button, select the AppendDB macro, click Run, and choose not to save the database.

Stop Macro button

8   Click the Stop Macro button, activate the Module1 sheet, and scroll to the bottom of the sheet to look at the new macro.

```
'
' DoAll Macro
' Macro recorded 4/7/94 by Tex Miller
'
'
Sub DoAll()
    Application.Run Macro:="LESSON2.XLS!FillLabels"
    Application.Run Macro:="LESSON2.XLS!AddDates"
    Application.Run Macro:="LESSON2.XLS!AddColumns"
    Application.Run Macro:="LESSON2.XLS!FixColumns"
    Application.Run Macro:="LESSON2.XLS!AppendDB"
End Sub
```

Following the standard rules for reading macros, you read the first statement as "With 'FillLabels' as the macro, run the application," and so forth for the rest of the statements. The DoAll macro runs each of the subtasks in turn. The subtasks, or submacros, are known as *subroutines*. You start macros with the word *Sub* so that you can turn them into subroutines simply by running them from another macro. (In Lesson 5, you will learn a more elegant way to run subroutines.)

Test the completed macro

1   Delete the Orders (2) worksheet and re-create it.

2   Click the Run Macro button, select the DoAll macro, click Run, and enter **Mar-94** into the input box.

Don't change the database so that you can review this lesson in the future.

3   When prompted to save changes to the database, click No.

4   Save the LESSON2.XLS workbook and exit Microsoft Excel. You've worked hard and deserve a rest. Take the rest of the day off.

Lesson Summary

To	Do this
Select blank cells in the current selection	Choose the Go To command from the Edit menu, click the Special button, and select the Blanks option.
Watch a macro execute one statement at a time	Select the macro name in the Macro dialog box and click Step. Click the Step Into button in the Visual Basic toolbar to execute the next statement.
Prompt the user of a macro for a value while the macro runs	Use the InputBox function.
Record movements relative to the active cell	From the Tools menu, choose the Record Macro submenu, and put a check mark next to the Use Relative References command.
Create a macro to run other macros	Turn on the macro recorder, run the other macros, and turn of the macro recorder.

For more information on	See
Editing Visual Basic macros	Chapter 2, "Editing Recorded Macros," in the *Microsoft Excel Visual Basic User's Guide*.
Stepping through a macro	Chapter 8, "Testing and Debugging Your Code," in the *Microsoft Excel Visual Basic User's Guide*.

Preview of the Next Lesson

In this lesson, you learned how to break a complex task into pieces, record and test each piece, and then pull all the pieces together into a single macro. You ended up with a macro that does a lot of work, but it was a lot of work to make the macro. In the next lesson you will learn how to record a single simple macro and then get lots and lots of work out of it.

Make a Macro Do Repetitive Tasks

Walk outside and stand in front of your car. Look down at the tread on the right front tire. See that little piece of gum stuck to the tread. Well, imagine you are that little piece of gum. Imagine what it feels like when the car first starts to move. You climb up, higher and higher, like a Ferris wheel. Whee! Then the pure thrill as you come back down the other side. Who needs Disneyland, anyway? But don't you think that just possibly by the five hundredth or the five thousandth or the five millionth revolution, you might start to get a little tiny bit bored? Thwack, thwack, thwack, thwack. It really could get old after a while.

Just about anything you do is interesting—the first few times you do it. Repetition, however, can bring boredom. When you start doing the same task over and over, you start wanting somebody—or something—else to do it. This lesson will teach you how to record repetitive tasks as Visual Basic macros, and then turn them into automatic machines that work relentlessly to improve your life.

You will learn how to:

- Make decisions with a macro.
- Run a macro multiple times in a loop.
- Format exception cells with a macro.
- Print multiple charts with a macro.

Estimated lesson time: 50 minutes

Start the lesson

▶   Start Microsoft Excel and close all open workbooks, including hidden workbooks such as the personal macro workbook. (Use the Unhide command from the Window menu or the File menu to find hidden workbooks.)

Creating a Pivot Table

In your capacity as bookkeeper and financial analyst for Miller Textiles, you've been wondering how the different shirt design lines are doing in different geographical areas and in different sales channels. You have an order history database that contains the information you need to analyze.

In the first part of the lesson, you will create a pivot table to show the order units by category. Then you will work through the pivot table, highlighting cells that contain exceptionally high sales figures. First you will highlight the exceptions by hand, and then you will create Visual Basic macros that do more and more of the work for you.

Later in the lesson, you will create a different pivot table and produce charts from the data in that table. Once again, you will create Visual Basic macros that will take care of the repetitive parts of the task for you.

Create a cross-tabulating pivot table

1   From the File menu, choose Open, change to the directory containing the files for this book, type **ORDERS.DBF** as the filename, and click Open.

The order history database opens.

2   From the Data menu, choose PivotTable.

In Lesson 5, you will learn how to use an external database directly as a source for a pivot table.

Step 1 of the PivotTable Wizard appears, with the Microsoft Excel List Or Database option selected as the default. Even though the order history database is a dBase file, once you open it into an Excel workbook, it acts like an Excel database.

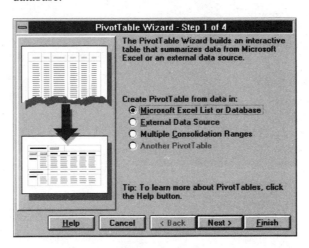

3   Click the Next button.

Step 2 of the PivotTable Wizard appears, with the name Database already entered as the default range. If the active workbook contains a range named Database, the PivotTable Wizard offers that range as the default.

4   Click the Next button.

Excel takes a few seconds to read the data from the database, and then Step 3 of the PivotTable Wizard appears with a list of field names.

5   Drag the Category field tile to the Column area; drag the State, Channel, and Price field tiles to the Row area; drag the Units field tile to the Data area; and click the Next button.

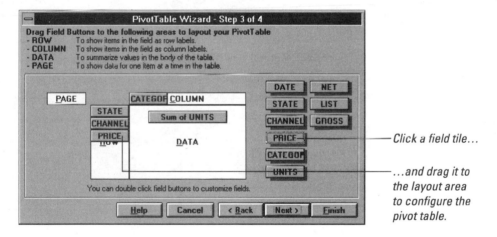

Click a field tile...

...and drag it to the layout area to configure the pivot table.

The final step of the PivotTable Wizard appears. The PivotTable Starting Cell box is blank. If you leave it blank, Excel will create a new worksheet for the new pivot table.

6 Leave the check boxes alone, and click Finish.

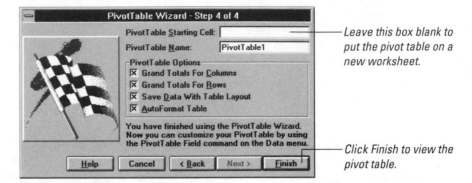

Leave this box blank to put the pivot table on a new worksheet.

Click Finish to view the pivot table.

After a few seconds, the pivot table appears, with the different states, channels, and price grades down the left, the categories across the top, and the units in each cell of the table.

	A	B	C	D	E	F	G	H
1	Sum of UNITS			CATEGORY				
2	STATE	CHANNEL	PRICE	Art	Dinosaurs	Environment	Humorous	Kids
3	AZ	Retail	High	337	0	0	0	0
4			Low	0	1368	245	431	532
5			Mid	1450	1049	431	116	403
6		Retail Total		1787	2417	676	547	935
7		Wholesale	High	2065	0	0	0	0
8			Low	0	2330	1470	780	850
9			Mid	1440	3445	1210	250	1235
10		Wholesale Total		3505	5775	2680	1030	2085
11	AZ Total			5292	8192	3356	1577	3020
12	CA	Retail	High	5402	0	0	0	0
13			Low	0	2205	1560	960	414
14			Mid	2445	2175	2280	1195	454
15		Retail Total		7847	4380	3840	2155	868

Sheet1 / ORDERS /

7 Double click the worksheet tab for the new pivot table worksheet, type **Categories** as the name for the sheet, and click OK.

8 Use the right mouse button to click the tab labeled ORDERS, the sheet with the original database. Choose the Delete command and confirm the deletion.

Once the pivot table has read the data from the original data source, it doesn't need the data source any more unless the data source changes and you want to refresh the data in the pivot table.

9 From the File menu, choose Save As, type **LESSON3** as the name for the file, select Microsoft Excel Workbook as the file type, and click OK. If the Summary Info dialog box appears, click OK.

Convert the pivot table to percentages

This pivot table displays a lot of information, but you still can't quickly see relationships among the different design categories. Part of the problem is that the variation in total units from state to state masks any patterns. Convert the pivot table to display percentages so that you can compare the relationships more easily.

1   Select cell A1, the cell with the label Sum of Units.

2   Click the PivotTable Field button on the Query And Pivot toolbar.

The PivotTable Field dialog box appears with information about the Sum of Units field.

3   Click the Options button to expand the dialog box.

4   From the Show Data As list, select the % Of Row option.

5   In the Name box, select the word *Sum* and replace it with **Percent**.

PivotTable Field button

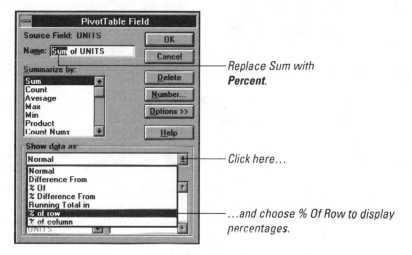

*Replace Sum with **Percent**.*

Click here...

...and choose % Of Row to display percentages.

Click OK to convert the pivot table to show percentages instead of absolute numbers.

Hide the Grand Total column

When the pivot table calculates percent-of-row values, the Grand Total column at the far right becomes, by definition, filled with 100%. You could tell the PivotTable Wizard not to display the Grand Total column, except that the pivot table needs the grand totals in order to calculate the percent-of-row values. If you remove the Grand Total column from the table, all the values in the table change to #NA. You can't remove the Grand Total column, but you can hide it.

1   Select any cell in column K, the Grand Total column.

2   From the Format menu, choose Column, Hide.

Now nobody has to see that the grand total is 100 percent of the total for the row.

Making Decisions with a Macro

Even with the numbers converted to percentages, the mass of data is so big that you still have a hard time deciphering relationships. Excel's formatting capabilities can be very useful. Change each cell in which the number is more than 30 percent of the total to yellow.

Highlight exceptions by hand

1   Select cell D3, the first value in the first column. Since the value in this cell is 43.04%, this cell qualifies for a new color.

Color button

2   Click the arrow on the Color button in the Formatting toolbar, and click the yellow color in the sixth box in the top row of the palette.

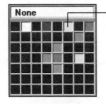

— *Click here to change the Color button default to yellow.*

3   Search down column D for the next cell that is greater than 30%. It is D5.

4   Select cell D5, and click the Color button. You don't have to open the palette any more, since yellow is now the default color for the Color button.

5   Find the next qualifying cell and format it. Find and format the next one after that. Find and format the next one after that.

Formatting a cell to get a special visual effect is really fun—the first two or three times. But once you start repeating any action over and over, even one as delightful as formatting a cell, a certain amount of boredom does seem to creep in.

Make a macro format a single cell

Record a macro that simplifies your task just a little. Without any macro, you look at each cell in the column, decide whether it qualifies for the formatting, format it if it does, and then move down to the next cell. Start by recording a macro that formats a cell and moves to the next cell down. (At this stage, you still have to find each qualifying cell yourself.)

Or choose the Toolbars command from the View menu and select the Visual Basic check box.

1   If the Visual Basic toolbar is not visible, use the right mouse button to click any toolbar, and choose Visual Basic.

2   Select the next cell that should be formatted. Do not select a cell that is already yellow.

3   Click the Record Macro button, type **FormatCell** as the name of the macro, and click the Options button.

Record Macro button

4   Set CTRL+SHIFT+A as the shortcut key for the macro, and click OK to start the macro recorder.

5   Click the Color button.

6   From the Tools menu, choose the Record Macro command. If the Use Relative References command does *not* have a check mark by it, choose that command. If the Use Relative References command already has a check mark, press ESC repeatedly to get out of the menus without executing a command.

Make sure this command has a check mark.

7   Press the DOWN ARROW key once.

8   Click the Stop Macro button.

Stop Macro button

9   Click the Module1 tab to look at the macro.

```
'
' FormatCell Macro
' Macro recorded 4/7/94 by Tex Miller
'
' Keyboard Shortcut: Ctrl+A
'
Sub FormatCell()
    With Selection.Interior
        .ColorIndex = 6
        .Pattern = xlSolid
    End With
    ActiveCell.Offset(1, 0).Range("A1").Select
End Sub
```

This macro sets the current cell, the *Selection*, to a solid yellow color. Since yellow is the sixth item in the color palette, the macro sets *ColorIndex* to 6 to get yellow. After setting the color of the current cell, the macro moves down one cell, relative to the original active cell.

Format a cell with the macro

1   Switch back to the Categories worksheet.

2   Scan down column D to find the next cell greater than 30%, and select it.

3   Press CTRL+SHIFT+A to run your macro.

Using this macro is slightly better, perhaps, than clicking the Color button. But you still have to find and select each qualifying cell manually.

Make the macro make a decision

When you color some cells yellow and leave other cells plain, you are making a decision. To automate this formatting task further, you need to get the macro to make the decision. The macro recorder cannot put decisions into your macro. You must add the decision yourself. You want the macro to decide whether the current cell qualifies for the color formatting.

After you rename a macro, the shortcut key may try to run the old macro name. If this happens, simply press the shortcut key again to run the macro.

1   Click the Module1 tab, double click the word *FormatCell* in the Sub statement, and type **ChooseFormat** to change the name of the macro.

2   Press END to move the insertion point to the end of the statement, press ENTER, and then press TAB.

Your screen should look something like this:

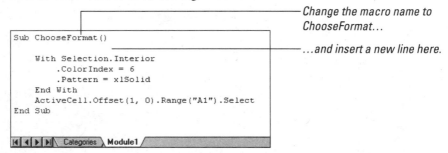

Change the macro name to ChooseFormat...

...and insert a new line here.

```
Sub ChooseFormat()

    With Selection.Interior
        .ColorIndex = 6
        .Pattern = xlSolid
    End With
    ActiveCell.Offset(1, 0).Range("A1").Select
End Sub
```

3   Type **If ActiveCell > .3 Then** to decide whether the active cell is greater than 30%.

Tip If you type keywords—such as If, ActiveCell, and Then—in all lowercase letters, Visual Basic changes appropriate letters of the keywords to uppercase letters when you press the DOWN ARROW key to leave the line. Seeing the words change is a good confirmation that you spelled them correctly.

The next four statements, which format the cell, should run only if the active cell is greater than 30%. If you indent them, you will be able to tell that they are controlled by the If statement.

4   Press DOWN ARROW, then HOME, and then TAB. Repeat this step four times to indent each of the next four lines.

Indenting the statements reminds *you* that these statements will run only if the cell qualifies, but indenting does not tell the *macro* how to run.

5   With the insertion point at the beginning of the End With statement, press END. Then press ENTER to create a new line, and press BACKSPACE to align the insertion point with the If statement.

6 Type **End If**.

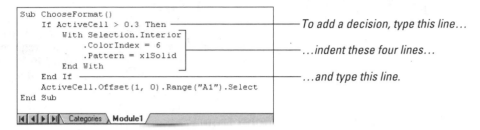

```
Sub ChooseFormat()
    If ActiveCell > 0.3 Then ──────────────────── To add a decision, type this line...
        With Selection.Interior
            .ColorIndex = 6
            .Pattern = xlSolid                    ...indent these four lines...
        End With
    End If ──────────────────────────────────── ...and type this line.
    ActiveCell.Offset(1, 0).Range("A1").Select
End Sub
```
Categories \ Module1 /

Now your macro will check the current cell, decide whether it qualifies for a color change, change the color if it does, and then select the next cell down.

Watch the macro make a decision

1 Switch back to the Categories worksheet, and select cell D26.

Cell D26 qualifies for formatting, but cell D27 below it does not.

Run Macro button

2 Click the Run Macro button, select ChooseFormat, and click Step.

3 Reduce the size of the Debug window so that you can see the worksheet.

The *Sub ChooseFormat( )* line of the macro has a box around it.

4 Click the Step Into button to move the box to the If statement.

5 Click the Step Into button again.

Step Into button

Because the value in cell D26—the active cell—is greater than 30%, the macro steps down into the indented lines to the With statement.

6 Click the Step Into button repeatedly until the end of the macro, or click the Resume Macro button to run the rest of the macro without stopping.

The active cell is now cell D27, which does not qualify for the formatting.

Resume Macro button

7 Once again, click the Run Macro button, select ChooseFormat, and click Step.

8 Step through all the lines of the macro.

When the macro gets to the If statement, it jumps directly to the End If statement because the active cell is not greater than 30%.

9 Press CTRL+SHIFT+A repeatedly until you get to the bottom of the values in column D.

The macro takes care of the formatting decision for the active cell and then moves into position to run again. This macro is significantly more convenient (and reliable) than manually searching through the cells looking for numbers to format. But formatting the cells is still a repetitive task. Running the macro over and over, 60 times for 60 rows, seems like a task that could be automated.

Repeating an Action with a Macro

If you write a macro in such a way that each time it ends you can run it again, you can put the macro into a loop. Probably the most important requirement for putting a macro into a loop is that the macro gets everything ready for the next time around before it quits. The ChooseFormat macro does get everything ready for the next time around, so put it into a loop.

Make the macro run around in circles

You learned earlier that the macro recorder cannot put decisions into your macro automatically. In the same way, you have to add loops to your macro without the assistance of the macro recorder. That's OK. You can handle it.

1   Click the Module1 tab, double click the word *ChooseFormat*, and type **FormatLoop**.

2   Press END to move the insertion point to the end of the statement, press ENTER, and then press TAB.

Your screen should look something like this:

```
Sub FormatLoop()

    If ActiveCell > 0.3 Then
        With Selection.Interior
            .ColorIndex = 6
            .Pattern = xlSolid
        End With
    End If
    ActiveCell.Offset(1, 0).Range("A1").Select
End Sub
```

Change the macro name to FormatLoop, and insert a new line below it.

3   Type **Do**.

The word *Do* tells the macro to start a loop.

You should indent each of the lines controlled by the Do statement to make the macro easy to read, just as you indented the lines controlled by the If statement.

4   Press DOWN ARROW, press HOME, and then press TAB. Repeat this step a total of seven times to indent each of the seven lines controlled by the loop. (Indent everything except the *End Sub* statement at the end.)

Indenting the statements helps you remember you that these statements are part of the loop, but you still have to tell the macro when to go back up to the top of the loop.

5   With the insertion point at the beginning of the *ActiveCell.Offset* statement, press END. Then press ENTER to create a new line, and press BACKSPACE to align the insertion point with the Do statement.

6   Type **Loop**.

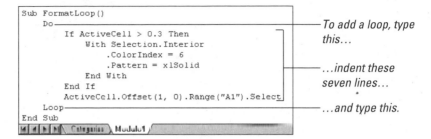

```
Sub FormatLoop()
    Do
        If ActiveCell > 0.3 Then
            With Selection.Interior
                .ColorIndex = 6
                .Pattern = xlSolid
            End With
        End If
        ActiveCell.Offset(1, 0).Range("A1").Select
    Loop
End Sub
```

To add a loop, type this...

...indent these seven lines...

...and type this.

Now the macro will run over and over all by itself.

Watch the macro run around in circles

Run Macro button

Step Into button

Resume Macro button

1   Activate the Categories worksheet and select cell E3, the first value in the Dinosaurs column.

2   Click the Run Macro button, select FormatLoop, and click Step.

3   Click the Step Into button repeatedly to watch the macro run down to the Loop statement and move back to the Do statement to continue.

4   When you are bored with watching the macro loop, click the Resume Macro button to let the macro run without stepping.

The macro quickly works through the rest of the cells—but then it just keeps on going and going. The macro really is running around in circles now!

5   Hold down the CTRL key and press BREAK.

6   Click the End button in the dialog box that appears, and scroll back up to the top of the worksheet.

The loop does exactly what you told it to do. It runs the original part of the macro over and over. Just like the magical brooms gone awry in the legend of the sorcerer's apprentice. This kind of loop is called an *infinite* loop. It keeps running until something like CTRL+BREAK stops it.

Make the macro stop gracefully

Your loop is like an albatross. It is beautiful, graceful, and powerful while it flies but looks like a clumsy, bumbling idiot when it lands. You need to tell your loop when to stop. How do *you* know when to stop? Well, you stop when you get to the bottom. But how do you know it's the bottom? It's the bottom when there's nothing else in the cells. So, you want the loop to keep going until the active cell has nothing in it.

1   Activate the Module1 sheet, select the name FormatLoop, and type **FormatColumn** as the new name for the macro.

2   Put the insertion point right after the word *Do*, and type a space.

3   Type **Until ActiveCell = ""**.

A set of quotation marks matches an empty cell.

```
Sub FormatColumn()
    Do Until ActiveCell = ""
        If ActiveCell > 0.3 Then
            With Selection.Interior
                .ColorIndex = 6
                .Pattern = xlSolid
            End With
        End If
        ActiveCell.Offset(1, 0).Range("A1").Select
    Loop
End Sub
```

To stop the loop, use the Until keyword.

TimeSeries / Categories \ **Module1** /

4   Activate the worksheet, select cell F3—the top cell in the next column—and press CTRL+SHIFT+A to run the macro.

The macro works down the whole column and then stops when it reaches the first blank cell at the bottom. Perfect.

5   Select cell G3, and press CTRL+SHIFT+A to run the macro again.

With this macro, you don't have to check each cell individually. Your job is reduced to selecting the top cell in each column and running the macro.

Make the macro find the next column

Moving the active cell up to the top of the next column is still somewhat bothersome. You can use the macro recorder to add the extra commands needed to move to the top of the next column.

1   Activate the Module1 sheet, position the insertion point at the beginning of the End Sub statement, and choose the Record Macro, Mark Position For Recording command from the Tools menu.

2   Activate the pivot table worksheet. Select the cell below the bottom of the last formatted column (cell G63), the same cell as when the macro stops.

3   From the Tools menu, open the Record Macro submenu. If the Use Relative References command does not have a check mark by it, choose that command; otherwise, continue to step 4.

4   From the Tools menu, choose the Record Macro, Record At Mark command.

5   Press the RIGHT ARROW key, and then press the UP ARROW key to get to the bottom value in column H (cell H62).

Press the END key, and then press the UP ARROW key to select the heading cell at the top of column H (cell I2).

6   Press the DOWN ARROW key to select the first cell in column H that contains a number (cell H3).

7   Click the Stop Macro button and activate the Module1 sheet to look at the macro.

The recorder added three new lines to the bottom of your macro, just above the *End Sub* statement.

Stop Macro button

```
Sub FormatColumn()
    Do Until ActiveCell = ""
        If ActiveCell > 0.3 Then
            With Selection.Interior
                .ColorIndex = 6
                .Pattern = xlSolid
            End With
        End If
        ActiveCell.Offset(1, 0).Range("A1").Select
    Loop
    ActiveCell.Offset(-1, 1).Range("A1").Select
    Selection.End(xlUp).Select
    ActiveCell.Offset(1, 0).Range("A1").Select
End Sub
```

The first new line moves the active cell one up and one to the right. The second new line moves the active cell to the top of the column. The third new line moves the active cell down one, ready to run the macro again. The way the recorder creates relative selections may be a little hard to understand, but you didn't have to write them, so as long as they work, who's to complain?

Run the macro to go to the next column

1   Activate the Categories worksheet.

The active cell should be cell H3.

2   Press CTRL+SHIFT+A to run the macro.

The macro formats the eligible cells in column H and makes cell I3 the active cell.

3   Press CTRL+SHIFT+A to run the macro again, then once more to format the rest of the table.

Make the macro format the entire block

The FormatColumn macro now formats a whole column and leaves the worksheet ready to run the macro again. Because you can run the FormatColumn macro over and over, you can put it into a loop so that it formats the entire block with one push of a button. First, think about how you know when to stop running the FormatColumn macro. Once again, you stop when you get to a blank cell— this time when you get to a column that has a blank cell at the top.

1   Click the Module1 tab, double click the word *FormatColumn*, and type **FormatAll**.

2   Insert the statement **Do Until ActiveCell = ""** as the first line in the macro.

3   Insert the statement **Loop** immediately before the End Sub statement in the macro.

4   Indent the 12 lines controlled by this loop.

The macro should look something like this:

```
Sub FormatAll()
    Do Until ActiveCell = ""
        Do Until ActiveCell = ""
            If ActiveCell > 0.3 Then
                With Selection.Interior
                    . ColorIndex = 6
                    . Pattern = xlSolid
                End With
            End If
            ActiveCell.Offset(1, 0).Range("A1").Select
        Loop
        ActiveCell.Offset(-1, 1).Range("A1").Select
        Selection.End(xlUp).Select
        ActiveCell.Offset(1, 0).Range("A1").Select
    Loop
End Sub
```

This macro is now able to format the entire block. Try it out.

Run the macro that formats the entire block

1   Activate the Categories worksheet.

The block is formatted already. You need to unformat it so that you can start over.

2   Select cell A1, hold down the CTRL key, and press the STAR key on the numeric keypad.

Color button

3   Click the arrow by the Color button to display the color palette, and click the box labeled None.

Note Field tiles in a pivot table are shaded using standard cell formatting. You can clear or change the formatting of pivot table field tiles. Whenever the field table recalculates, the formatting of the field tiles changes back to the default.

---

4   Select cell D3, the first cell with a value, and press CTRL+SHIFT+A.

The macro formats all the appropriate cells in all the columns and then quits when it gets to the first blank column. The macro even formats all the cells in the Grand Total column (they all are greater than 30%), but since the Grand Total column is hidden, that doesn't really matter.

By starting with a simple recorded macro and adding decisions and loops, you can make a powerful machine for eliminating repetition—and errors.

You also learned that your Humorous line of shirts is not selling very well anywhere. Maybe that's because your funny shirts just aren't very funny. Or maybe the problem is that the Humorous line is your newest line—you've been selling it for only a year. Make some charts to compare orders for the different categories over time.

Copying Rows from a Database

You need to make a presentation to the owner of Miller Textiles, and you want to have a set of overhead transparencies to use during the presentation. You want one chart for each category of shirt designs, showing the month-by-month orders over time.

Create a time series pivot table

First you need to create a new pivot table that displays the orders by category over time. You could just modify the existing pivot table, but you want to keep the current one, too. You could reopen the database and start over with a new pivot table, but Excel provides an easier way. When the PivotTable Wizard created the first pivot table, it copied all the data from the database into a special storage area for that pivot table. You can create a second pivot table that shares that same backstage storage area.

PivotTable Wizard button

1 Activate the Categories worksheet and select cell M2—or any cell that is *not* part of the current pivot table.

2 Click the PivotTable Wizard button.

3 In Step 1 of the PivotTable Wizard, select the option labeled Another PivotTable, and click Next.

4 In Step 2, the name of the current pivot table—probably PivotTable1—should already be highlighted. Click Next.

5 In Step 3, drag the Date field tile to the Column area, drag the Category field tile to the Row area, drag the Net field tile to the Data area, and click Next.

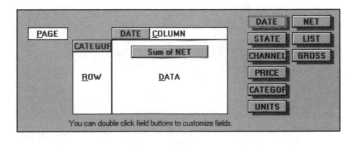

6 In Step 4, clear the box labeled PivotTable Starting Cell, clear the check box labeled Grand Total For Rows, and click Finish.

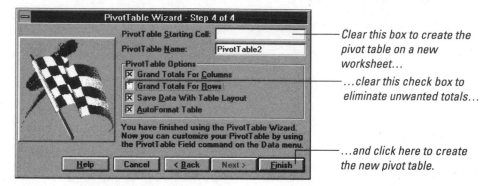

Clear this box to create the pivot table on a new worksheet...

...clear this check box to eliminate unwanted totals...

...and click here to create the new pivot table.

With the PivotTable Starting Cell box left blank, the PivotTable Wizard creates a new worksheet for the new pivot table.

7 Double click the worksheet tab for the new sheet, type **TimeSeries** as the name of the worksheet, and click OK.

This pivot table shows the total net order dollars for each category by month over the last few years. You want to print a chart for each row in this table.

Create a staging area

The easiest way to chart various rows from a list is to create a single "staging area" range—a range where you copy the data needed to make one chart. You then link a single chart to the staging area range and change from one chart to the next by copying the appropriate values into the staging area.

1 Select cell A2, the cell with the Category tile.

2 While holding down the SHIFT key, press the DOWN ARROW key, then press the END key, and then press the RIGHT ARROW key.

The selection should extend from cell A2 through cell AK3.

3 Press CTRL+C to copy the selection.

Select this range, and press CTRL+C to copy it.

4 Select cell A15—a few rows under the pivot table—and press ENTER to paste the dates and the Art category values.

This copy is not linked to the pivot table in any way. It is simply a copy suitable for charting. It is your staging area. You will paste values from different rows of the pivot table into the second row of the staging area. To make the staging area easier to use, name the second row.

5   Select the range A16:AK16.

6   In the Reference area to the left of the formula bar, type **Stage,** and press ENTER.

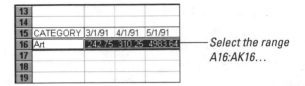

*Select the range
A16:AK16...*

*and type a name for
the range here.*

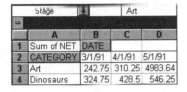

With the staging area prepared and named, you can now build a macro to put values from a different category row into it.

Copy the next row into the staging area

You can copy a row from the pivot table into the staging area, and the chart will automatically change. You don't need to copy the dates, because each row uses the same dates. You do need to copy the category name, because each row has a different category name.

You want to create a macro you can run again each time it stops. First work through the steps without the macro recorder turned on.

1   Select cell A3, the cell with Art as the category heading. You will want to start running the macro from this position.

2   Select all the values in the current row (the range A3:AK3).

3   Press CTRL+C to copy the selection.

4   From the Edit menu, choose the Go To command, select the range Stage, and click OK to change the selection to the staging area.

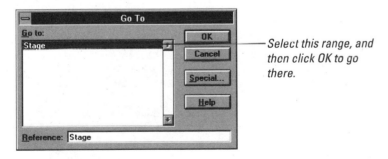

*Select this range, and
then click OK to go
there.*

5   Press ENTER to paste the values.

6   From the Edit menu, choose the Go To command, and click OK without making any changes in the dialog box.

The default reference in the Go To dialog box is the range that was selected before you last used the Go To command.

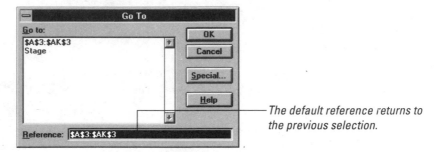

The default reference returns to the previous selection.

7   Press the DOWN ARROW key to select the next category label.

Make the macro copy the next row

The steps in the previous section allow you to copy the current row to the staging area and get into position to copy the next row. Now record those steps into a macro.

1   From the Tools menu, choose the Record Macro command and make sure that the Use Relative References command has a check mark.

2   Click the Record Macro button, type **CopyToStage** as the name of the macro, and click Options.

Record Macro button

3   Enter CTRL+SHIFT+C as the shortcut key for the macro, and click OK.

4   Carry out steps 2 through 7 from the previous section.

5   Click the Stop Macro button, activate the Module1 sheet, and look at the macro.

Stop Macro button

```
'
' CopyToStage Macro
' Macro recorded 4/7/94 by Tex Miller
'
' Keyboard Shortcut: Ctrl+C
'
Sub CopyToStage()
    ActiveCell.Range("A1:AK1").Select
    Selection.Copy
    Application.Goto Reference:="Stage"
    ActiveSheet.Paste
    Application.CutCopyMode = False
    Application.Goto Reference:="R3C1:R3C37"
    ActiveCell.Offset(1, 0).Range("A1").Select
End Sub
```

Most of this macro should be reasonably familiar—or at least somewhat decipherable. A few lines warrant some discussion. The statement

```
ActiveCell.Range("A1:AK1").Select
```

appears to select the range A1:AK1. Of course, it really doesn't. (I don't know *how* you could *possibly* think that this statement selects the range A1:AK1.) What it really does is treat the current active cell (which was cell A3 when you recorded the macro) as if it is the top left cell of a new *virtual* worksheet, and then it selects the range A1:AK1 of that virtual worksheet, which ends up being range A3:AK3 of the real worksheet. As you run the macro from different starting locations, the virtual worksheet changes, but the macro stays the same.

The statement

```
Application.Goto Reference:="Stage"
```

In Lesson 9 you will learn about the Application object.

is equivalent to selecting the Go To command from the Edit menu. You can read it as "With 'Stage' as the reference, go to." Sometimes when a statement in a macro starts with the word *Application*, you just have to ignore that word.

You might wonder why the macro doesn't say something like

```
Range("Stage").Select
```

instead of using Goto. In fact, you could replace the statement *Application.Goto Reference:="Stage"* with the statement *Range("Stage").Select*, and this part of the macro would still work fine. The problem with using Select instead of Goto is that when you use the Goto command, Excel stores the address of the range you started with. When you use the Goto command again, you can go back to the same range. When you use Select, Excel does not save the address of the range you came from. The Goto command's ability to remember where it came from makes it a powerful secret weapon when making macros that have to switch back and forth between two ranges.

For more information about R1C1 notation, see "References Make Formulas More Powerful" in the Microsoft Excel User's Guide.

The statement

```
Application.Goto Reference:="R3C1:R3C37"
```

is much like the earlier Goto statement. This Goto statement goes back to the range in the pivot table. The address *R3C1:R3C37* is an absolute address in R1C1 notation. It means the same as "A3:AK3" in A1 notation. The Goto command always records with absolute addresses, even when you set the recorder to use relative references. Changing the Use Relative References setting won't help in this case. Both absolute and relative references are wrong for this statement. You don't want the absolute range A3:AK3, and you don't want the relative range always 12 rows above the staging area. You want the macro to go *back* to wherever it came from.

Make the macro return to where it came from

When you record the Goto command, you always get an absolute reference. Interactively, if you use the Goto command without typing or selecting a reference, the command goes back to the previous location. But the macro recorder has no way of knowing whether you typed the cell address into the dialog box or whether you used the default previous location. So the recorder assumes you typed in the address. You just need to tell the macro that you don't want a specific address.

▶ Delete the argument *Reference:="R3C1:R3C37"* from the Goto statement in the macro. The resulting line should be simply *Application.Goto*.

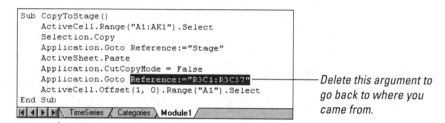

Delete this argument to go back to where you came from.

```
Sub CopyToStage()
    ActiveCell.Range("A1:AK1").Select
    Selection.Copy
    Application.Goto Reference:="Stage"
    ActiveSheet.Paste
    Application.CutCopyMode = False
    Application.Goto Reference:="R3C1:R3C37"
    ActiveCell.Offset(1, 0).Range("A1").Select
End Sub
```

When you remove the reference argument from the Goto statement, it uses the saved address of the previous location. Of course, in order for the Goto command to have a previous location, you have to have used the Goto command at least once before.

Run the CopyToStage macro

Now the macro is ready to copy one line at a time.

1   Select cell A3, the label for the Category row.

2   Press CTRL+SHIFT+C to run the macro once.

The macro should copy the Art row to the staging area and then return to the Dinosaurs row.

3   Press CTRL+SHIFT+C to run the macro again. Repeat this step for each remaining row in the table.

Each time you run the macro, it gets everything ready to run again before it quits.

Put the macro into a loop

When you run the macro once for each row, you quit when you get to a blank cell. You can make the macro watch for the blank cell.

1   Activate the Module1 sheet, select *CopyToStage*, and replace it with **CopyAll** to rename the macro.

2   Insert the statement **Do Until ActiveCell = ""** as the first statement in the body of the macro.

3   Indent each line in the body of the macro.

4   Insert the statement **Loop** before the *End Sub* statement.

The finished macro should look like this:

```
Sub CopyAll()
    Do Until ActiveCell = ""
        ActiveCell.Range("A1:AK1").Select
        Selection.Copy
        Application.Goto Reference:="Stage"
        ActiveSheet.Paste
        Application.CutCopyMode = False
        Application.Goto
        ActiveCell.Offset(1, 0).Range("A1").Select
    Loop
End Sub
```

Run the CopyAll macro

1   Activate the TimeSeries worksheet, and select cell A3.

2   Press CTRL+SHIFT+C to run the macro.

The macro quickly copies each row in turn into the staging area. The macro runs very fast. Maybe too fast. You don't have anything to remember it by when it is finished. What you really want is a set of printed transparencies, with a chart for each category. This macro copies values to the staging area nicely, but it doesn't produce any charts.

Creating Charts from the Database

Now that the macro can loop through the categories, copying the values for each category to the staging area, creating a set of charts from the pivot table will be easy.

Link a chart to the staging area

First link a chart to the staging area. You don't need to include this in the macro because you need to do it only once for the whole loop.

1   Select cell A15 and press CTRL+STAR to select the entire staging area.

You can create a chart as a new sheet in one step by pressing F11.

2 From the Insert menu, choose the Chart, As New Sheet command, and click the Finish button in the first ChartWizard dialog box.

Select this range, choose Chart, As New Sheet from the Insert menu...

...and click Finish.

This is the chart. The default format is good enough for this presentation.

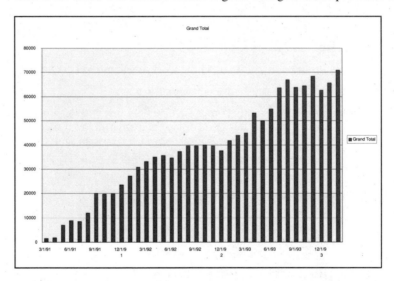

3 Click the TimeSeries worksheet tab to activate the worksheet with the pivot table.

Now you have the chart. You just need to add the steps to the macro to switch to the chart page, print it, and switch back to the pivot table.

Make the macro print several charts

1 Activate the Module1 sheet, and change the name of the CopyAll macro to **PrintCharts**.

2   Put the insertion point at the beginning of the second *Application.Goto* statement.

```
Sub PrintCharts()
    Do Until ActiveCell = ""
        ActiveCell.Range("A1:AK1").Select
        Selection.Copy
        Application.Goto Reference:="Stage"
        ActiveSheet.Paste
        Application.CutCopyMode = False
        Application.Goto
        ActiveCell.Offset(1, 0).Range("A1").Select
    Loop
End Sub
```

— *Put the insertion point here.*

Chart1 / TimeSeries / Categories \ **Module1** /

3   From the Tools menu, choose Record Macro, Mark Position For Recording.

4   Activate the TimeSeries worksheet, and choose Record Macro, Record At Mark from the Tools menu.

5   Press CTRL+PAGE UP to switch to the chart sheet.

6   Click the Print Preview button to simulate printing the chart, and then click the Close button.

7   Press CTRL+PAGE DOWN to switch back to the TimeSeries worksheet.

8   Click the Stop Macro button.

9   Activate the Module1 sheet to look at the macro.

Print Preview button

Stop Macro button

This is what your newly revised macro should look like:

```
Sub PrintCharts()
    Do Until ActiveCell = ""
        ActiveCell.Range("A1:AK1").Select
        Selection.Copy
        Application.Goto Reference:="Stage"
        ActiveSheet.Paste
        Application.CutCopyMode = False
    ActiveSheet.Previous.Select
    ActiveSheet.PrintPreview
    ActiveSheet.Next.Select
        Application.Goto
        ActiveCell.Offset(1, 0).Range("A1").Select
    Loop
End Sub
```

The three new lines are not indented as much as the other lines. You can indent them to match if you want your macro to look nice.

Using CTRL+PAGE UP and CTRL+PAGE DOWN to toggle between two adjacent sheets in a workbook is an effective way to avoid having to put the names of the sheets into the macro. If you rename one or both sheets, the macro will keep working as long as the chart sheet is immediately in front of the pivot table worksheet.

Run the PrintCharts macro

Try out the PrintCharts macro. You may want to start close to the bottom of the Category list so that you can test whether the macro will stop without waiting for all the categories to display.

1 Activate the TimeSeries worksheet and select cell A8, the Seattle category, three rows from the bottom.

2 Press CTRL+SHIFT+C to run the macro.

The macro creates a chart for the Seattle category and display the print preview.

3 Click Close to continue running the macro.

Tip Instead of skipping the first categories in the table, you can also speed up testing the macro by putting an apostrophe at the beginning of the *ActiveSheet.PrintPreview* statement to keep it from executing. Since an apostrophe indicates a comment in a macro, temporarily disabling a statement by adding an apostrophe is called "commenting out" the code.

Convert print preview to print

Once the looping and copying part of the macro works the way you want, you can change the print preview statement to print the chart to the printer.

1 Activate the Module1 sheet.

2 Select the word *PrintPreview,* and type **PrintOut** to replace it.

3 Activate the TimeSeries worksheet, and select cell A3.

4 Press CTRL+SHIFT+C to run the macro and print the charts for your presentation.

5 Save the workbook.

Hurry, the meeting is ready to start.

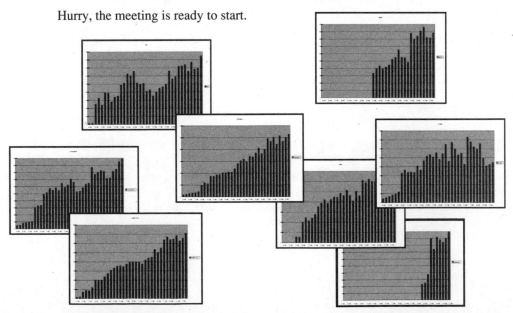

Lesson Summary

To	Do this
Run a block of statements only if a certain condition is true	Add If and End If statements around the block of statements.
Run a block of statements repeatedly	Add Do and Loop statements around the block of statements.
Indicate when to stop repeating a block of statements	Add an Until clause to the Do statement of the loop.
Move back and forth between two ranges	Use the Application.Goto method without any arguments.
Stop a macro while it is running	Press CTRL+BREAK.

For more information on	See
Controlling how macro statements run	Chapter 7, "Controlling How Your Code Runs," in the *Microsoft Excel Visual Basic User's Guide*.

Preview of the Next Lesson

In Part 1, you have learned how to create simple macros, complex macros, and repeating macros, all using the macro recorder. In Part 2, you will learn how to use some of Excel's tools for making macros easy to use. Some of the tools that make macros easy to use can also be used to make worksheets easy to use. For example, in Lesson 4 you will use dialog box controls to make a worksheet model easy for yourself and others to use.

2 Making Tools Easy to Use

Use Dialog Box Controls

Microsoft Excel is a great program. Many people purchase Excel for use at work. Or at least the *excuse* people use for buying Excel is that they're going to use it at work. Do you want to know the real, ulterior reason 97.32 percent of Excel users have when they buy it?

You buy Excel, spend a lot of time learning how to use Excel, buy lots of books about Excel, even get a job somewhere so you can have an excuse for having Excel, just so that you can calculate loan payments for that new car you want. Try to deny it if you wish, but I know—absolutely, positively—that the car loan payment problem was the reason you bought Excel. All right, all right. Maybe I'm wrong. Maybe you *are* part of that incredible 2.68 percent of users who actually bought Excel so they could do something besides figure out their car payments. You bought it so you could figure out your *house* payment.

Now, say you have a friend who just bought Excel but doesn't really know how to use it very well yet. You want to help him out by building a little model so that he can immediately start calculating the payments for a used car he wants to buy. You want him to be able to try out several possible prices, interest rates, and repayment periods, but you want to minimize the chance for mistakes. Excel has some very powerful tools to help you make a nice model for your friend.

You will learn how to:

■ Add dialog controls to a worksheet.

■ Link a list box to a worksheet range.

■ Link results from dialog controls to worksheet cells.

Estimated lesson time: 15 minutes

Start the lesson

▶ Start Excel with a new, fresh workbook, and save the workbook with the name LESSON4.XLS.

Creating a Car Loan Calculator

When you interact with Excel, you do so through Excel's graphical user interface. A graphical user interface includes menus, dialog boxes, list boxes, scroll bars, buttons, and other graphical images. A graphical user interface makes a program easier to learn and also helps reduce errors by restricting choices to valid options.

Historically, creating a graphical user interface has been the domain of professional computer scientists. More recently, users of advanced applications could add graphical controls to custom dialog boxes. Now, with Excel 5, you can take advantage of dialog box-style controls directly on the worksheet, without doing any programming at all.

In this lesson, you will build a worksheet model to calculate a car loan payment amount, and you will add graphical controls to make it easy to use for a friend who is unfamiliar with worksheets. You won't create macros in this lesson, but you will become familiar with how dialog box controls work, which will be useful when you build a full-featured dialog box in Lesson 14.

Create a payment model

1   Type these labels into cells B2 through B7 of a blank worksheet: **Price**, **Down**, **Loan**, **Interest**, **Years**, and **Payment**.

2   Type **$5,000** in cell C2 (to the right of Price), type **20%** in cell C3 (to the right of Down), type **8%** in cell C5 (to the right of Interest), and type **3** in cell C6 (to the right of Years).

3   In cell C4 (to the right of Loan), type **=C2*(1-C3)** and press ENTER. The value 4000 appears in the cell.

4   In cell C7 (to the right of Payment), type **=PMT(C5/12,C6*12,C4)** and press ENTER. The payment amount $125.35 appears in the cell. The red text color and the parentheses around the number in the worksheet indicate a negative number: you don't receive this amount, unfortunately; you pay it. This is the monthly payment amount for this hypothetical car.

	A	B	C	D
1				
2		Price	$5,000	
3		Down	20%	
4		Loan	4000	
5		Interest	8%	
6		Years	3	
7		Payment	($125.35)	
8				

Make the model look nice

Since you're creating this model for your friend, you want to make the fonts a little larger and more inviting.

1   Select cell B2 and press CTRL+STAR to select all the cells in the model.

2   In the Font Size box on the Formatting toolbar, select 16.

3   From the Format menu, choose Column, AutoFit Selection.

Currency Style button

4   Select cell C4 (the cell next to the Loan label), and click the Currency Style button on the Formatting toolbar. Click twice on the Decrease Decimal button to show only dollars with no cents.

Decrease Decimal button

5   Select cell C5 (the cell next to the Interest label), and click twice on the Increase Decimal button so that you can see fractional interest rates.

Increase Decimal button

Now the model is easier to read.

	A	B	C	D
1				
2		Price	$5,000	
3		Down	20%	
4		Loan	$4,000	
5		Interest	8.00%	
6		Years	3	
7		Payment	($125.35)	
8				

Try out the model

1   In cell C2 (to the right of Price), enter **$12,000**. The loan amount should change to $9,600 and the payment amount should change to $300.83.

This simple model calculates monthly loan payments for a given set of input variables. You change the input variables to anything you like and the payment changes. You can even enter outlandish values.

2   As the price of the car, enter **$1,500,000**. This is a very expensive car. The payment formula bravely calculates the monthly payment, but you can't read it because it is too big.

3   Press CTRL+Z to change the price back to something more reasonable. (The monthly payment for the expensive car, in case you are interested, was $37,603.64.)

One of the problems with this model is that it is too flexible. You can enter ridiculously large prices and ridiculously high interest rates. (Try 500%—I hope 500% is a ridiculous interest rate.) You can even enter, as the number of years, something totally useless, such as "Dog". The wide spectrum of choices available—only a few of which are meaningful—may confuse your friend as he uses the model.

Creating an Error-Resistant Loan Calculator

Excel has tools that enable you to make an error-resistant loan calculator. By restricting options to valid items, you can make your model less likely to produce erroneous results, and also much easier to use.

Make a list of cars

You know that your friend has been looking through the want ads and has come up with a list of used cars he's thinking of buying. Put a list of the cars and their prices onto the worksheet as a reference.

1   Starting in cell K2, off out of the way, type this table of cars and prices into the worksheet, and adjust the column widths so that you can see all the values.

	J	K	L	M
1				
2		Car	Price	
3		91 Mercury Sable	10500	
4		88 Nissan Pulsar NX	6350	
5		90 Toyota Camry	8950	
6		88 Dodge Lancer ES	6299	
7		87 BMW 325	7950	
8		91 Chev Camaro	6795	
9		88 Mazda MX6	8500	
10				

2   Select cell K2 and press CTRL+STAR to select the entire block of cells.

3   From the Insert menu, choose the Name, Create command. Select the Top Row check box, clear any other check boxes, and click OK. This gives the name Car to the list of cars and the name Price to the list of prices.

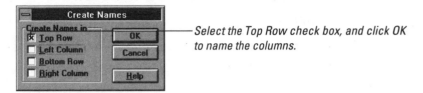

Select the Top Row check box, and click OK to name the columns.

4   Use the right mouse button to click any toolbar, and choose the Forms toolbar.

Drop-Down button

5   Click the Drop-Down button and drag a rectangle from the top left corner of cell E2 to the bottom right corner of cell G2.

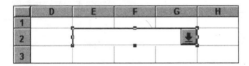

6   Double click the new drop-down control to display the Format Object dialog box, and select the Control tab.

7   Type **Car** in the Input Range box, type **H2** in the Cell Link box, and click OK.

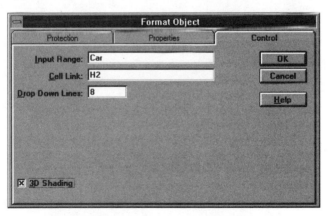

8   Press ESC to deselect the drop-down control.

9   Click the arrow on the right of the drop-down control, and select 90 Toyota Camry from the list.

The name for the Toyota appears in the drop-down control, and the number 3 appears in cell H2.

	D	E	F	G	H	I
1						
2		90 Toyota Camry		↧	3	
3						

You just created an on-screen drop-down list box control. You linked the list box to the list of cars on the worksheet, and you linked the result of the list box to cell H2. Cell H2 displays the number 3 because 90 Toyota Camry is item number 3 in the list. (If you type 4 in cell H2, the car in the drop-down control automatically changes to 88 Dodge Lancer ES. If you try this, change the number back to 3.)

Retrieve the price from the list

1 Select cell C2.

2 Type **=INDEX(Price,H2)** and press ENTER.

The price of the Toyota—$8,950—appears in the cell. This formula finds the third item in the Price list because cell H2 contains the number 3.

3 Select the 87 BMW from the drop-down list of cars.

The number in cell H2 changes to 5 and the price changes to $7,950.

	A	B	C	D	E	F	G	H	I
1									
2		Price	$7,950		87 BMW 325		↧	5	
3		Down	20%						
4		Loan	$6,360						
5		Interest	8.00%						
6		Years	3						
7		Payment	($199.30)						
8									

Now your friend will not accidentally try to find the payment for a million dollar car. He can just select various cars from the list—thinking in terms that are meaningful to him—and the price is guaranteed to be correct.

Restrict the down payment to valid values

Unfortunately, your friend can still enter an invalid down payment percentage—such as -50% or "Dog". You need to help him out.

Spinner button

1   Click the Spinner button in the Forms toolbar.

2   Drag from the top left corner of cell E3 down to the bottom center of cell E3.

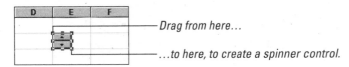

           Drag from here...

           ...to here, to create a spinner control.

3   Double click the new spinner control.

4   Type **20** in the Maximum Value box, type **H3** in the Cell Link box, and click OK.

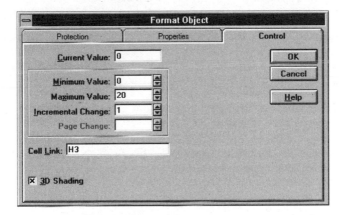

5   Press ESC to deselect the spinner control, and click the top and bottom parts of the control to see how the value in cell H3 changes within the range 0 through 20. Finish with the number 15 in cell H3.

6   Select cell C3, type **=H3/100,** and press ENTER.

    The value 15% appears in the cell.

The spinner control can increment only in whole numbers, but the down payment needs to be entered as a percentage. Dividing the value in cell H3 by 100 allows the spinner control to use whole numbers and still allows you to specify the down payment as a percentage.

Make the spinner count by fives

Your spinner control now disallows invalid inputs like -50% and "Dog", but your friend might legitimately want to put more than 20 percent down on a car—50 percent, for example, or even 80 percent. In principle, he should be able to choose any whole-number percentage from 0% through 100%. But getting from 0% to 100% by clicking 100 times on a spinner control could be unpleasant. Incrementing 5 percent at a time is a good solution.

1   Hold down the CTRL key and click the spinner control to select it.

   If you don't hold down the CTRL key, clicking the spinner control changes the value in cell H3.

2   Double click the spinner control.

3   Type **100** in the Maximum Value box, type **5** in the Incremental Change box, and click ENTER.

4   Press ESC to deselect the spinner control.

Now you can try a wide variety of car model and down payment percentage combinations.

Restrict the interest rate to valid values

The next input value your friend might make a mistake with is the interest rate. The interest rate is similar to the down payment rate. Both are percentages. You probably want to allow interest rates to vary by as little as a quarter of a percent, and within a range from 0% through about 20%. Because you're allowing fractional percentages, you will have many more steps than with the down payment rate, so use a scroll bar control instead of a spinner control.

Scroll Bar button

1   Click the Scroll Bar button in the Forms toolbar.

2   Drag from the top left corner of cell E5 to the bottom right corner of cell G5.

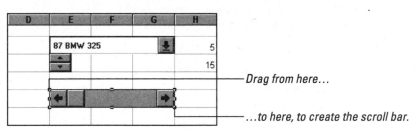

Drag from here...

...to here, to create the scroll bar.

3   Double click the new scroll bar control.

4 Type **0** in the Current Value box, type **2000** in the Maximum Value box, type **25** in the Incremental Change box, type **100** in the Page Change box, type **H5** in the Cell Link box, and click OK.

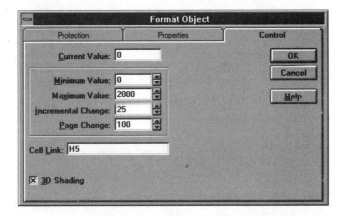

5 Press ESC to deselect the scroll bar control.

6 Try out the scroll bar control. If you click one of the arrows on either end, the number in cell H5 changes by 25. If you click between the box and the end, the number changes by 100.

7 Select cell C5, type **=H5/10000**, and press ENTER.

You divide by 100 to turn the number into a percent and by another 100 to allow for hundredths of a percent.

Now your friend can easily modify the car's price (selecting the car by name from the drop-down control), the down payment percentage (using the spinner control), or the interest rate (using the scroll bar control). The only input value left to improve is the number of years. A simple spinner control should work for this one.

Restrict the years to a valid range

1 Click the Spinner button on the Forms toolbar.

2 Drag from the top left corner of cell E6 to the bottom center of cell E6.

Spinner button

3 Double click the new spinner control.

4 Type **1** in the Minimum Value box, type **6** in the Maximum Value box, type **H6** in the Cell Link box, and click OK.

5   Select cell C6, type **=H6**, and press ENTER.

The completed model looks like this.

	A	B	C	D	E	F	G	H
1								
2		Price	$ 7,950		87 BMW 325		⬇	5
3		Down	15%		▲▼			15
4		Loan	$ 6,758					
5		Interest	8.00%		←		➡	800
6		Years	4		▲▼			4
7		Payment	($164.97)					
8								
9								

Now your friend can experiment with various scenarios as much as he wants without having to worry about typing invalid inputs into the model. In fact, he won't have to worry about typing anything into the model. He can do everything he wants by just clicking controls with the mouse. One of the greatest benefits of a graphical user interface is the ability to restrict choices to valid values. In an Excel worksheet, you can create a graphical interface without writing any code at all.

Protect the worksheet

The only remaining problem with your model is that your friend might forget to use the nice tools you have given him. For example, he might accidentally select the cell with the payment formula, type the payment he wants, and destroy the formula. You can protect the worksheet against accidental changes to formulas.

1   Select the cell range H2:H6.

2   From the Format menu, choose the Cells command and then activate the Protection tab.

Before you can protect the entire worksheet, you have to unlock these cells so that the controls will still be able to change them.

Note   When you create a new worksheet, all the cells are already locked. You can still enter values into the cells, however. That is because locking a cell has no effect unless the worksheet is protected. Having locked cells is like having mice in your basement: you don't see them until you turn the light on.

---

3   Clear the Locked check box, and click OK.

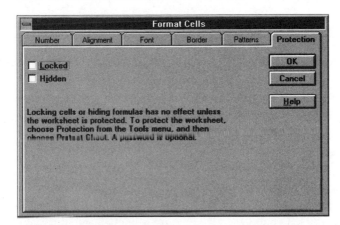

4   Select the cell range H2:L2. You want to hide the columns containing these cells.

5   From the Format menu, choose the Column, Hide command.

Once you hide these columns, they won't be a distraction for your friend.

6   From the Tools menu, choose Protection, Protect Sheet.

7   Accept the default options for the dialog box and click OK.

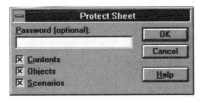

Now the worksheet model is ready to give to your friend. He doesn't need to know anything about formulas, worksheets, or entering values in a worksheet to use the model. I wish I could be there to see the happy look on his face when you give it to him.

8   Delete any unneeded sheets from the LESSON4.XLS workbook, and save and close it.

You have been very helpful to your friend, but if you don't hurry and get back to doing something for Miller Textiles, your boss will notice and then you won't have a job and then you won't have an excuse for playing with Excel any more. Hurry—back to work!

Lesson Summary

To	Do this
Add dialog box-style controls to a worksheet	Use the right mouse button to click any toolbar, and choose the Forms toolbar. Click a control button and drag a place for it on the worksheet.
Select a control without running it	Hold down the CTRL key and click the control.
Link the value of a control to a cell	Double click the control and type the cell address in the Cell Link box.
Link the list for a list box control to a worksheet range	Double click the list box control and type the range address in the Input Range box.
Set limits for spinner and scroll bar controls	Double click the control and type values in the Minimum and Maximum boxes.
Limit changes on a worksheet to selected cells	Unlock the cells you want to change (using the Protection tab of the Format Cells dialog box), and protect the worksheet (using the Protection, Protect Sheet command from the Tools menu).

For more information on	See
Using graphic objects on a worksheet	Chapter 13, "Creating Graphic Objects on Worksheets and Charts," in the *Microsoft Excel User's Guide*.
Using dialog box-style controls on a worksheet	Chapter 11, "Controls and Dialog Boxes," in the *Microsoft Excel Visual Basic User's Guide*.

Preview of the Next Lesson

In this lesson, you used Excel's dialog box controls to make a worksheet model easy to use—without even writing any macros. In the next lesson, you will use dialog box controls to make easy-to-use macros for retrieving information from the order history database. Your macros will create a pivot table and a chart, retrieving information directly from an external database without opening the database as an Excel worksheet.

Make an Enterprise Information System

My grandmother used to use her sewing machine to embroider names on outfits for us. She had a powerful old sewing machine, with lots of pulleys and levers and loops. When she changed the thread, she had to poke the thread up and over and through what seemed like countless turns and spools and guides, even before getting to the needle. I still don't know how she managed embroidering the names. She would move levers and twist the fabric and the name appeared. She was very good, and the result was beautiful. Very few people could create embroidered names the way she did.

Now, even I can embroider names onto clothes. You flip the thread around a couple of guides and the machine is threaded. You type in the name, select the lettering style, and push another button to embroider the name. The machine sews in all directions so you don't have to turn the fabric. No longer do you have to be an expert to use a sewing machine.

In Microsoft Excel, you may be an expert at retrieving data from a database, producing a summary report, and creating a chart. Others in your organization, however, may not have the same expertise. The purpose of an Enterprise Information System (EIS) is to allow people from all parts of the enterprise to find the information they need—without having to become specialists at retrieving and formatting data. In this lesson, you will build a simple EIS application that anyone in the organization can use.

You will learn how to:

- Build a pivot table with data from an external database.

- Create a simple EIS application, with a graphical start-up screen.

- Create a custom menu for your macros.

Estimated lesson time: 45 minutes

Start the lesson

▶ Start Excel and change to the directory containing the sample files for this book.

Creating a Simple Enterprise Information System

Even at work you sometimes need to create simple tools for others to use. One common request around Miller Textiles is a simple way for people in the company to see how orders are doing for the different shirt categories in the different states. So you decide to build a simple Enterprise Information System (EIS) for them to use to browse the order history database.

Set up the database as a data source

In Lessons 2 and 3, you worked with the order history database by opening the database file directly into Excel. Excel is able to convert a dBase format database file directly into an Excel worksheet. When Excel opens a database file as a worksheet, it has to load the entire file into memory. That is fine for small databases with only a few thousand records, like your order history database, but as your database grows to hundreds of thousands, or even millions of records, you will undoubtedly manage the database with a specialized database program such as Oracle or SQL Server.

You can connect to your small order history database as an external database using the same tools and techniques as you would use to connect to a large database. Then, as the company grows, your EIS application will continue to work without modification. Excel communicates with external databases using Open Database Connectivity (ODBC) drivers that you set up in the operating system. The first step in using the order history database as an external database is to set it up as an ODBC data source.

1   Activate the Windows Program Manager, open the Main group, and start the Control Panel application.

If the ODBC icon is not in the Control Panel, run Excel Setup and add the Data Access component. Be sure to install the dBase driver option in order to use the sample database.

One of the icons in the Control Panel is labeled ODBC. This is the control panel for ODBC drivers.

2   Double click the ODBC icon to display the Data Sources dialog box.

Open ODBC in the Control Panel.

You can have data sources for single databases or for types of databases. The specific data sources in the list depend on what databases have been already added to your system. Excel's setup program adds some sample data sources for you. You will set up a new data source specifically for the Miller Textiles databases.

3 In the Data Sources dialog box, click the Add button.

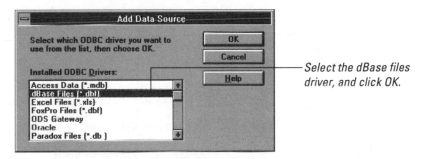

Click the Add button to add a new data source.

The Add Data Sources dialog box appears, showing a list of the installed ODBC drivers.

4 Since the order history database is a dBase file, select the driver labeled dBase Files (*.dbf), and click OK.

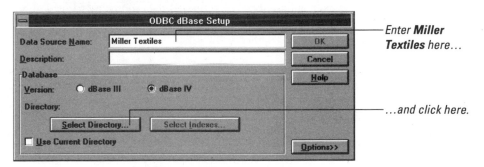

Select the dBase files driver, and click OK.

The ODBC dBase Setup dialog box appears. This is where you enter information for the specific database you want to use as a data source.

5 Type **Miller Textiles** in the Data Source Name box, and click the Select Directory button.

Enter **Miller Textiles** here...

...and click here.

The Select Directory dialog box appears. This dialog box is similar to the standard dialog box for opening files in Windows.

6   Change to the directory that contains the sample files for this book.

The filename, ORDERS.DBF, should appear, grayed, on the left side of the dialog box.

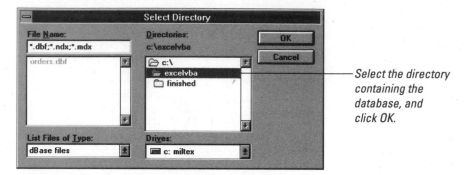

Select the directory containing the database, and click OK.

7   Click OK to return to the ODBC dBase Setup dialog box, click OK to return to the Data Sources dialog box (where Miller Textiles is now in the list of data sources), and click Close to return to the main Control Panel.

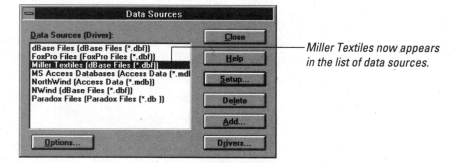

Miller Textiles now appears in the list of data sources.

8   Close the Control Panel, and activate Excel.

Your order history database is now added as an ODBC data source in Windows. Now you can use the Miller Textiles data source by name without specifying the location of the database files. If you move the database to a new location, or even change to a different database format, you need only to change the definition of the Miller Textiles data source.

Setting up a new data source may seem complicated at first, but giving a name to the data source can simplify the task of upgrading from a local database to a LAN-based client-server database, if you ever decide to make that change.

Look at the finished product

In this part of the lesson you will build a simple EIS for your associates at work. This will be a simple EIS, but it still requires a number of pieces to get it all to work. The pieces will make more sense if you have a vision of what you will end up with. Take a look at the finished product before you start building it yourself.

1   From the File menu, choose Open, change to the FINISHED subdirectory, select the file LESSON5.XLS, and click OK.

The start-up screen for the EIS appears.

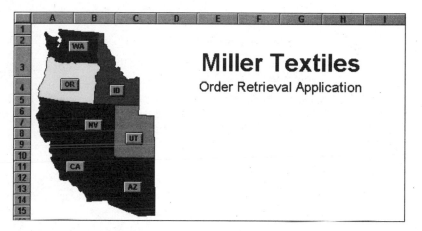

2   Click the button on the map for Oregon.

The screen flashes a little and then you see the orders by category for Oregon, along with a simple chart.

Depending on your system configuration, your chart may look slightly different than this one.

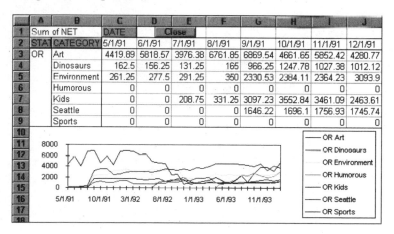

3   Click the Close button.

You are back at the start-up screen. In addition to clicking the states on the map, you can also retrieve the same order information from the custom EIS menu.

4   From the EIS menu, choose California.

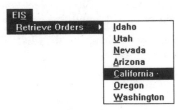

You see the table and chart showing orders for California.

5   Click the Close button and choose the Close command from the File menu to close the LESSON5.XLS file.

This is a very simple order history review tool. (You will learn how to make a more packaged application in Part 5.) But almost everything about this EIS was done using the macro recorder and other simple tools in Excel.

Make a start-up screen

Every good EIS must have a start-up screen. At first, you will just have a simple button on this screen, but later you will add the map so that you can let users of the application click buttons on maps of the states.

New Workbook button

1   Click the New Workbook button to create a new workbook, change back to the directory containing the sample files for this book, and save the workbook as LESSON5.XLS.

2   Double click the Sheet1 worksheet tab, type **EIS** as the worksheet name, and then click OK.

Drawing button

3   Click the Drawing button on the Standard toolbar to display the Drawing toolbar.

Create Button button

4   Click the Create Button button and drag a rectangle for a button in the middle of the worksheet.

5   In the Assign Macro dialog box that appears, click Cancel.

6   Canceling the Assign Macro dialog box does not cancel the creation of the button. It just closes the Assign Macro dialog box without assigning a macro to the button. You don't have a macro ready yet, so you will assign the macro later.

7   With the new button still selected, type **Retrieve Orders**, and click cell A1 to deselect the button.

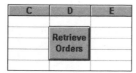

Now you are ready to retrieve the data and start building the application.

Launch Microsoft Query

For the EIS application, you will retrieve the data directly from an external database without opening the database file into Excel. You can use Excel's PivotTable Wizard to help you retrieve the data. First practice creating a pivot table without creating a macro, and turn on the macro recorder while you build another one.

1   From the Data menu, choose the PivotTable command.

2   Select the External Data Source option and click Next.

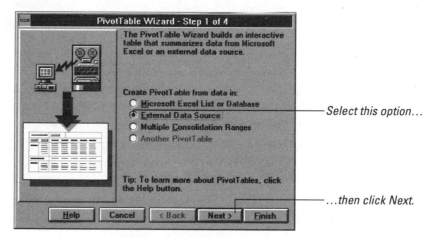

Step 2 of the PivotTable Wizard appears.

3   Click the Get Data button.

4   The Microsoft Query application appears on the screen, possibly with a Cue Card window on top. (If the Cue Card window is visible, close it.)

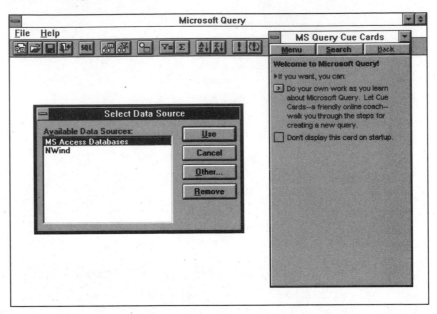

The Select Data Source dialog box is displayed on the screen. Even though you added Miller Textiles as an ODBC data source in the Control Panel, this list only shows data sources previously installed in Query.

5   Click the Other button.

The ODBC Data Sources dialog box appears. The Miller Textiles data source is in this list.

6   Select Miller Textiles and click OK to return to the Select Data Source dialog box.

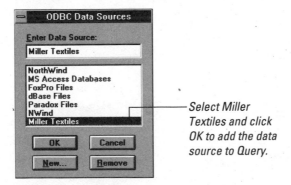

Select Miller Textiles and click OK to add the data source to Query.

Miller Textiles is now in the list of data sources for Query. The next time you use Query, Miller Textiles will already be in the list.

Create the query

The Select Data Source dialog box is on the screen, with Query in the background. The next time you click the Get Data button in the PivotTable Wizard, that is how the screen will appear.

1   Select Miller Textiles as the data source, and click Use.

2   Select ORDERS.DBF as the table name, click Add, and then click Close.

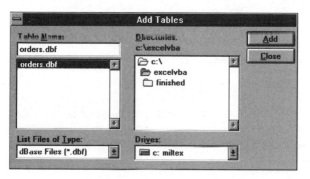

Query allows you to include more than one table in a query. For this query, you need only the one table.

3   In the list of fields, double click Date, then double click State, then double click Category, and finally double click Net.

As you double click each field name, that field appears in the query table.

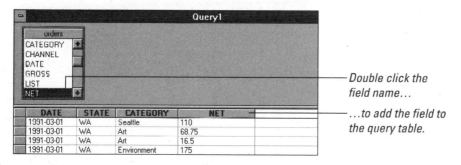

Double click the field name...

...to add the field to the query table.

4   Click the first cell under the State heading, the cell containing *WA*.

Criteria Equals button

5   Click the Criteria Equals button in the toolbar under the menus, to restrict the query to only orders from Washington.

6   From the File menu, choose Return Data To Microsoft Excel.

After a few seconds, you are back in Step 2 of the PivotTable Wizard and the text next to the Get Data button changes to *Data Retrieved*.

That's the process for retrieving data from an external database into the PivotTable Wizard. Now you can create the pivot table from the retrieved data.

Create the pivot table

You were in Step 2 of the PivotTable Wizard when you started Microsoft Query to retrieve the data. Now that you have retrieved the data, you are back in Step 2, ready to continue creating the pivot table.

1   In Step 2 of the PivotTable Wizard, with the data retrieved, click Next.

2   In Step 3 of the PivotTable Wizard, drag the Date field tile to the Column area, drag the State and the Category field tiles to the Row area, and drag the Net field tile to the Data area.

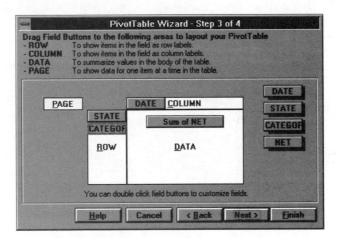

3   Click Next to accept the pivot table layout.

4   In Step 4 of the PivotTable Wizard, clear the PivotTable Starting Cell box, clear both Grand Totals check boxes, and click Finish.

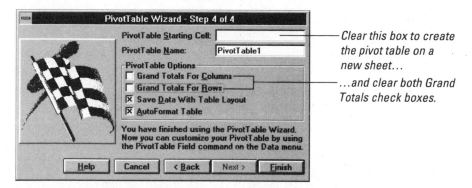

Clear this box to create the pivot table on a new sheet...

...and clear both Grand Totals check boxes.

Even though you cleared the Grand Totals For Columns check box, the pivot table has a row of totals at the bottom. These totals are really for the State field. Since you have data for only one state, the total by state seems to be a grand total. Get rid of it.

5   Double click the State field tile, select the None option in the Subtotals group, and click OK.

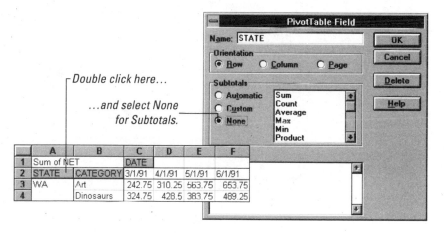

Double click here...

...and select None for Subtotals.

You have now completed all the steps necessary to create a pivot table from an external data source. When you repeat the steps to create a macro, you won't need to define a new data source.

Create a pivot table with a macro

1   Delete the sheet containing the pivot table.

2   If the Visual Basic toolbar is not visible, use the right mouse button to click any toolbar, and choose Visual Basic.

Record Macro button

3   Click the Record Macro button, type **MakePivot** as the name for the macro, and click OK.

4   From the Data menu, choose PivotTable, select the External Data Source option, and click Next.

5   Click the Get Data button to launch Microsoft Query.

6   Repeat the steps from the "Create the query" and the "Create the pivot table" sections earlier in this lesson.

Stop Macro button

7   Click the Stop Macro button to stop the recorder.

You now have a macro that will access the external database and create a pivot table displaying monthly orders by category.

Assign the macro to the button

Before testing the macro, assign it to the button on the EIS worksheet to make it easier to run.

1   From the Edit menu, choose Delete Sheet and confirm that you do want to delete the worksheet.

You should be back on the EIS worksheet.

2   Use the right mouse button to click the Retrieve Orders button, and choose the Assign Macro command.

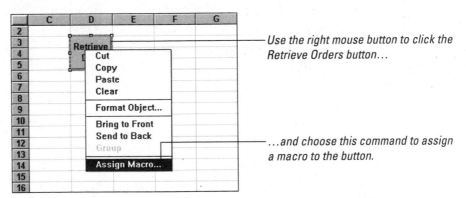

Use the right mouse button to click the Retrieve Orders button...

...and choose this command to assign a macro to the button.

3   Select MakePivot from the list (hard choice, isn't it?), and click OK.

4   Click cell A1 to deselect the button, and then click the Retrieve Orders button to test the macro.

5   Delete the new pivot table worksheet to get back to the EIS worksheet.

Now you can produce a new pivot table of Washington state orders at the click of a button. Of course, Washington *is* the most important state—even if you sell more designs elsewhere—but there is a slight possibility that some of your associates at Miller Textiles might conceivably want to look at orders for a different state. In order to modify the macro, you have to look at it.

Look at the MakePivot macro

Before you look at the macro that creates the pivot table, I want to tell you some bad news and some good news. The bad news is that the macro looks terrible. It is almost completely indecipherable. The good news is that you don't need to decipher it. You can make the macro retrieve data for any state you want simply by following the simple steps that I will show you.

▶   Click the Module sheet tab and look at the macro.

Note The macro on your screen might look slightly different than the macro here because some of the lines on the screen are too long to fit on a single printed page in a book. You don't need to read the macro that closely anyway, though, so don't worry about it.

```
Sub MakePivot()
    ActiveSheet.PivotTableWizard SourceType:=xlExternal, SourceData:= _
        Array("DSN=Miller Textiles;DBQ=C:\excelvba;FIL=dBase4;", _
        "SELECT orders.DATE, orders.STATE, orders.CATEGORY, orders.NET
            FROM c:\excelvba\orders.dbf orders
            WHERE (orders.STATE='WA')"), _
        TableDestination:="", TableName:="PivotTable2", RowGrand _
        :=False, ColumnGrand:=False
    ActiveSheet.PivotTables("PivotTable2").AddFields RowFields:=Array( _
        "STATE", "CATEGORY"), ColumnFields:="DATE"
    ActiveSheet.PivotTables("PivotTable2").PivotFields("NET"). _
        Orientation = xlDataField
    ActiveSheet.PivotTables("PivotTable2").PivotFields("STATE"). _
        Subtotals = Array(False, False, False, False, False, False, _
        False, False, False, False, False, False)
End Sub
```

You can probably figure out that all the statements have something to do with pivot tables. In Lesson 12, you will work directly with this kind of code. For now, all you need to do is make the macro prompt the user for a state. You want to touch as little as possible, while still learning how to customize recorded statements like this.

Make the macro prompt the user for a state

When you created the pivot table, the entire request for external data was sent to Query as a single long text string. The characters *WA* were in the middle of that text string because you used Washington as the sample state. Now you need to replace those characters with a state code that changes each time you run the macro.

1   Put the insertion point at the end of the statement *Sub MakePivot( )*, press ENTER, and then press TAB. You are now ready to type a new line in the macro.

2   Type **myState = InputBox("Enter State Code")** and press ENTER to get a new blank line.

In Lesson 10 you will learn more about variables.

This statement prompts the user for a state code and then puts that state code into a storage place—into a variable—named myState. The name *myState* is simply a word that I made up. When you put a value into a variable, you get to invent the variable's name. In this case, you could just as well use *NewStateCodeVariable*. (But don't. Why not? Because I'm the author, and I said not to.)

3   From the Edit menu, choose the Find command.

4   Type **WA** in the Find What box, select the Match Case check box and also the Find Whole Words Only check box, and click Find Next.

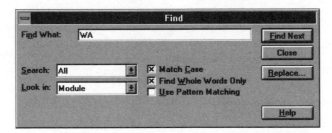

When you created the original query, you used WA as the sample state code. Now you need to find where that state code appears in the mass of Visual Basic code.

5   Click Close to dismiss the Find dialog box.

The Find command found the text *WA* in the middle of the phrase *(orders.STATE='WA')*, which is in the middle of a long quoted text string.

You need to replace the text *WA* with the myState variable that you created at the beginning of the macro. Since the constant is in the middle of a text string, you have to close the text string, add your variable, and then continue the text string.

6   With WA selected, type **"**, type a space, type **&**, type another space, type **myState**, type a third space, type **&**, type a fourth space, and type **"**. The phrase within the parentheses should be *(orders.STATE= '" & myState & "')*. Think of what you're adding as the variable myState, bracketed by ampersands to "add" it to the rest of the statement, with quotation marks on each end to close and then to continue the original text string.

7 Switch back to the EIS worksheet, click the Retrieve Orders button, and enter **CA** when prompted for a state name.

The macro produces a new pivot table, this time with California orders.

8 Delete the new pivot table worksheet.

The macro recorder records all the instructions for creating the pivot table, including the criteria for retrieving the records. As long as you are careful about starting and stopping text strings, you can replace constants in the macro with variables, without having to understand very much about the pivot table macro statements themselves.

Try canceling the macro

Try running the macro again, imagining you are a naive user who has never seen it before.

1 Click the Retrieve Orders button.

The input box prompting you for the state code appears. You are not sure what you should put in for a state code.

2 You don't want to risk entering the wrong value, so click the Cancel button.

The macro does not stop, as you might expect. It continues, blinking and clicking and making you very nervous. Finally, a strange, malicious-looking dialog box with several buttons appears.

3 Click the End button. (Remember that it is the End button you click to stop the macro from running any more. You will see the word *End* again later.)

Thankfully, the macro stops. You hope you didn't hurt anything. You certainly never want to use this macro again.

Of course, you don't want your associates to feel like that. You need to fix the macro.

Make the macro quit when canceled

1   Activate the Module1 sheet.

2   In the blank line you inserted right after the statement that prompts the user for the state code, type **If myState = "" Then End**

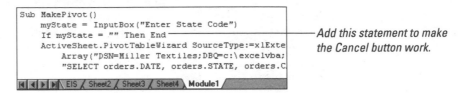

Add this statement to make the Cancel button work.

Now if a user of the macro clicks Cancel—or just clicks OK without entering a state code—the InputBox function assigns an empty text string to the myState variable. Putting the word *End* into the macro stops the macro, the same as the button on the error dialog box did.

3   Run the macro again, and click Cancel in the input box to see the macro quit.

Adding a Close Button to the EIS Application

Each time you run the macro, it creates a new worksheet for the new pivot table, but the macro does not get rid of any old worksheets. You can't just delete the worksheet as part of the MakePivot macro, because the worksheet would disappear before the users had a chance to see the information they requested. You need to give them a Close button to delete the worksheet. First, make a macro to delete the worksheet, and then make a macro that actually puts a Close button onto the EIS worksheet.

Create a macro to delete a worksheet

1   Select a blank, expendable worksheet. (If you don't have one handy, insert one.)

Record Macro button

2   Click the Record Macro button, type **DeleteSheet** as the name for the macro, and click OK.

3   From the Edit menu, choose the Delete Sheet command, confirm that you want to delete the worksheet, and click the Stop Macro button.

Stop Macro button

4   Activate the Module1 sheet and scroll to the bottom to see the macro.

```
Sub DeleteSheet()
    ActiveWindow.SelectedSheets.Delete
End Sub
```

The macro prompts you and then deletes the selected worksheet. You can make the macro delete the worksheet without asking for confirmation.

Make the DeleteSheet macro work quietly

▶   Below the *Sub DeleteSheet( )* statement, insert the statement
    Application.DisplayAlerts = False.

You will learn more about the Application object in Lesson 9.

One of the properties of the Excel application is whether it displays alert
messages. If you set the DisplayAlerts property to False, the macro will not
prompt the user when it deletes the worksheet.

The finished macro should look like this:

```
Sub DeleteSheet()
    Application.DisplayAlerts = False
    ActiveWindow.SelectedSheets.Delete
End Sub
```

Now you can run the macro to quickly—and quietly—delete any selected worksheet.

Assign the DeleteSheet macro to a button

1   Activate another blank, expendable worksheet.

Create Button button

2   Click the Create Button button in the Drawing toolbar, and while holding down
    the ALT key drag a rectangle for a new button in cell D1, the same size as the cell.
    Holding down the ALT key when you move or size an object makes the object
    borders snap to the edges of the worksheet cells.

3   In the Assign Macro dialog box that appears, select DeleteSheet as the macro
    name, and click OK.

4   With the new button still selected, type **Close**, and click cell A1 to deselect the
    button.

5   Click the button.

    It worked—the worksheet is gone, without a whisper. Great job! Three cheers!
    Uh, oh. The button is gone too.

Make a macro to make a button

If the button to delete the worksheet disappears along with the worksheet, you
obviously need an easier way to make the button.

1   Activate another expendable worksheet.

Record Macro button

2   Click the Record Macro button, type **AddDeleteButton** as the name for the
    macro, and click OK.

3   Repeat steps 2 through 4 in the preceding section, "Assign the DeleteSheet macro
    to a button."

Stop Macro button

4   Click the Stop Macro button.

5 Activate the Module1 sheet and scroll to the bottom to look at the macro.

```
Sub AddDeleteButton()
    ActiveSheet.Buttons.Add(144, 0, 48, 12.75).Select
    Selection.OnAction = "DeleteSheet"
    Selection.Characters.Text = "Close"
    With Selection.Characters(Start:=1, Length:=5).Font
        .Name = "Arial"
        .FontStyle = "Bold"
        .Size = 10
        .Strikethrough = False
        .Superscript = False
        .Subscript = False
        .OutlineFont = False
        .Shadow = False
        .Underline = xlNone
        .ColorIndex = xlAutomatic
    End With
    Range("A1").Select
End Sub
```

The most complex part of this macro is the part between the *With* and *End With* statements. Actually, those lines are there just in case you added any extra formatting to the button. Since you used the default settings for the button, you can delete everything from the *With* statement through the *End With* statement. Of course, you can also leave the macro as it is. You don't have to understand it for it to work.

Now you can add a Close button to any worksheet just by running this macro.

Add the Close button with the MakePivot macro

The MakePivot macro creates a new worksheet with a new pivot table. The best time to add the Close button to the worksheet is when you create it. Since the MakePivot macro and the AddDeleteButton macro do two separate tasks, leave them as two separate macros, and add a third macro that runs both of them as subroutines. You could use the recorder to create this new macro, but you are probably comfortable enough with Visual Basic now to just type it in yourself.

1 At the top of the module sheet, type **Sub RetrieveOrders** and press ENTER.

A *Sub* statement is supposed to end with open and close parentheses. If you press ENTER without typing the parentheses, Visual Basic adds them for you.

2 Press TAB, type **MakePivot**, and press ENTER.

3 Type **AddDeleteButton** and press ENTER.

4 Press BACKSPACE, type **End Sub**, and press ENTER.

That's your main macro that calls two subroutine macros. Here's what the whole thing looks like:

```
Sub RetrieveOrders()
    MakePivot
    AddDeleteButton
End Sub
```

If you created the main macro by turning on the macro recorder and running the two subroutine macros (as you did in Lesson 2), you would end up with a main macro that looked like this:

```
Sub RetrieveOrders()
    Application.Run Macro:="MakePivot"
    Application.Run Macro:="AddDeleteButton"
End Sub
```

Sometimes you can write a simpler macro than the macro recorder can create. To run a subroutine macro from another macro, all you really have to do is type the name of the macro you want to run.

Try out the RetrieveOrders macro

Your RetrieveOrders macro will now prompt the user for the state code, create the pivot table, and add the Close button. Try it out. First change the Retrieve Orders button on the EIS worksheet to run the RetrieveOrders macro.

1   Switch to the EIS worksheet, use the right mouse button to click Retrieve Orders, and choose the Assign Macro command.

2   Select RetrieveOrders, click OK, and then press ESC to deselect the button.

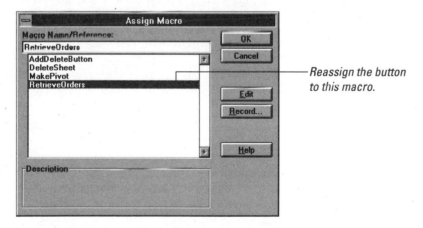

Reassign the button
to this macro.

3   Click the Retrieve Orders button and type a state code.

The macro retrieves the data, builds the pivot table, and adds the Close button.

4   Click the Close button to close the pivot table worksheet.

Adding a Chart to the EIS Application

Big blocks of tabular numbers are hard for most people to decipher. You want to add a chart to the EIS application so that your associates can more easily interpret whether orders are improving.

Chart the pivot table

1   Click the Retrieve Orders button and type **WA** as the state code. Do not click the Close button.

Record Macro button

2   Click the Record Macro button, type **MakeChart** as the name of the macro, and click OK.

3   Select cell A1, the top left cell in the pivot table, and press CTRL+STAR to select the entire pivot table.

In the Reference area to the left of the formula bar, type **ChartRegion** as the name for the range, and press ENTER.

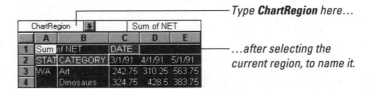

Type **ChartRegion** here...

...after selecting the current region, to name it.

Note Some states have more dates or more categories than other states. For example, Washington orders start much sooner than Idaho orders. When you create the sample chart, you are using Washington orders, but later you will want your macro to create a chart of Idaho orders. Even though you don't need to name the range to create a chart, giving a name to the range will simplify the process of making the macro work with different states.

---

4   Click the ChartWizard button and drag a place for the chart from the top left corner of cell A10 to the bottom left corner of cell K18.

ChartWizard button

5   In the ChartWizard, click Next in Step 1, double click Line for the chart type in Step 2, double click option 2 as the format in Step 3, and click Finish in Step 4.

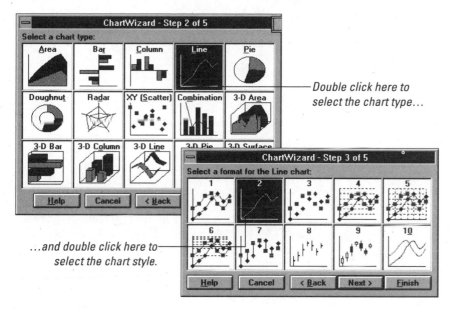

Double click here to select the chart type...

...and double click here to select the chart style.

6   Press ESC to deselect the chart.

7   Click the Stop Macro button.

Stop Macro button

Test the MakeChart macro

You need to try out the MakeChart macro to see if it works properly.

1   Click the Close button to close the Washington state pivot table.

2   Click the Retrieve Orders button, type **NV** as the state code, and click OK.

3   When the pivot table is ready, click the Run Macro button, select MakeChart from the list, and click Run.

The macro should create the chart, but the chart doesn't look right. The lines stop about halfway across the chart.

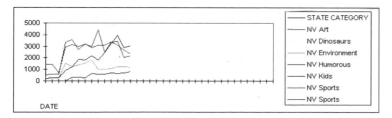

4   Click the chart to select it and press DELETE. You can try creating the same chart again after looking at the macro.

5   Activate the Module1 sheet and scroll to the bottom to see the MakeChart macro.

```
Sub MakeChart()
    Range("A1").Select
    Selection.CurrentRegion.Select
    ActiveWorkbook.Names.Add Name:="ChartRegion", RefersToR1C1:= _
        "=Sheet8!R1C1:R9C38"
    ActiveSheet.ChartObjects.Add(0, 114.75, 420.75, 114.75).Select
    Application.CutCopyMode = False
    ActiveChart.ChartWizard Source:=Range("A1:AL9"), Gallery:=xlLine, _
        Format:=2, PlotBy:=xlRows, CategoryLabels:=1, SeriesLabels _
        :=2, HasLegend:=1
    Range("A1:AL9").Select
End Sub
```

You may not understand everything in every statement in the macro, but you can get a general sense of what it is doing: "Select cell A1, select the current region, define the name ChartRegion, create a chart, turn off copy mode (who knows why), adjust the chart with the settings from the ChartWizard, and select range A1:AL9 on the worksheet."

Make the chart plot the current selection

Notice in the ChartWizard method that the macro recorder created the chart pointing at a specific range of cells: A1:AL9. That was the range for the Washington state pivot table. Since you haven't been selling designs in Nevada as long as you have in Washington, the chart extends way past the current data.

Fortunately, when you recorded the macro, you had the foresight to define the name ChartRegion right after selecting the current region of the table. Unfortunately, the statement that defines ("Adds") the name seems to use a specific cell address range also. The range Sheet8!R1C1:R9C38 in the statement with the Add method is equivalent to the range A1:AL9 in the statement with the ChartWizard method.

Instead of giving the name ChartRegion to the same range each time you run the macro, you need to make the name ChartRegion refer to the current selection. To make a name refer to the current selection, you assign the name to the Name property of the selection.

Once the name ChartRegion refers to the correct range, you can change the ChartWizard method to use the ChartRegion range.

1   Delete the entire statement *ActiveWorkbook.Names.Add Name:="ChartRegion", RefersToR1C1:= "=Sheet8!R1C1:R9C38"*.

2   In the place of the deleted statement, type **Selection.Name = "ChartRegion"**.

This statement sets the name of the current selection to ChartRegion. The size of this named range can change depending on the number of months and categories for a particular state.

3   After the word *Range* in the statement with the ChartWizard method, select the reference A1:AL9, and delete it. (Do not delete the quotation marks.)

4   In the place of the reference, type **ChartRegion**.

The first part of the statement will look like this:

```
ActiveChart.ChartWizard Source:=Range("ChartRegion")
```

With these two changes, the ChartWizard will create a chart based on the current selection.

Run Macro button

5   Activate the worksheet with the Nevada pivot table, click the Run Macro button, and run the MakeChart macro.

The chart lines should fill the whole chart.

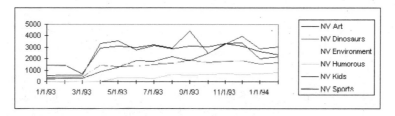

6   Click the Close button to remove the worksheet.

You will learn more about working with charts in Lesson 9.

Giving a name to the selection and then using that defined name is the easiest way to get the ChartWizard to create a chart from the current selection. At least, that's the easiest way to do it until you understand more about Excel objects and references, which you will learn about in Part 3. Once you understand how Excel objects really work, you can simplify many of these recorded macros. (Just a little sales pitch for the next few lessons.)

Add the MakeChart macro to the EIS button

You want the chart to appear whenever a user clicks the Retrieve Orders button, so add the MakeChart subroutine to the RetrieveOrders macro.

1   Activate the Module1 sheet, scroll to the top, and insert the statement **MakeChart** after the statement *MakePivot*.

2   Activate the EIS start-up worksheet, click the Retrieve Orders button, enter a state code, and watch the magic.

Linking the EIS Application to a Map

Your EIS macro can do a lot. Simply by clicking a button and typing a state code, a user of your macros can see the orders for a state, both as tabular data and as a chart. But what if one of your associates types an invalid state code, or accidentally types *AX* for Arizona instead of *AZ*. The pivot table will not be able to retrieve the data from the database, and the macro will halt with an error.

You can prevent the problem of entering an invalid state—and at the same time create a more appealing start-up screen—by allowing the user to click a button on a map of a state to retrieve the orders for that state.

Add a map to the start-up screen

1   Activate the worksheet named EIS and select cell A1

2   From the Insert menu, choose Picture, select MAP.CGM, and click OK.

3   From the Zoom Control's list, choose Selection.

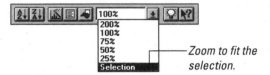

Zoom to fit the selection.

The window zooms out until you can see the whole map.

4   Hold down the SHIFT key and drag the bottom right corner of the map up and to the left until the bottom of the map lines up with row 17 of the worksheet.

When you hold down the SHIFT key while you resize an object, the object maintains the same height and width ratio. You want the map to still be in proportion after you shrink it.

5   Get rid of the border on the picture: From the Format menu, choose Object, select the Patterns tab, set the Border option to None, and click OK.

6   Enter **Miller Textiles** in cell E3, and then enter **Order Retrieval Application** in cell E4.

7   Change the zoom back to 100%, change the font size of cell E3 to 28 points, and change the font style to bold. Then change the font size of cell E4 to 16 points.

Center Across Columns button

8   Select the range E3:H4, and click the Center Across Columns button to center the labels on the right side of the screen.

9   Get rid of the gridlines on the worksheet: From the Tools menu, choose Options, select the View tab, clear the Gridlines check box, and click OK.

Your screen should look like this.

Now your start-up screen looks very nice. Next you need to add buttons to each of the states so that a user can retrieve orders for a state by clicking a button. But before you can add buttons that run macros, you need to create macros for the buttons to run.

Make the macro fill in the blank

Currently, you have one RetrieveOrders macro that prompts the user for a state code. You don't want your associates to have to remember and type in the state codes; you want the macro to fill in the state code. Start by changing the RetrieveOrders macro to fill in the state code for Washington.

1   Activate the Module1 sheet and scroll to the RetrieveOrders macro.

2   Change the name of the macro from RetrieveOrders to **RetrieveWA**.

At the end of the MakePivot statement, type a space, and then type **myState:="WA"**. (Type both a colon and an equal sign.)

The finished statement should be *MakePivot myState:="WA"*.

You can give arguments to built-in Excel commands by adding the argument name, a colon plus an equal sign, and then the value of the argument. In the same way, you can give arguments to your own subroutine macros. Read this statement like this: "With 'WA' as my state, make pivot."

3   Between the parentheses at the top of the MakePivot macro, type **myState**.

The finished statement should be *Sub MakePivot(myState)*.

In Lesson 10 you will learn more about using arguments with subroutines.

You always have to put parentheses at the end of a Sub statement so that the parentheses will be ready if you ever want to add arguments to the subroutine. The name you put inside the parentheses is the link between the value in the subroutine and the value back in the RetrieveWA macro. You must spell the name inside the parentheses (*myState*) exactly the same as you spell the argument name in the statement that calls the subroutine (*MakePivot mystate:="WA"*).

4   Delete the statement *myState=InputBox("Enter State Code")*.

You don't need to prompt the user for a state code any more.

```
Sub RetrieveWA()
    MakePivot myState:="WA"
    MakeChart
    AddDeleteButton
End Sub

'
' MakePivot Macro
' Macro recorded by Tex Miller
'
Sub MakePivot(myState)
    myState = InputBox("Enter State Code")
    If myState = "" Then End
    Sheets.Add
    ActiveSheet.PivotTableWizard SourceType:=xlExternal
```

Sheet1 / EIS \ **Module1**

Select this line and press DELETE. *It is no longer necessary.*

Put a button on the map

1   Activate the EIS worksheet, use the right mouse button to click the Retrieve Orders button, and choose the Assign Macro command.

2   Select RetrieveWA from the list and click OK.

3   Type **WA** as the new label for the button.

4   Press ESC to stop typing, which reselects the button.

From the Format menu, choose Object, select the Alignment tab, select the Automatic Size check box, and click OK to shrink the button to fit the label.

5   Use the Font Size control on the Formatting toolbar to change the font size on the label to 8 points.

The label shrinks and the button shrinks with it.

6   Drag the button on top of the map of Washington state and press ESC to deselect the button.

The button disappears because you created the button before you created the map. The button is behind the map.

7   Click the map to select it, and from the Format menu, choose Placement, Send To Back.

8   Click the WA button to try out the macro, and click Close after you have finished perusing the resulting information.

Make seven macros for seven states

1   Activate the Module1 sheet, and select the entire RetrieveWA macro.

2   Press CTRL+C to copy the RetrieveWA macro.

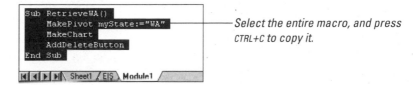

Select the entire macro, and press CTRL+C to copy it.

3   Press UP ARROW and then DOWN ARROW to change the selection to a single insertion point.

4   Press CTRL+V six times to paste six copies of the RetrieveWA macro onto the module sheet.

5   Put the insertion point at the beginning of the second RetrieveWA macro, and choose the Replace command from the Edit menu.

6   Type **WA** in the Find What box, type **OR** in the Replace With box, clear any selected check boxes, and click the Find Next button to select the next occurrence of the letters *WA*.

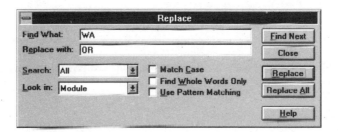

7   Click the Replace button twice to replace two occurrences of *WA* with *OR*.

8   Type **CA** in the Replace With box and click the Replace button twice. Replace the state code two times in each of the remaining macros, using **NV**, **AZ**, **UT**, and **ID** as the Replace With values.

9   Press ESC to dismiss the Replace dialog box.

Now you have seven very simple macros, each of which runs the MakePivot macro with the appropriate state code and then runs the MakeChart and AddDeleteButton subroutines.

Link seven buttons to seven macros

Now you just need to add buttons to the other states to run the individual state macros.

1   Activate the EIS start-up worksheet.

2   Hold down the CTRL key and drag a copy of the WA button onto the middle of the map of Oregon. Repeat this step five times, dragging a copy of the button onto the map of each remaining state.

3   Use the right mouse button to click the button on the map of Oregon, and choose the Assign Macro command.

4   Select RetrieveOR from the list of macros, click OK, and then type **OR** as a new label for the button.

5   Repeat steps 3 and 4 to assign and relabel each of the remaining state buttons.

Creating separate macros and separate buttons for each of the states can make running the macro much more intuitive. Your associates will be less likely to make mistakes and more likely to say nice things about you for creating such an easy to use application.

Adding the EIS Application to a Menu

A big, splashy start-up screen with a big map and lots of buttons is easy to understand and use: Just point at the state you want and click. The problem with big, splashy start-up screens with a big maps and lots of buttons is that they take up the whole screen. What if one of your associates wants to be able to take a look at the orders at any time, even when working with another worksheet in Excel? If you create a custom menu for your application, that associate will be able to review the orders anytime.

Add macros to a menu

Menu Editor button

1   Activate the Module1 sheet and click the Menu Editor button in the Visual Basic toolbar.

The Menu Bars list should display Worksheet as the default menu bar.

2   In the Menus list, select (End Of Menu Bar) at the bottom of the list—notice that the Caption box is grayed out—and click Insert. This inserts an empty line into the Menus list—notice that the Caption box is now available.

3   In the Caption box, type **EI&S**. (Do not press ENTER.)

The ampersand in a caption tells Excel where to put the underline for the keyboard accelerator character. The keyboard accelerator character allows you to choose a menu item with the keyboard by typing the underlined letter. You don't have to use accelerator characters in your menu, but every other Windows-based application in the world does, so you might succumb to peer pressure if nothing else. The letters *E* and *I* are already used (for Edit and Insert, respectively) so use *S* as your accelerator character.

4   Select the (End Of Menu) label in the Menu Items list and click Insert. EI&S now appears in the Menus list.)

5   In the Caption box, type **&Retrieve Orders**.

6   Select the (End Of Menu) label in the Submenu Items list and click Insert. Retrieve Orders now appears in the Menu Items list.

7   In the Caption box, type **&Washington**, select RetrieveWA from the Macro list, and click Insert.

8   Repeat steps 7 and 8 for each of the other six states, using the first letter of the state name as the accelerator character, and then click OK.

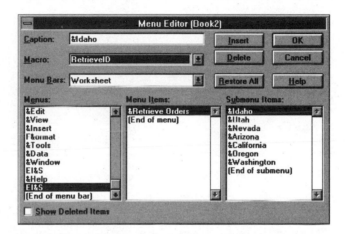

Your menu is finished and operational. Look on the menu bar, between the Window and Help menus. What? You don't see it? You're sure?

Try out the menu bar

When you add a new menu to a menu bar, you typically add the menu to the Worksheet menu bar. If the active sheet is a Module or a Chart sheet, you won't see the new menu.

1   Activate the EIS worksheet.

With a worksheet active, the EIS menu appears, with the *S* appropriately underlined.

2   From the EIS menu, choose Retrieve Orders, Nevada.

The macro runs, retrieving Nevada's orders.

3   Click Close.

4   Click the New Workbook button.

The EIS menu is still visible. The workbook containing the macro does not have to be active for the menu to work.

5   From the EIS menu, choose Retrieve Orders, Arizona.

The macro works just as well with a different workbook active. The workbook containing the macro just has to be open for the new menu to work.

Your simple EIS application is finished. It may not be as full featured as some EIS applications you can imagine, but *you* created it! Give it to your associates. I can't wait to hear them ooh and aah.

Lesson Summary

To	Do this
Set up an external data source	Open the ODBC control in the Windows Control Panel, select the database driver, and add the data source.
Assign a macro to an existing button in a worksheet	Use the right mouse button to click the button, and choose the Assign Macro command.
Make a macro stop	Enter the *End* statement in the macro.
Insert a variable in a text string	Replace the constant in the text string with *" & Variable & "*.
Prevent statements in a macro from displaying a warning message	Use the statement *Application.DisplayAlerts = False*.
Make a chart of the current selection	Make the macro name the selection, and then set the ChartWizard method's Source argument to use the name of the range.
Give the name NewName to the current selection	Use the statement *Selection.Name = "NewName"*.
Import a picture from a file onto a worksheet	From the Insert menu, choose the Picture command and select the picture file.
Attach a macro to a menu command	Click the Menu Editor button in the Visual Basic toolbar, type a caption for the menu item, and select a macro from the Macro list.

For more information on	See
Buttons and other worksheet controls	Chapter 11, "Controls and Dialog Boxes," in the *Microsoft Excel Visual Basic User's Guide*.
Menus and custom menu commands	Chapter 12, "Menus and Toolbars," in the *Microsoft Excel Visual Basic User's Guide*.

Preview of the Next Lesson

In the lessons of Part 2, you have learned how to use graphical user interface tools to make worksheet models and macro applications easy to use. When you have needed macros, you have still largely utilized the macro recorder to build the macros.

If you want to create macros that are faster, more flexible, and easier to read, however, you need to understand more about how Excel and Visual Basic work together. In the lessons of Part 3, you will learn what Excel objects are and how to work effectively with them.

3 Exploring Objects

Explore Object Collections

Think back on your third grade classroom. Your wooden frame desk, decorated with decades of crudely carved names, was fourth from the front, over in the last row next to the windows. Remember those big stairs down to the main floor, with that magnificent banister you would always watch for a chance to slide down? The main hallway was papered with drawings clustered around each classroom door. Each door led to a classroom, and each classroom was filled with kids.

A Microsoft Excel workbook is a lot like a school. The cells in a worksheet appear in rows and columns like students in a classroom. Worksheets are grouped into workbooks, like classrooms in a school. And Excel can have several open workbooks, just as a city can have several schools. Just as you were able to move around freely in the rooms and halls of your old elementary school, you will soon be able to move around freely in Excel objects with your macros.

Visual Basic interacts with Excel by working with Excel objects. Everything in Excel that Visual Basic can control—workbooks, worksheets, cells, menus, text box controls—all of these are objects. In order to effectively control Excel from Visual Basic, you must understand what objects are and how they work in Excel.

You will learn how to:

- Manipulate collections of workbooks and worksheets.

- Manipulate individual workbook and worksheet items.

- Manipulate module sheets and other sheet types.

- Use properties and methods with objects

Estimated lesson time: 30 minutes

Start the lesson

▶   Open Microsoft Excel, with a clean, blank workbook. If you have other workbooks open, such as PERSONAL.XLS, close them. (To find hidden workbooks, choose Unhide from the Window menu.)

What Is an Object?

The easiest way to understand objects in Excel is to compare them to objects in the real world. In the real world, cities, schools, classrooms, and students are all objects. A city is dotted with schools, a school is lined with classrooms, a classroom is packed with students—and all the students are arranged in tidy rows of tidy desks, smiling happily and listening attentively to the kind, wise, firm, but patient teacher. Well, maybe not *all* the desks are tidy.

Objects come in collections

Look around you. The world consists of objects in collections, which are in turn objects in other collections: rooms in apartments in buildings in complexes, flowers in beds in yards in neighborhoods, rocks on crags on mountains in ranges, children in households in extended families in clans. Each object—each city, each student, each flower, each mountain, each family—is an individual item, yet each also belongs to a collection of similar objects, and each collection of objects is itself an individual item within a larger collection.

If you're a city official thinking about the collection of School objects, you may refer to the collection of schools as a group: "All the schools have asbestos problems." Or you may refer to an individual school: "We need to replace the light fixtures at Jefferson Elementary School."

When you do refer to an individual school, you may refer to the school by name: "Jefferson Elementary School, as you may know, was named for the esteemed author of the Declaration of Independence." Or you may refer to it by its position in the collection: "The first school built in our city, back in 1887, is the one I attended as a child." Or (if you are conducting a driving tour) you may refer to the individual school by pointing: "Notice the classic architecture of this magnificent school building."

An Excel workbook is like a school. Just as you can have more than one school in a city, you can have more than one workbook open in Excel. Each workbook is individual and unique, yet each is a Workbook object. You can refer to the entire collection of open workbooks as a group ("Close all the open workbooks"), or you can refer to individual workbooks. If you refer to an individual workbook, you can specify the workbook by name ("Open LESSON1.XLS"), by position ("What is the first workbook in the list of recently opened files?"), or by pointing ("Save the active workbook").

A worksheet in a workbook is like a classroom in a school, and worksheet cells are like students in a classroom, arranged in neat little rows and columns. Excel also has other collections of objects: menu items in menus in menu bars, columns in a series in a layer in a chart, items in fields in rows in a pivot table. You can refer to each collection, whether in Excel or in the natural world, as a whole or as a single item. If you refer to a single item within the collection, you can refer to it by name, by position, or by pointing.

Objects have properties

Do you see that little boy in Mrs. Middlefields's class—the one on the third row, the fourth seat over? He's about four feet seven inches tall. His hair is short. The color of his shirt is blue. His name is Jared. And his eyes are closed.

The boy's height, hair length, shirt color, name, and eye state are *properties* of that one particular Student object. The little girl sitting behind him also has Height, Hair Length, Shirt Color, Name, and Eye State properties, but the *values* of her properties are different. The boy is a different object from the girl, but each is a Student object.

The desk the boy is sitting at is also an object, a Desk object. A Desk object has a Height property, as does a Student object, but a Desk object does not have a Hair Length property. Likewise, a Student object does not have the Manufacturer's Name property that a Desk object has. Because the boy and the desk have different lists of properties, they are different types, or *classes*, of objects. Because the boy and the girl share the same list of properties—even though they have different values for the properties—they both belong to the same class of object. They both belong to the Student object class. Sharing the same list of properties is what makes two objects belong to the same object class.

Just as Jared is an object—a *Student* object—Mrs. Middlefield's entire collection of students is also an object—a *Students* object. The collection has its own properties; the properties of the collection are not the same as the properties of the individual objects contained within it. For example, you don't really care to know the Hair Length property of the entire collection of students. Would that be total hair length or average hair length? But the collection object does have properties of its own. For example, the number of students in the collection is a property of the Students object. The Students object class is different from the Student object class because the two object classes have different lists of properties.

Some properties are easy to change. You could perhaps change Jared's Eye State property with a good, sharp rap with a ruler on his desk. (And of course, he can change the property right back after you look the other way.) You might even change Jared's name to Gerard temporarily for the French language instruction. But changing the boy's height, weight, eye color, or gender probably falls outside the scope of a normal school activity.

Excel objects have properties too. A workbook has an author. A worksheet has a name. A cell has a width, a height, and a value. A menu has a caption. A collection of worksheets has a count of the worksheets in the collection. Changing some of the properties—such as the name of a worksheet or the height of a cell—is easy. Changing other properties—such as the count of cells on a worksheet—probably falls outside the scope of a normal macro activity.

Objects have methods

Look, Mrs. Middlefield is telling the class to stand up. She's leading them in a stirring rendition of "Row, Row, Row Your Boat." Student objects can sing songs. Singing a song is an activity. Student objects also do other activities. Student objects eat. Student objects draw pictures. One student may sing, or eat, or draw well, and another student may sing, or eat, or draw badly, but they both share the ability to do the action. Desk objects, on the other hand, do not sing songs or eat or draw pictures. Desk objects may squeak, perhaps, whereas Student objects generally don't. In the same way that different classes of objects have different lists of properties, they also have different lists of activities they can do. The activities an object can do are called *methods*. Objects that belong to the same class can all do the same methods.

A collection object has a separate list of methods from the methods that belong to the individual items in it. One of the most important methods for most collections is adding a new item to the collection. When a new student moves into the class, you are executing the Add method on the Students object, not on an individual Student object. When the construction bond passes and the school gets a new wing, you are executing the Add method on the Classrooms object. You don't add the new classroom to an individual classroom; you add it to the collection of classrooms.

Another important method for a collection is selecting a single item out of the collection. If Mrs. Middlefield wants to communicate with Jared so that she can ask him to sing a solo, she will establish a communication link with him by calling his name, "Jared." The action of singling out an individual Student object and establishing a communication link with that individual is a method of the Students collection.

Most Excel collection objects have an Add method for adding a new item to the collection, and they all have an Item method for establishing a link to an individual item in the collection. Excel worksheet objects also have a Calculate method for causing all the cells to recalculate, and Excel charts have a ChartWizard method that quickly changes various attributes of a chart.

Sometimes the distinction between a method and a property is vague. When Jared opens his eyes, is he carrying out the Open Eyes method (an action), or is he assigning a new value to his Eye State property? Here are some concepts that may help:

Methods can change properties   Some methods do change properties. When Jared carries out the Fingerpaint method, the action happens to change his Shirt Color property. Then, when he goes home and carries out the Wash Clothes method, the Shirt Color property changes back (with perhaps a few residual stains). Likewise, in Excel, the ChartWizard *method* can change several *properties* of the chart.

Properties can involve actions Setting a property does sometimes involve some kind of action. When you change the classroom's Wall Color property, you do get out the paint rollers and the ladders and start working, but you are more concerned about the finished attribute of the wall than about the action that changed the attribute. In Excel, hiding a worksheet is setting a property (because the worksheet is still there and you may want to change the property back). But closing a file is a method because there's no trace of the file left in memory after you are done.

Note Most of the time you don't need to worry about the difference between properties and methods. Excel has on-line tools to help you find the methods and properties for objects, and you may not need to know which is which. For example, you can turn on the macro recorder, carry out a task, and then copy or modify the code the macro recorder produced—without ever really knowing whether Excel used a property or a method for any given task.

In summary, an individual item is an object from one object class, while a collection of those items is an object from a different object class. A single item from one collection can contain an entire collection of other objects. For example, a single school from the district's collection of schools can contain an entire collection of classrooms. Each object belongs to an object class that has a unique list of properties and methods. Many different individual objects (Student objects) can belong to a single object class (the Student object class), in which case they all share the same list of properties and methods, while retaining their own individuality. In these lessons in Part 3, you will learn how to work with many kinds of Excel objects.

Understanding Workbooks

Workbooks are the major structural unit in Excel. You can learn much about how objects and collections work in Excel by experimenting with workbooks.

Excel also has a powerful tool to help you experiment with objects, properties, and methods: the Immediate pane of the Debug window. You can use the Immediate pane to explore Workbook objects.

Add a workbook

1 If the Visual Basic toolbar is not visible, use the right mouse button to click any toolbar, and choose Visual Basic.

2 Click the Insert Module button, and then click the Module1 sheet tab to activate the module.

Insert Module button **3** From the View menu, choose the Debug Window command.

The Debug window appears. This is the same window that appears when you step through a macro.

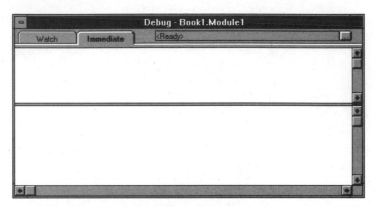

4   Resize the Debug window so that you can see the workbook behind it, and click in the top half of the Debug window.

The top half of the Debug window is called the Immediate pane (as long as the tab labeled Immediate is selected).

5   In the Immediate pane, type **Workbooks.Add**, and press ENTER.

A new workbook appears. The Add method added a new workbook to the collection, and you watched it happen. In the Immediate pane, you type macro statements and see the effect immediately. The Immediate pane is an effective tool for finding out immediately what happens when you execute a statement.

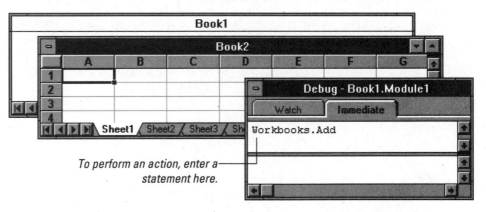

To perform an action, enter a—
statement here.

6   Press the UP ARROW key so that the insertion point is back in the *Workbooks.Add* statement, and press ENTER.

The Add method creates another Workbook object.

To reexecute a statement in the Immediate pane, put the insertion point anywhere in the line and press ENTER.

The word *Workbooks* is a link to the Workbooks object—the collection of workbooks currently open in Excel. The word *Add* is a method for the Workbooks object that adds a new item to the collection. A method follows an object, separated by a single period (*object.method*). Most collections in Excel have an Add method for adding new items to the collection.

Count the workbooks

You have now used a method—the Add method—with a Workbooks object. The Workbooks object also has properties. One of the properties—the Count property—tells you how many items are in the collection. The Count property returns a value. You can display that value in the Immediate pane.

1   In the Immediate pane, type **?Workbooks. Count** and press ENTER.

The number 3 (or however many workbooks are currently open) appears.

In the Immediate pane, typing a question mark followed by anything that returns a value displays that value on the next line. Since the Count property returns a number value, you can display that value using the question mark.

2   Press UP ARROW to get back to the *Workbooks.Add* statement, press ENTER to add a new workbook, and then press ENTER again in the *?Workbooks.Count* statement to see the new workbook count.

The count should now be 4 (or one greater than whatever it was before).

The word *Count* is a property. You attach a property to its object with a period in the same way that you attach a method to its object. When you execute the Add method, you don't put a question mark in front of it because it returns an object rather than a value. You can see the effect of the Add method by looking at the screen. When you use the Count property, you want to find out the value of the property. Putting a question mark in front of the property displays the property's value.

Note   You cannot change the number of workbooks by changing the Count property. You must use the Add method to add a new workbook to the collection. A property where you cannot assign a new value, but can only read the current value, is called a *read-only* property.

Close the workbooks

The Add method works on the Workbooks object by adding one item to it. The Workbooks object has an additional method—the Close method—that can close the entire collection.

1   Type **Workbooks.Close**, press ENTER, and click No when asked to save changes.

All the open workbooks disappear. Using the Close method on the Workbooks object closes the entire collection. The Close method closes everything so fast that you may want to see it work again.

2   Reexecute the *Workbooks.Add* line six or seven times to create a few new workbooks.

3   Reexecute the *?Workbooks.Count* line to see how many workbooks are in the collection.

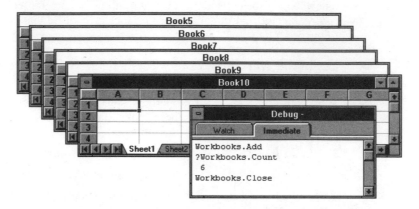

4   Reexecute the *Workbooks.Close* line to close all the workbooks.

Doesn't that give you a great sense of power? One keystroke and all those workbooks are utterly annihilated.

5   Reexecute the *?Workbooks.Count* line to see how many workbooks are in the collection.

The number zero appears because you destroyed all the workbooks.

Add and Close are both methods of the Workbooks object. Count is a property of the Workbooks object. The Add and the Close methods indirectly change the value of the Count property and are, in fact, the only ways you can change the Count property. The Count property is *read-only*.

Refer to a single workbook

Closing the entire Workbooks collection all at once is a powerful experience, and possibly occasionally useful, but usually you want more control over which workbooks disappear. To close a single workbook, you need to specify a single item out of the Workbooks collection.

1   Run the *Workbooks.Add* statement at the top of the Immediate pane several times to create a few new workbooks.

2   Press CTRL+END to get to the first blank line at the bottom of the Immediate pane.

3   Type **?Workbooks.Item(1).Name** and press ENTER.

The name of the first workbook—the first of the current set of workbooks to be opened (probably something like Book12)—appears.

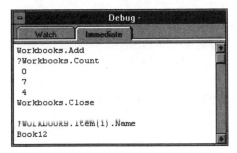

Reading from right to left, this statement asks: "The name of the first item in the workbooks collection is what?"

The word *Name* is a property of a single workbook. Since Name is a property, you can display its value by using the question mark at the beginning of the statement. The Name property is not available for a Workbooks object because a collection of workbooks doesn't have a name.

The word *Item* is a method. Like the teacher establishing a communication link by addressing an individual student, the Item method creates a link to an individual item in a collection. The Item method requires a single argument: the position number of the item you want.

Note   Retrieving a single item from a collection is so common that you can leave out the word *Item* (and its accompanying period) and put the parentheses right after the name of the collection. The statement *?Workbooks(1).Name* accomplishes the same task as *?Workbooks.Item(1).Name*. Using the Item method explicitly at first can help you remember to use the plural word *Workbooks* even though you are referring to a single workbook item.

The word *Workbooks* establishes a link to the entire collection of workbooks—the Workbooks object. Once you have a link to the Workbooks object, the word *Item(1)* switches the link to the specified item within the collection—a Workbook object. Once you have a link to a Workbook object, the word *Name* returns the name of that object.

4   Type **Workbooks.Item(1).Close** and press ENTER.

The first workbook disappears.

5   Reexecute the *?Workbooks.Item(1).Name* statement.

The name of the new first workbook appears. (If the first workbook was Book12 before, the new first workbook is probably Book13.)

6   Reexecute the *Workbooks.Item(1).Close* statement to close the new first workbook in the collection.

The word *Workbooks* has two meanings in Excel: First, the word *Workbooks* is the name of an object class, the Workbooks object class; it is a noun, a thing. Second, the word *Workbooks* is a method that establishes a link to the collection of workbooks; it is a verb, an action. You cannot put the actual Workbooks object "thing" into your macro. (The Workbooks object is inside Excel; you can see it on your computer display.) What you put into your macro is the verb, the Workbooks "action" that establishes a link to the Workbooks "thing."

Once the Workbooks method establishes a link to the Workbooks object, you can "talk" to the object using methods and properties from the list that a Workbooks object understands. You can use the Count property to look at the number of items in the collection. You can use the Add method to add a new item to the collection. You can use the Close method to close the entire collection of workbooks. *Count*, *Add*, and *Close* are three of the words that a Workbooks object can understand.

A Workbooks object can also understand the Item method. The Item method is an "action" that establishes a link to an individual Workbook "thing." Excel does not have a Workbook method to link to a single Workbook object. You use the Item method of the Workbooks object to establish the link to an individual object.

Once the Item method establishes a link to an individual Workbook object, you can "talk" to the object using methods and properties that a Workbook object understands. You can use the Name property to look at the workbook's name. You can use the Close method to close the one workbook.

All collection objects in Excel share the same name as the method that establishes a link with the object. The Workbooks object shares its name with the Workbooks method. The Workbooks method establishes a link with the Workbooks object. As you learn more about objects, you will see that the Worksheets object shares its name with the Worksheets method, the Windows object shares its name with the Windows method, the Charts object shares its name with the Charts method, and so forth.

In Visual Basic code, you never refer to an individual item from a collection by leaving the letter *s* off the name of the collection. For example, you never refer to an individual workbook in a macro by using the word *Workbook*. Every collection object class has an Item method that you use to establish a link to an individual item in the collection.

Refer to a workbook by name

So far when you have used the Item method to establish a link to an individual workbook, you have specified the workbook you want by number, its position in the collection. A workbook's position number is determined by the order in which you open the workbooks. You can also refer to an item in a collection by its name.

1   If you are running out of workbooks, scroll back to the top of the Immediate pane and execute the *Workbooks.Add* statement a few more times.

2   Scroll to the bottom of the Immediate pane.

Look at the name of one of the workbooks, preferably one in the middle of the stack. Perhaps you see a workbook named Book17.

3   Type **Workbooks.Item("Book17").Activate** and press ENTER.

The workbook you specified moves to the top of the stack of workbooks. The word *Activate* is a method. It is a message that a single Workbook object understands. The Activate method moves the workbook to the top of the stack of workbooks.

You can refer to a workbook either by name or by position number. If you use the name, you must put it in quotation marks. If you use the position number, you must not use quotation marks.

When you refer to an item in a collection by name, you always get the same item—as long as it still exists.

Type **Workbooks.Item("Book17").Close**, and press ENTER to close the workbook.

4   Reexecute the *Workbooks.Item("Book17").Close* statement.

Excel displays an error message because the workbook with that name no longer exists.

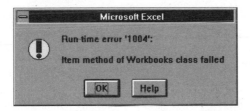

5   Click OK to remove the error message.

You can use either the name or the position number to refer to an item in a collection. If you use the position number, you may get a different item each time you use the Item method; if you use the name, you may get an error if the item no longer exists.

Refer to a workbook by pointing

Suppose you want to refer to the top workbook on the stack, but you don't know either its name or its position number. Because it is the active workbook, you can refer to it by pointing.

▶   On a blank row at the bottom of the Immediate pane, type **ActiveWorkbook.Close** and press ENTER.

The top workbook in the stack disappears.

The word *ActiveWorkbook* establishes a link directly to the active workbook. ActiveWorkbook bypasses the Workbooks object and establishes the link directly. If the first workbook opened happens to be the active workbook, *Workbooks.Item(1)* establishes a link to the same Workbook object as *ActiveWorkbook*. Once you have a link to the workbook, you can look at its name or close it. Once you have a link to an object, the process by which you established that link is not important.

Change a workbook property value

Both the Count property of a Workbooks object and the Name property of a Workbook object are *read-only* properties. You can look at the value returned by the property, but you cannot change it. A workbook has other properties, *read-write* properties, that you can change as well as look at.

1   In the Immediate pane, type **?ActiveWorkbook. Saved** and press ENTER.

The word *True* appears because the workbook hasn't had any changes made to it.

Note When you close a workbook, Excel uses the value of the Saved property to decide whether to prompt you to save changes. If the Saved property is True, Excel does not prompt you. If the Saved property is False, Excel does prompt you.

Normally, you change the Saved property to False by typing something into a cell, and you change the Saved property to True by saving the workbook. You can, however, change the Saved property directly.

2   Type **ActiveWorkbook.Saved = False** and press ENTER.

Nothing seems to have happened, but you just changed the value of the property.

3   Reexecute the *?ActiveWorkbook.Saved* statement to see the new value for the property.

The word *False* appears. Now Excel thinks that the worksheet has unsaved changes in it.

4   Reexecute the *ActiveWorkbook.Close* statement.

Because you set the Saved property to False, Excel asks if you want to save changes.

5   Click the Cancel button to leave the workbook open.

6   At the bottom of the Immediate pane, type **ActiveWorkbook.Saved = True** and press ENTER.

7   Reexecute the *ActiveWorkbook.Close* statement.

The workbook closes without a whisper.

Tip If you write a macro that modifies a workbook and you want to close the workbook without saving changes (and without displaying a warning prompt), make the macro change the Saved property of the workbook to True.

The Saved property is a *read-write* property. You can display its current value, and you can also change its value.

Look at the return value of the Close method

Normally, you execute a method and you change the value or retrieve the value of a property. Methods do return values, however, and you may want to see the value that a method returns. For example, when you use the Close method on a workbook, the effect of the method is to close the workbook, but the method also returns a value to the macro.

1   If you are running out of workbooks, scroll back to the top of the Immediate pane, execute the *Workbooks.Add* statement a couple more times, and then scroll to the bottom of the Immediate pane.

2   Type **?ActiveWorkbook.Close** and press ENTER.

The active workbook closes, and the word *True* appears after the statement.

When the Close method carries out its task, it returns the value True if it completes the task successfully. The closing of the workbook is the *effect* of the method. The word *True* that appears in the Immediate pane is the *return value* of the method.

If the Close method cannot accomplish the desired effect, it produces a different return value.

3   Type **ActiveWorkbook.Saved = False** and press ENTER.

This makes Excel think the current active workbook has been changed.

4   Type **?ActiveWorkbook.Close** and press ENTER. Click Cancel when asked if you want to save changes.

The word *False* appears after the statement. This time, the Close method did not complete the task of closing the workbook, so it returns the value False. You can often look at a method's return value to find out whether it completed its task.

All methods always return something. Some methods (like Close) return either True or False, depending on whether they are successful at the task. Some methods (like Activate) always return True because if they do not accomplish the desired effect, the macro refuses to continue. Some methods (like Item) establish a link to an object and return that link so that you can use methods and properties to communicate with the object.

Quit Microsoft Excel

You have done a lot of experimenting using the Immediate pane. Before you continue, close Microsoft Excel. You can close Excel directly from the Debug window.

▶   In the Immediate pane, type **Application.Quit** and press ENTER. Click No if prompted to save changes to any workbooks.

In this section, you learned how to use the Add method and the Close method on a Workbooks object, and you learned how to use the Activate method and the Close method on a Workbook object. You saw how to read the value of the Count property of a Workbooks object and the Name property of a Workbook object. You also saw how to change the value of the read-write Saved property of a Workbook object.

You learned how to use the Workbooks method to establish a link to the Workbooks object, how to use the Item method of the Workbooks object to switch the link to a single Workbook object, and how to use the ActiveWorkbook property to set a link directly to the active Workbook object.

Along the way, you learned how to use the Immediate pane of the Debug window to read the value of properties, set the value of read-write properties, watch the effect of executing methods, and display the return value of some methods.

Understanding Worksheets

Worksheets come in collections just as workbooks do. By manipulating worksheets in the Immediate pane, you will see some similarities—and also some differences—between different classes of collections.

Add a new worksheet

Insert Module button

1   Start Microsoft Excel, display the Visual Basic toolbar, click the Insert Module button to add a new module, and then delete all the other sheets in the workbook. (Click the Sheet1 tab, scroll the sheet tabs until you can see the last worksheet, hold down the SHIFT key, and click the last worksheet tab. Choose Delete Sheets from the Edit menu, and click Yes to confirm.)

2   With the Module1 sheet active, choose Debug Window from the View menu. Resize the Debug window so that you can see the sheet tab in Book1.

3   In the Immediate pane, type **Worksheets.Add** and press ENTER.

A new worksheet appears before Module1.

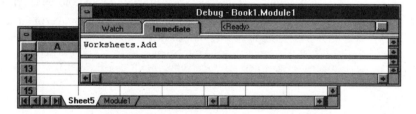

You add a new worksheet to the current workbook the same way that you add a new workbook to Excel: with the Add method. The name *Worksheets* is used for both the Worksheets object and the Worksheets method. When you enter the word *Worksheets* into your code, you are using the Worksheets method, which establishes a link to the Worksheets object that exists inside Excel somewhere. You never enter an object name directly into your code; you always enter a method or property that establishes a link to the object.

4   Reexecute the *Worksheets.Add* statement three times so that you have four total worksheets (plus one module sheet) in the workbook.

5 Type **?Worksheets.Item(1).Name** and press ENTER to display the name of the first worksheet.

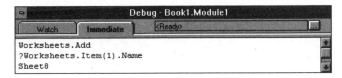

```
Worksheets.Add
?Worksheets.Item(1).Name
Sheet8
```

In the same way that you use the Item method on a Workbooks object to establish a link to a single Workbook object, you use the Item method on a Worksheets object to establish a link to a single Worksheet object. Once you have the link to a Worksheet object, you can use Worksheet object properties, such as Name.

The name of a work*book* is a read-only property. (You have to save a file to change its name.) The name of a work*sheet* is a read-write property. You can change the name directly.

6 Type **Worksheets.Item(1).Name = "Input Values"** and press ENTER.

The name of the worksheet changes.

As with workbooks, you can refer to a single worksheet by name, by number, or by pointing. Now that the first worksheet has the name *Input Values*, the expressions *Worksheets.Item("Input Values")*, *Worksheets.Item(1)*, and *ActiveSheet* all establish a link to the same Worksheet object.

Look at the result of the Add method

Earlier in this lesson, you saw that the Close method returns either True or False depending on whether it achieves the desired effect. The Add method also has an effect: It creates a new item in the collection. But the Add method does not return True or False. The Add method returns a link to the newly created object. You can use that link the same way you use the link created by the Item method or by the ActiveSheet property.

▶ Type **?Worksheets.Add.Name** and press ENTER.

A new worksheet appears in the workbook, and the default name of the new worksheet, possibly Sheet9, appears in the Debug window.

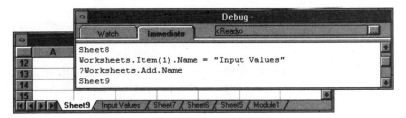

The Add method has an effect: It creates the new worksheet. It also returns a link to the new object. If you don't use the link immediately—as part of the same statement—the link is discarded. If you then want to communicate with the new worksheet, you must reestablish a link using ActiveSheet or the Item method. Usually, you don't bother using the link returned by Worksheets.Add because using ActiveSheet to establish a new link is as easy as shouting "Jared" to get a slumbering student's attention.

Copy and move a worksheet

1 Type **Worksheets.Item("Input Values").Copy** and press ENTER.

A new workbook appears in front of the original workbook, containing the copy of the Input Values worksheet.

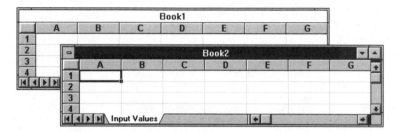

The word *Copy* is a worksheet method. If you don't tell the Copy method where to put the copy of the worksheet, it creates a new workbook for the copy.

2 Type **Workbooks.Item(1).Activate** to put the original workbook back on top.

3 Type **Worksheets.Item("Input Values").Copy Before:=Worksheets.Item(2)**, and press ENTER to create a copy of the Input Values worksheet.

You can tell the Copy method where to put the copy by using the Before argument. As the value of the Before argument, use a link to a single Worksheet object. (The Copy method also has an After argument that you can use instead of the Before argument to specify a location for the copy.)

4 Type **Worksheets.Item(2).Name = "Variant Values"** and press ENTER to change the name of the new worksheet.

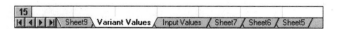

A worksheet does not have to be active for you to change its properties. All you need is a link to the Worksheet object you want to change.

5 Type **Worksheets.Item(2).Move Before:=Worksheets.Item(1)** and press ENTER to move the second worksheet to the first position.

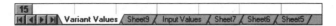

The word *Move* is another method that applies to a worksheet. You must give the Move method either a Before argument or an After argument. When you use the name of an argument, you separate the argument name from the argument value with a colon and an equal sign (:=).

6 Type **Workbooks.Item(2).Worksheets.Item(1).Name = "Old Values"** and press ENTER.

The name of the worksheet in the second workbook changes. (The second workbook is the one that was created when you copied the worksheet without giving it a location.)

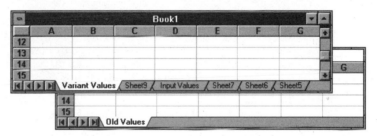

You can manipulate objects in workbooks that are not active, the same as you can manipulate objects in the active workbook. You just establish a link to the object you want to work with.

Manipulate multiple worksheets

When you were exploring workbooks, you closed all the workbooks at the same time using the statement *Workbooks.Close*, and you closed a single workbook from the collection using the statement *Workbooks.Item(1).Close*. Most of the time when working with a collection, you want to use either the entire collection or a single item from the collection. Sometimes, however, you want to create a subcollection: a new collection that includes some, but not all, the items in the original collection.

1 Type **Worksheets(3).Select** and press ENTER to select the third worksheet in the workbook, the Input Values worksheet.

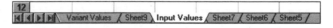

The Select method allows you to select a new worksheet within the workbook.

2   Type **Worksheets(Array(1,3,4)).Select** and press ENTER to select the first, third, and fourth worksheets.

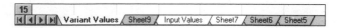

The word *Array* is a function that lets you treat multiple values as one. With the Array function, you can select more than one worksheet at the same time. (When you are not in a macro, you select multiple worksheets by holding down the CTRL key and clicking the sheet tabs.)

3   Type **Worksheets(3).Activate** and press ENTER to activate the third worksheet in the workbook, the Input Values worksheet, while leaving all three worksheets selected.

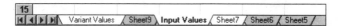

When you select more than one worksheet, one of the worksheets is on top, as the active worksheet. All three worksheets are selected, but only one is active. You use the Activate method to specify which worksheet should be the active worksheet. If only one worksheet is selected, the Select method and the Activate method act the same: They select and activate a single worksheet. You can run methods or set properties using the entire subcollection of worksheets at once.

4   Type **?Worksheets(Array(1,3,4)).Count** and press ENTER.

The number 3 appears. When you select items from a collection with the Array function, the selected items form a new collection.

5   Type **Activesheet.Select** and press ENTER to select only a single worksheet.

Select a type of sheet

So far, you have worked exclusively with the Worksheets collection. Excel workbooks can also contain other types of sheets. The other types of sheets in a workbook have their own collections.

1   Type **Modules.Add** and press ENTER to add a new module sheet.

Modules, like worksheets, are contained in a workbook, but modules are a different collection from worksheets, and they have their own Modules object. Using the Add method on the Modules object adds a new module to the workbook.

2 Type **?Modules.Count** and press ENTER.

The number of modules appears. The Modules object is similar to the Worksheets object: You can add a module, count the modules, hide modules, or establish a link to a single module. The Module object is similar to the Worksheet object: You can copy one, move one, delete one, or give a new name to one. You use the Workbook object's Modules method to establish a link to the Modules object (the collection). You use the Modules object's Item method to establish a link to the Module object (an individual item).

3 Type **?Sheets.Count** and press ENTER.

The total count of worksheets and module sheets appears.

The word *Sheets* is a method that establishes a link to a Sheets object. The Sheets object is a special collection that includes worksheets, modules, chart sheets, and dialog sheets. Use the Sheets object if you want to refer to all the sheets regardless of type.

In addition to worksheets and modules, Excel workbooks can contain chart sheets and dialog sheets. Each type of sheet has its own collection object: the Worksheets object, the Modules object, the Charts object, or the DialogSheets object. Each of those objects has a method with the same name that you use to establish a link to the collection. As a result, you can establish a link to all the sheets in the workbook, all the sheets of one type, or one or more individual sheets.

Quit Microsoft Excel

▶ In the Immediate pane, type **Application.Quit**, and click No when asked to save changes to any workbooks.

Lesson Summary

To	Do this
Create a new workbook	Use the statement *Workbooks.Add*.
Add a new worksheet to the active workbook	Use the statement *Worksheets.Add*.
Close the active workbook	Use the statement *ActiveWorkbook.Close*.
Give the name NewSheet to the first worksheet in a workbook	Use the statement *Worksheets.Item(1).Name = "NewSheet"*.
Select multiple worksheets	Use the Array function to specify items from the collection. For example, use the statement *Worksheets(Array(1,3)).Select*.
Quit Microsoft Excel	Use the statement *Application.Quit*.

For more information on	See
Microsoft Excel objects	Chapter 5, "Working with Objects," in the *Microsoft Excel Visual Basic User's Guide*.

Preview of the Next Lesson

In this lesson, you have seen how collections, properties, and methods work with worksheets. Collections, whether worksheets, modules, or workbooks, all work basically the same. The fact that all collections work very consistently will be useful to you as you learn how to work with Excel objects.

In the next lesson, you will learn how to use Excel's Object Browser tool to find out methods and properties for an object. In the process, you will learn how to work with one of the most important objects in Excel: the Windows object.

Explore Window Objects

Modern electronic equipment uses remote controls extensively. Viewers are too busy to get up and walk across the room to select one of the hundreds of cable channels available on the television, so the television manufacturer puts direct access buttons onto a remote control. The result is convenience, beauty, and elegance.

The problem is that each piece of equipment uses a different remote control. You don't need very many components in your entertainment system to have a coffee table that looks like your four-year-old niece abandoned a building-block construction project.

Excel objects are like electronic equipment, and each object class has its own unique remote control. The methods and properties for an object class are like the buttons, displays, and knobs on its remote control. Fortunately, many of the specific controls are similar among different object classes. Also fortunately, Excel provides extensive on-line tools to help you use the controls—the methods and properties—correctly.

You will learn how to:

- Manipulate Window objects with Visual Basic code.

- Use the Object Browser to find out about objects, properties, and methods.

- Use named Excel constants to make your code easy to read.

Estimated lesson time: 20 minutes

Start the lesson

Restore button

▶ Open Microsoft Excel with a blank workbook. If the workbook window is maximized, click the Restore button so that you will be able to adjust the size of the window.

Managing Objects

Microsoft Excel has more than 120 different classes of objects, approximately 500 properties, and 300 methods. Even after you get comfortable with the concepts involved in manipulating objects, properties, and methods, you still have to find the ones you want, when you want them. Trying to memorize lists of objects, properties, and methods is probably futile.

Excel's on-line tools can help you find the object class you need and the methods and properties you need to manipulate it. The on-line tools include the Object Browser, the Visual Basic Reference in Help, and the macro recorder. In this lesson, you will learn how to use the Object Browser resource and also how to manipulate windows.

Exploring Windows Using the Object Browser

You can learn how to use the Object Browser by exploring the Windows object. Like the Workbooks object and the Worksheets object, the Windows object is a collection. Each item in the Windows object is a separate Window object.

Create windows interactively

First create some windows interactively. In Excel you create a new window every time you create a new workbook. You can also create multiple windows for a single workbook.

When you first open Excel, you see a blank workbook, Book1. This workbook has its own window, and the name of the workbook appears as the caption of the window.

New Workbook button

1   Click the New Workbook button.

A second workbook appears—again with its own window and with the workbook name as the caption of the window.

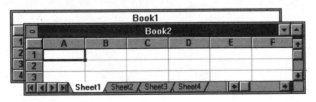

2   From the Window menu, choose the New Window command.

Another new window appears. The window caption shows the workbook name, followed by a colon, followed by the number 2, since this is now the second window for the workbook.

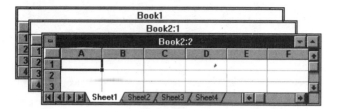

You now have three windows and two workbooks. A workbook always has at least one window, but it can have many more than one. Many of the attributes you may think of as belonging to a workbook—such as its size and location on the screen or its caption at the top—are actually attributes of the workbook's window.

Create a new workbook using the Object Browser

In Lesson 6, you created a new workbook by typing the *Workbooks.Add* statement. Now construct that same statement using the Object Browser to see how the Object Browser works.

Insert Module button

1   Click the Insert Module button in the Visual Basic toolbar, choose the Debug Window command from the View menu, resize the Debug window so you can see the windows behind it, and activate the Immediate pane.

Object Browser button

2   Click the Object Browser button in the Visual Basic toolbar.

The Object Browser dialog box appears. The name of the active workbook is in the box labeled Libraries/Workbooks at the top.

Tip   You can also press F2 to activate the Object Browser.

3   Select Excel from the Libraries/Workbooks list.

The list labeled Objects/Modules changes to show the names for all Excel's object classes.

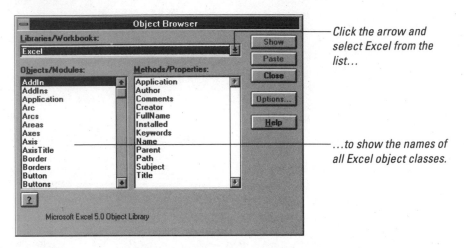

Click the arrow and select Excel from the list...

...to show the names of all Excel object classes.

4   Select Workbooks from the list of object names.

The Methods/Properties list changes to show the methods and properties available for Workbooks. Notice that Add is at the top of the list. This is the same Add method that you used in Lesson 5 to create a new workbook.

5   Select the Add method from the Methods/Properties list.

A brief description of the Add method appears at the bottom of the dialog box, and the text on the Paste button changes from gray to black because the button is now available. You can paste only words that appear in the Methods/Properties list because you never put object class names directly into your macros.

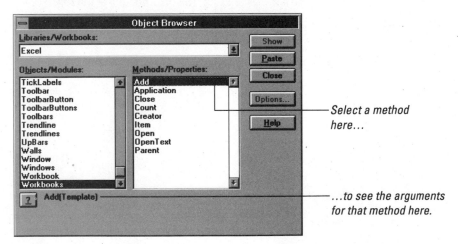

Select a method here...

...to see the arguments for that method here.

6   Click the Paste button.

If you are not familiar with workbook templates, search Help for "AutoTemplates."

The Add method of the Workbooks object allows you to specify a template for the new workbook.

7   Delete the argument (including the parentheses).

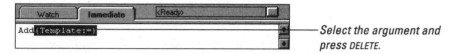

— *Select the argument and press DELETE.*

Create a link to an object

The Object Browser pastes the method (*Add*), along with any arguments (*Template:=*), but it does not paste the name of the object. You never enter the name of an object class directly into your code. You always get an object by a method or a property. To put a Workbooks *object* into your macro, you need to use the Workbooks *method*. Workbooks is a method of the Application object.

Object Browser button

1   Click in front of the word *Add*, click the Object Browser button, and select Application from the Objects/Modules list on the left.

2   In the Methods/Properties list on the right, select Workbooks, and click Paste.

The words *Workbooks(Index:=)* appear before the word *Add*. The word *Workbooks* is the Workbooks method, which establishes the link to—or *returns*—the Workbooks object. The word *Index* is an argument that allows you to specify a single workbook from the colleciton.

3   Select the argument *(Index:=)* and delete it. (Be sure to delete the parentheses with the argument name.)

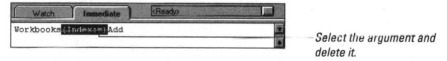

—*Select the argument and delete it.*

4   Type a PERIOD (.) to separate the Workbooks method (which returns a Workbooks object) from the Add method (which can be used with the Workbooks object), and press ENTER.

The new workbook appears.

Obviously, typing the statement *Workbooks.Add* directly is easier than going through the Object Browser—provided that you know the names of the methods or properties you need to type. The Object Browser helps you find properties and methods you may not already know.

The Object Browser can help you understand the difference between the name of an object class and the process you use to refer to a specific object in your macro. In the Object Browser, the Objects/Modules list (on the left) is a list of object class names. You never put the name of an object class from this list directly into a macro statement. If you need to put an object into your code, you must use a method or property from the Methods/Properties list (on the right). The Object Browser pastes words only from the list on the right.

Create a new window using the Object Browser

Most collections—like Workbooks, Worksheets, Modules, and Charts—have an Add method that you use to add an item to the collection. The Windows collection, however, does not have an Add method because creating a new workbook automatically creates a window for that workbook. You can use the Object Browser to help you find how to add a new window to an existing workbook.

Object Browser button

1 Click the Object Browser button, and then select Windows from the Objects/Modules list.

The list of methods and properties for the Windows collection contains six entries, but none of them seems to be useful for adding a new window to an existing workbook. Since you are adding a new window to a workbook, see if the Workbook object has a potentially helpful method.

2 Select Workbook from the Objects/Modules list and scroll down the list of methods and properties.

One of the entries in the list is *NewWindow*. Interactively, you created a new window for an existing workbook by choosing the New Window command from the Window menu, so maybe this is the method you want.

3 Select the NewWindow method and click Paste.

The word *NewWindow* appears in the Immediate pane, but it doesn't have an object in front of it. Since NewWindow is a method for a Workbook object, you need to put a Workbook object in front of it.

4 Press HOME to get to the start of the line, type **ActiveWorkbook.** (with the period), and press ENTER.

The new window appears. The colon in the caption lets you know that this is a new window for the same workbook.

When you don't know the exact name of the method you need, sometimes browsing through the Object Browser can provide a needed clue.

Look at the Windows object

Most collections have similar methods and properties. Once you learn how to use the remote control for one collection object, you can easily use the remote control for most other collections. By browsing through the list of methods and properties for the Windows object, you can learn more about all collections.

In the Object Browser, you can select the Windows object quickly by pressing W three times.

1   Click the Object Browser button, and select Windows from the list of object names. Look at the list of properties and methods.

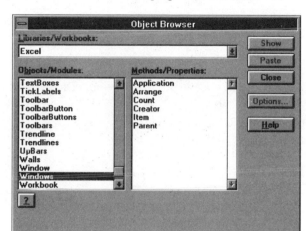

You used the Count property and the Item method when working with workbooks in Lesson 6. All collections have a Count property and an Item method.

The word *Application* is the first entry in the list of properties and methods. Every object in Excel has an Application property; the Application property returns the Application object, which is Microsoft Excel. The Application property is useful when you write applications that cross application boundaries.

The words *Parent* and *Creator* are unfamiliar items in the list:

Every object has a Parent property. The Parent property returns the next higher object in the hierarchy. Using the school analogy, the parent of a Student object is a Classroom object, and the parent of a Classroom object is a School object. In Excel, the parent of a Worksheet object is a Workbook object, and the parent of a Workbook object is the Application object, which is Microsoft Excel. For every object, the chain of parent objects continues up to the Application object.

Every object also has a Creator property. The Creator property is a number that uniquely identifies the Microsoft Excel application in a Macintosh environment.

2   Press ESC to close the Object Browser.

Three of the properties for the Windows object—Application, Creator, and Parent—are common to every object in Excel. In addition, the Count property and the Item method are common to every collection in Excel. (Most collections also have the Add method.) That leaves one method—Arrange—that is unique to a Windows object.

Arrange windows

Object Browser button

1   In the Immediate pane, type **Windows.** (with the period), and click the Object Browser button.

The word *Windows* is the Windows method. The Windows *method* returns the Windows *object*, which is a collection of all the open windows in the application.

2   In the Object Browser, select Windows from the list of object names, select Arrange as the method, and click Paste.

The word *Windows* on the left side of the Object Browser is the Windows object class name. You choose Windows from the list of names because you are looking for methods and properties that you can use with a Windows object.

When you paste the Arrange method, the word *Arrange* appears in the Immediate pane, followed by a long list of arguments. These arguments correspond to settings in the Arrange dialog box from the Window menu.

In Lesson 9, you will learn about when to remove and when to leave parentheses around arguments.

3   Type **1** as the value for ArrangeStyle, and delete all the other arguments. Delete the parentheses around the arguments. You should end up with the statement *Windows.Arrange ArrangeStyle:=1*.

4   Press ENTER.

The windows change to a tiled pattern, filling the screen.

5   Change the value of the ArrangeStyle argument to 2, then 3, and then 7, executing the *Windows.Arrange* command for each value.

The windows are arranged horizontally, vertically, and cascading down the screen, depending on which argument value you use.

The values for the ArrangeStyle argument correspond to the different options available in the Arrange dialog box.

Find a named constant using the Object Browser

The Object Browser tells you that ArrangeStyle is an argument for the Arrange method, but it does not tell you to use 1, 2, 3, and 7 as values for the ArrangeStyle argument. Excel actually provides named constants that can help you understand what the values for the arguments are, and the Object Browser can help you find a named constant.

1   In the statement *Windows.Arrange ArrangeStyle:=7*, select the number 7 and delete it.

2   Without moving the insertion point, click the Object Browser button.

3   In the list of object names, select Constants.

The word *Constants* is not really the name of an object class, but it appears in the Object Browser as a convenience to you.

When you select Constants from the Objects/Modules list, a list of all the named constants in Excel appears in the Method/Properties list.

4   From the list of constants, select xlTiled and click Paste.

The word *xlTiled* appears where the number 7 had been.

5   Press ENTER to arrange the worksheets in a tiled pattern.

The xlTiled constant is equivalent to the number 1. The constants xlHorizontal, xlVertical, and xlCascade are equivalent to the numbers 2, 3, and 7.

Note   To find the constants that can be used with a particular method, look for that method in Help. In Lesson 8 you will learn more about using Help to explore Excel objects.

6   Type **Windows.Arrange ArrangeStyle:=xlCascade**, and press ENTER to leave the windows cascading before you continue.

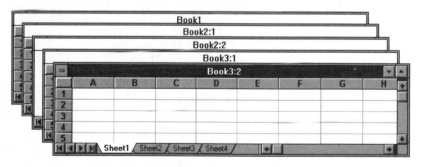

In Lesson 8, you will use Help to find argument values for specific methods.

The list of constants in Excel is very large. You probably could not find a completely unknown constant using the Object Browser. The Object Browser can be very helpful, however, if you are trying to remember a constant or if you are trying to remember how to spell a constant.

Activate windows

When working with several windows on the screen, you sometimes need to control which window is on top, or active. Interactively, you select the name of the window from the Window menu to activate it. In a macro, you use methods. In Lesson 5, you used the Activate method with Worksheet objects. The Object Browser can help you find whether a Window object also has an Activate method.

1   Click the Object Browser button, and select Window from the list of object names.

The list of methods and properties is much longer for a Window object than it was for a Windows object. The Activate method does appear in the list. (While you're in the Object Browser, notice that just below Activate are two other items that may be of interest: ActivateNext and ActivatePrevious.)

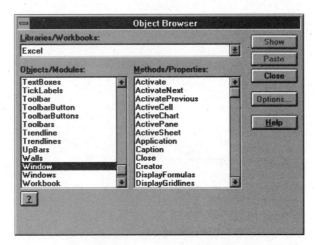

2   Select Activate from the list of methods and properties, click Paste, press HOME to get back to the start of the line, type **Windows.Item(2).** in front of the word *Activate*, and press ENTER.

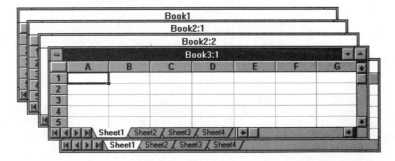

The second window becomes the first window. The position numbers in the Windows collection correspond to the current order of the stack of windows on the screen. When you activate Windows.Item(2), it becomes Windows.Item(1). The Window object returned by the *ActiveWindow* property is always identical to the one returned by Windows.Item(1).

3   Reexecute the *Windows.Item(2).Activate* statement.

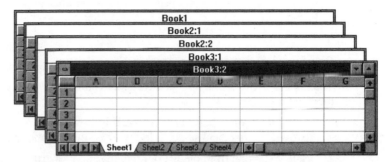

The original Windows.Item(1) comes back to the top. If you repeatedly activate the second window, you toggle between the two top windows. If you have five windows and you repeatedly activate window number 5, you cycle through all the windows in turn.

When you were in the Object Browser looking for the Activate method, you also noticed ActivateNext and ActivatePrevious in the list of methods and properties. Now you'll see what they do.

4   Type **ActiveWindow.** (with the period), click the Object Browser button, select Window from the list of object names, select ActivateNext from the list of methods and properties, and click Paste. (The resulting statement is *ActiveWindow.ActivateNext.*) Press ENTER.

The top window on the stack moves to the bottom of the stack.

5   Reexecute the *Windows.Arrange ArrangeStyle:= xlCascade* statement to see the Book3:2 window at the bottom of the stack.

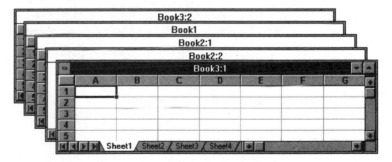

The position number you use to refer to an item in the Windows collection is the item's position in the stack. When the top window moves to the bottom, the position number of each of the other windows moves up one.

In the same way that the ActivateNext method moves the top window to the bottom of the stack, the ActivatePrevious method moves the bottom window to the top of the stack.

Sometimes when you are pasting entries from the Object Browser, you may notice a related entry that you haven't used before. Sometimes these newly discovered methods and properties turn out to be very useful. Think of the Object Browser as a pool of Excel object tips.

Change the window caption

The Object Browser can help you find interesting properties of an object that you can modify.

Object Browser button

1 In the Immediate pane, type **ActiveWindow.** (with the period), click the Object Browser button, and select Window from the list of object names.

2 Select Caption from the list of methods and properties, and click Paste.

The Object Browser does not tell you whether the word is a method or a property. If it is a method, you can simply execute it. If it is a property, you can assign a value to it or read the value from it. Try executing Caption as a method and see what happens.

3 Press ENTER.

An alert message informs you that Window does not have a Caption method. That might be a good clue that Caption is a property.

4 Click OK to dismiss the alert message. Then press HOME to get to the start of the line, type **?** (resulting in *?ActiveWindow.Caption*), and press ENTER.

The caption from the top of the window—perhaps Book3:1—appears. Caption is a property of the window. Find out if it is a read-write property by trying to change it.

5   Type **Let ActiveWindow.Caption** = **"My Own Window"** and press ENTER.

The caption changes.

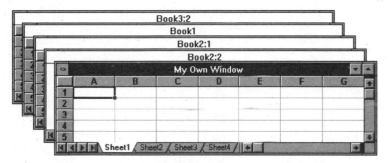

If you can disguise which workbook you are working in, maybe you can also disguise the fact that you are working in Excel.

6   Type **Let Application.** (with the period), click the Object Browser button, select Application from the list of object names, select Caption as the property, and click Paste.

7   Type = **"My Important Application"**, and then press ENTER to change the caption of the Excel application.

You can disguise the fact that you are working in Microsoft Excel. You can make your friends think that you created this whole application by yourself.

Window objects have many useful and fun properties and methods. The Object Browser can help you find those of interest to you. Once you find a useful property or method for one object class, you can often use the same property or method with other object classes as well.

Close Microsoft Excel

▶   In the Immediate pane, type **Application.Quit**, and click No when asked to save any workbooks.

Lesson Summary

To	Do this
Add a new window to the active workbook	Use the statement *ActiveWorkbook.NewWindow*.
Arrange windows in a cascading pattern	Use the statement *Windows.Arrange Style:=xlCascade*.
Activate the third window	Use the statement *Windows(3).Activate*.
Move the top window to the bottom of the stack of windows	Use the statement *Windows.ActivateNext*
Change the caption of the active window to "My Window"	Use the statement *ActiveWindow.Caption = "My Window"*.
Open the Object Browser	With a module sheet active, click the Object Browser button in the Visual Basic toolbar.
Paste a method or property from the Object Browser	Open the Object Browser and select Excel in the Workbooks/Libraries list. Select the object class from the Objects/Modules list. Select the method or property name from the Methods/Properties list. Then click Paste.
Paste a named constant from the Object Browser	With Excel selected as the library in the Object Browser, select Constants from the Objects/Modules list. Select the constant from the Methods/Properties list and click Paste.

For more information on	See
Working with windows	Chapter 7, "Working in Workbooks," in the *Microsoft Excel User's Guide*.

Preview of the Next Lesson

In this lesson you learned how Excel Window objects work and how to use the Object Browser to find properties and methods for an object. In the next lesson, you will learn how to use Range objects—one of the most important classes of objects in Excel—and how to use Excel's extensive on-line Help facilities to find out details about objects.

Explore Range Objects

The world would be much simpler if everybody were the same size. Cars would not need adjustable seats; heads would never get bumped on door frames; feet would never dangle from a chair. Of course, some new complexities would probably arise. When exchanging that ghastly outfit you received for your birthday, you would not be able to claim it was the wrong size.

If your worksheets and data files are all the same size, you don't need to worry about Range objects. If you never insert new lines into a budget, if you always put yearly totals in column M, if every month's transaction file has 5 columns and 120 rows, the macro recorder can take care of dealing with ranges for you.

In the real world of humans, people are different sizes, and clothes and cars have to adjust to fit them. In the real world of worksheets, models and data files are different sizes, and you want your macros to fit them. Excel provides many methods and properties for working with Range objects. In this lesson you will explore Range objects, and along the way you will find out how to use tools that will help you learn more about all objects, properties, and methods.

You will learn how to:

- Manipulate Range objects from Visual Basic statements.
- Use the Help reference to learn about objects, properties, and methods.
- Put formulas and values into cells.

Estimated lesson time: 30 minutes

Start the lesson

► Open Microsoft Excel with a blank workbook.

Exploring Ranges Using the Help Reference

The Object Browser is a convenient and quick tool for finding names of properties, methods, and object classes. But sometimes you need more information than just a name. For example, you may need to find out valid settings for arguments to a method, or you may want to find out if other object classes share a particular property. Excel's Help system contains a complete reference guide to all of Excel's object classes, properties, and methods. In this section, you will learn how to navigate through the Help system as you explore one of the most important classes of objects in Excel: the Range object.

Find the Range object in Help

Insert Module button

1   Start Excel, click the Insert Module button in the Visual Basic toolbar, choose Debug Window from the View menu, resize the Debug window so that you can see the workbook behind it, and activate the Immediate pane.

2   Type **Worksheets.Item(1).Select** and press ENTER to activate a worksheet.

You need to activate a worksheet since you will be exploring Range objects and Visual Basic modules don't have ranges.

3   From the Help menu, choose Contents.

The main Microsoft Excel Help window appears. One of the main headings is *Programming With Visual Basic*.

Programming with Visual Basic
Complete reference information about the Visual Basic macro language

4   Click the Programming With Visual Basic heading.

The main Visual Basic Reference Help screen appears. A main part of the screen has the heading *Programming Language Summary*.

If you start Help while a worksheet is active, you see the main Microsoft Excel Help Contents screen. If you start Help while a module sheet is active, you go directly to the Visual Basic Reference in Help.

5   Click Programming Language Summary.

Programming Language Summary
An alphabetical listing of all programming language topics including functions, methods, objects, properties, and statements.

Functions	An alphabetical listing of functions.
Methods	An alphabetical listing of methods.
Objects	An alphabetical listing of objects.
Properties	An alphabetical listing of properties.
Statements	An alphabetical listing of statements.
Keywords by Task	A functional listing of keywords by programming task.

Click this to jump to a list of all available keywords.

A new window, captioned Visual Basic Reference Index, appears.

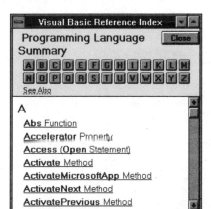

This Index contains an alphabetical list of all the important words—the keywords—you can use while writing macros in Excel, including the names of all the object classes, properties, and methods. These keywords are bold, colored, and underlined because each one is linked to the topic for that keyword. Clicking a colored keyword switches you to that topic. In the new topic you will find other linked keywords. Because these topic keywords form an interlinked topic network, I will refer to them as *hyperlinks*.

Since the complete index of keywords is so long, you can view different subsets of it.

6   Click the See Also hyperlink, and then click the Objects hyperlink in the pop-up window.

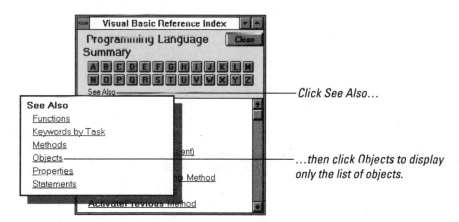

Click See Also...

...then click Objects to display only the list of objects.

The index now displays an alphabetical list of only object names. (You can also display lists of only property names or only method names.) The list is still long, so you can click a letter button at the top of the index to go directly to that part of the list.

7 Click the R button.

The list scrolls to object names beginning with *R*, and the Range Object hyperlink is now at the top of the list.

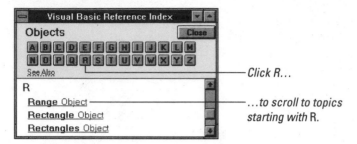

— *Click R...*

...to scroll to topics starting with R.

8 Click the Range Object hyperlink.

A reference window appears that contains useful information about ranges.

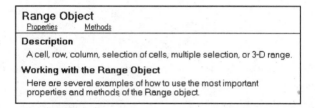

The topic defines a Range object, "a cell, row, column, selection of cells, multiple selection, or 3-D range," and displays hyperlinks to lists of properties and methods for the Range object.

All topics that describe objects have a description along with hyperlinks to lists of properties and methods. The topic for the Range object, because it is so crucial, also describes some of the most important methods, including the Cells method, the Range method, and the Offset method.

Explore the Cells method

1 In the Range Object topic in Help, click the Methods hyperlink.

The list of hyperlinks for all methods that apply to the Range object appears.

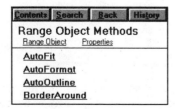

At the top of the list are two additional hyperlinks: one back to the main topic for the object and one to the list of properties.

The Help system is a little different from the Object Browser. In the Object Browser, you see a combined list of methods and properties for each object class. In Help, the method list and the property list are separate.

2   Click the Cells hyperlink from the list of methods.

The Cells Method topic appears. The description says that the Cells method returns either a single cell or a collection of cells. Using the Cells method to return a single cell is the same as using the Item method to get a single item from a collection.

Use the Immediate pane in Excel to explore how the Cells collection works:

3   Switch back to Microsoft Excel. (Hold down the ALT key and press TAB.) The Immediate pane should still be active.

4   Type **Cells.Select** and press ENTER.

All the cells in the worksheet are selected. The Cells method establishes a link to the collection of all the cells in the worksheet, just as the Workbooks method establishes a link to the collection of all open workbooks. The Select method selects the collection of cells returned by the Cells method.

5   Type **Cells.Item(1).Select** and press ENTER.

The selection shrinks to cell A1. The expression *Cells.Item(1)* establishes a link to a single item in the collection of cells, using the position number of the item within the collection. You can then use the Select method with that single item.

Cell 1

6   Type **Cells.Item(5).Select** and press ENTER.

The selection changes to cell E1. Position numbers within the collection of cells go from left to right across a row.

Cell 5

7   Type **Cells.Item(257).Select** and press ENTER.

The selection changes to cell A2. Position numbers within the collection of cells continue from the last cell of one row to the first cell of the next row down. Since the worksheet is 256 cells across, the 257th cell on the worksheet is in row 2, column 1.

— *Cell 257*

8   Type **Cells.Item(4194304).Select** and press ENTER.

The selection changes to cell IV16384.

— *Cell 4,194,304*

Most collections in Excel have only a dozen or two items at most, so indexing into the collection with a position number is no problem. An Excel worksheet, however, has millions of cells. Also, cells in a worksheet have a natural row and column orientation. Accordingly, the Cells method allows you to specify an individual cell using either a single position number or a combination of two position numbers.

9   Type **Cells.Item(3,2).Select** and press ENTER.

The selection changes to cell B3. When you use two position numbers with the Cells method, you always put the row number first and the column number second.

— *Cell 3,2*

Note   For Excel developers familiar with the R1C1 notation used by Excel 4 macros, the Cells method with two arguments provides the same benefits as R1C1 notation, without the requirement of combining the row and column numbers into a single text string.

The Cells method is very effective when you need to work with cells as a collection: either to access all the cells in the collection or to access a single cell from the collection. But many times you need to specify more flexible ranges.

Explore the Range method

Like the Cells method, the Range method is an important way of working with ranges in Excel. Find out how the Range method can specify a range.

1   Return to the Cells Method topic in the Help system.

2   Click the See Also hyperlink, and click the Range Method hyperlink in the pop-up window.

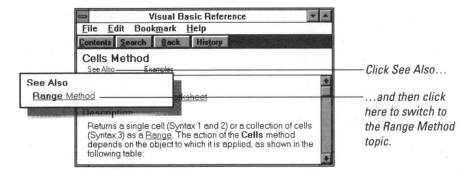

The Range Method topic appears. The description says that the Range method returns a cell or a range of cells, and the detail states that the reference must be in A1 notation but can use colons and commas as well as defined names on the worksheet.

Switch back to the Debug window in Excel, type **Range("B4").Select**, and press ENTER to change the selection to cell B4.

To select a specific cell address, use the cell address (in quotation marks) as the argument to the Range method.

3   Type **Range("B3:D8").Select** and press ENTER to select the range B3:D8.

You can use any valid Excel reference (in quotation marks) as the argument to the Range method. The Range method returns a Range object, which you can manipulate with any methods or properties that apply to the Range object class, such as the Select method.

4   Type **Range("B3,D8,E4,A6").Select** and press ENTER to create a single Range object consisting of four separate cells.

	A	B	C	D	E	F
2						
3		☐				
4					▬	
5						
6	▬					
7						
8				▬		
9						

The commas between the cell addresses do not mean separate arguments. All four cell addresses are part of a single text string, and that one text string is a single argument.

5   Type **Range("B3","D8").Select** and press ENTER.

The Range method can accept two arguments. When you use two arguments, they must be the corner points of a rectangular block of cells. A rectangular block of cells, defined by opposite corner cells, is the traditional definition of a range.

6   Type **Range(Cells.Item(3,2),Cells.Item(8,4)).Select** and press ENTER.

This statement also selects the range B3:D8.

Since the Cells method can return a single cell range object, you can use that single cell object as one or both of the corner points of a range.

The Range method is a flexible way of establishing a link to an arbitrary Range object. As arguments to the Range method, you can either use a text string that contains any valid reference, or you can use two cells to define a rectangular range.

Note The word *Range* is both the name of the method that returns a Range object and the name of the Range object class itself. In the Object Browser, you will find the word *Range* as an object name (on the left) and also as a method name for a Worksheet object (on the right).

The word *Cells*, however, is only the name of a method. The Cells method returns a Range object. In the Object Browser, you will *not* find the word *Cells* in the list of object names (on the left), but you will find it as a method name for a Worksheet object (on the right).

Exploring Advanced Range Objects

Most ranges in Excel are either single cells or rectangles. Therefore, the Cells method and the Range method will probably be the methods that you use most frequently in dealing with ranges. Ranges, however, are ubiquitous in Excel, and as you develop macro applications, you will often find yourself working with ranges in new ways. Excel has a wide variety of methods that return Range objects. This section introduces you to some of the most useful.

Explore the Columns method

The Cells method returns a Range object as a collection of cells. Since rows and columns are so important in a worksheet, they have their own collections, too. Use Help to find out more about the Columns collection.

1   Switch back to the Range Method topic in the Help system.

Towards the top of the Range Method topic are the names of all the object classes the method applies to. Each name is a hyperlink to the Help topic for that object. In Help, every method and property topic begins with the names of the objects that support the method or property.

2   Click the Range hyperlink to jump to the Range Object topic, and click the Methods hyperlink to jump to the list of methods for the Range object.

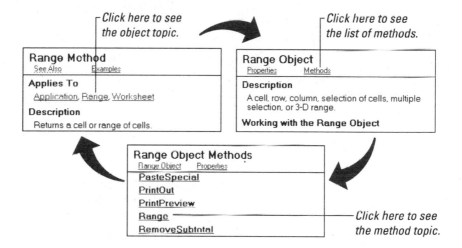

From any individual method or property topic, you can jump back to the main topic for the object class and from there jump to the list of methods or properties.

3   Click the Columns method hyperlink.

The Columns Method topic appears. According to the description, this method returns either a single column or a collection of columns. In the same way that the Cells method returns a Range object as a collection of cells, the Columns method returns a Range object as a collection of columns. The collection returned by the Columns method follows the standard rules for a collection: You can count the items or return a single item from the collection.

4   Switch back to Excel, type **Columns.Item(5).Select**, and press ENTER.

All of column E is selected. The expression *Columns.Item(5)* returns a single column range, just as the expression *Cells.Item(5)* returns a single cell range.

	A	B	C	D	E	F
1						
2						
3						
4						

5 Type **?Cells.Count** and press ENTER.

The number 4194304 appears. That's how many cells are in the worksheet.

6 Type **?Columns.Count** and press ENTER.

The number 256 appears. That's how many columns are in the worksheet.

As you might expect, the Rows method works like a transposed Columns method. The two most important reasons for using the Rows method or the Columns method instead of the Cells method are to count the number of rows or columns and to select an entire row or column.

Explore the Rows method of a range

Just as you can use the Columns method to return the collection of columns on an entire worksheet, you can use the Rows and Columns methods with ranges. Look at the Help topic for Rows to see how similar the Rows method is to the Columns method, and also to learn how to use both these collections with smaller ranges.

You can also click the See Also hyperlink to go directly to the Rows Method topic.

1 Switch back to Help, to the Columns Method topic. Click the See Also Range hyperlink to get back to the Range Object topic, click the Methods hyperlink to get to the list of methods for the Range object, and then click the Rows hyperlink to get to the Rows Method topic.

According to the Help topic, the Rows method applies to the Application object, to a Range object, or to a Worksheet object. When you use the the Rows method with the Application object, or without any object, it returns the collection of rows on the active worksheet. As a result, the expression *Rows* is the same as *Application.Rows,* which is the same as *ActiveSheet.Rows*, and all three apply the Rows method to the entire Worksheet object. The Rows method can also apply to a specific Range object.

When you use a method such as Rows with a Range object, think of the starting range as if it were a worksheet—a *virtual worksheet*.

2 Switch back to Excel, type **Range("A1:E3").Select**, and press ENTER to select the rectangular range from A1 through E3. Think of this range as a virtual worksheet.

	A	B	C	D	E	F
1						
2						
3						
4						

See what happens when you use the Rows method with this small range.

3 Type **Range("A1:E3").Rows.Item(3).Select** and press ENTER.

This selects the third row of the starting range—cells A3:E3.

	A	B	C	D	E	F
1						
2						
3						
4						

4 Type **Range("A1:E3").Rows.Item(4).Select** and press ENTER.

This selects the fourth row of the starting range, even though it has only three rows! Because a Range object is like a *virtual* worksheet, its boundaries are not as absolute as those of a *real* worksheet. Selecting rows or columns slightly outside a range is perfect for adding titles or totals to a block of numbers.

	A	B	C	D	E	F
1						
2						
3						
4						

5 Type **Range("C4:E6").Select** and press ENTER.

The range C4:E6 is a rectangular range that doesn't start at the corner of the worksheet.

	A	B	C	D	E	F
3						
4						
5						
6						
7						

6 Type **Range("C4:E6").Rows.Item(0).Select** and press ENTER.

This selects the zeroth row of the starting range. You can also select the minus one row, the minus two row, and so forth.

	A	B	C	D	E	F
3						
4						
5						
6						
7						

The Range method is useful when you want to access a specific cell range. The Cells, Columns, and Rows methods are useful when you want to retrieve a single cell, column, or row from a worksheet or a rectangular range. Excel has other methods for working with ranges that can be useful in many situations.

Calculating flexible ranges

Excel has several methods that can calculate a new range based on an existing range. One of the methods mentioned in the Range Object topic in Help as particularly useful is the Offset method. The Offset method takes one Range object (virtual worksheet) and calculates a new Range object (virtual worksheet) from it.

1   Type **Range("B3:D6").Select** and press ENTER to select a starting range.

2   Type **Selection.Offset(RowOffset:=-1, ColumnOffset:=2).Select** and press ENTER to select a new range (D2:F5) one cell up and two cells to the right of the starting selection.

This statement consists of three methods: Selection, Offset, and Select:

The Selection method returns a Range object consisting of the starting range—B3:D6.

The Offset method operates on that range and calculates a new Range object, shifted one row up and two columns to the right of the original range—D2:F5.

The Select method operates on that range and makes it the new selection.

3   Type **Selection.Offset(RowOffset:=4, ColumnOffset:=-3).Select** and press ENTER to select a new range (A6:C9) four rows down and three columns to the left of the starting selection.

4   Type **Selection.Offset(RowOffset:=-2, ColumnOffset:=1).Select** and press
ENTER to select a new range (B4:D7) three rows up and one column to the right of
the starting selection, one cell below the original range.

The Offset method is a powerful tool for calculating a new range from a starting
range. You give the Offset method two arguments: the number of rows to shift the
selection down and the number of columns to shift the selection to the right. To
shift the selection up or to the left, use negative numbers for the arguments. The
expression *Selection.Offset(RowOffset:=0, ColumnOffset:=0)* returns the same
range as the original selection.

Another method, the Resize method, allows you to change the number of rows
and columns in a range. Like the Offset method, the Resize method takes one
Range object (virtual worksheet) and calculates another Range object (virtual
worksheet) from it. Combining the Resize method with the Offset method gives
you almost unlimited control over a range.

5   With the range B4:D7 as the starting selection, type
Selection.Offset(RowOffset:=0, ColumnOffset:=3).Resize(ColumnSize:=2).Select
and press ENTER to select a new range (E4:F7) two columns wide and shifted three
columns to the right of the starting range.

In this statement, the Offset method calculates a new range by shifting the top left
cell of the starting selection three columns to the right. Then the Resize method
calculates a second new range, changing the number of columns. Finally, the
Select method selects the range returned by the Resize method.

Tip Rather than thinking of a range as a rectangle defined by a top left cell and a
bottom right cell, think of it as a rectangle defined by a starting position (the top
left cell) and a size (the width and height). The Offset method calculates a new
starting position for a range, and the Resize method calculates a new size.

You can give the Resize method two arguments: the number of rows (the "row size") and the number of columns (the "column size"). If you omit an argument, the Resize method retains the same size for that dimension as the original range.

You can get very elaborate calculating range sizes. Here's how to select a range that extends one cell further on all sides than the original selection:

6   Type **Selection.Offset(RowOffset:=-1, ColumnOffset:=-1) .Resize(RowSize:=Selection.Rows.Count+2, ColumnSize:=Selection .Columns.Count+2).Select** (all on one line) and press ENTER.

Note   The combined functionality of the Offset and Resize methods is equivalent to that of the OFFSET function available on worksheets and in Excel 4 macros.

Often, as in the examples in Lesson 2, you need to select all the cells in the current selection, minus the first row. For example, with the range A1:I119 selected, you may need to select the range A2:I119. You can easily calculate the needed range using the Offset and Resize methods. To select all but the top row of the current selection:

7   Type **Selection.Offset(RowOffset:=1, ColumnOffset:=0) .Resize(RowSize:=Selection.Rows.Count-1).Select**, and press ENTER.

These are long expressions, but each piece is not complicated. Using the argument names helps you learn what the methods are doing, but they contribute to making the expressions long. Here's the statement from step 7, omitting the argument names: *Selection.Offset(1, 0).Resize(Selection.Rows.Count-1).Select*.

Note You can omit argument names as long as you keep the argument values in the correct order. For example, the expression *Offset(-1,2)* is equivalent to *Offset(RowOffset:=-1, ColumnOffset:=2)*. While you are first learning to use methods, you may want to use the argument names to remind yourself what the argument values mean.

Sometimes you need to extend a selection to include an entire row or column. The EntireRow property and the EntireColumn property of a Range object calculate that range extended to the entire row or column.

8   Type **Selection.EntireRow.Select** and press ENTER.

The current selection now includes the entire rows of the original selection.

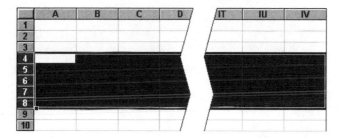

The Offset and Resize methods, along with the EntireRow and EntireColumn properties, provide you with flexible tools for calculating new Range objects based on an original starting range.

Exploring the Contents of Ranges

Selecting ranges helps you understand how to manipulate Range objects, but to get real work done, you must format cells, put values and formulas into cells, retrieve values from cells, retrieve formulas from cells, and retrieve formatted values from cells. This section will show you how.

Put values and formulas into a range

1   Type **Range("B2:B6").Select** and press ENTER to select a starting range of cells.

2   Type **Let Selection.Formula = 100** and press ENTER.

The number 100 fills all the cells of the selection. Formula is a property of the range. When you set the Formula property for the selection, you change the formula for all the cells in the selection.

	A	B	C	D
1				
2		100		
3		100		
4		100		
5		100		
6		100		
7				

The number 100 is not a formula; it is a constant. But the Formula property is equivalent to whatever you see in the formula bar when the cell is selected. The formula bar can contain constants as well as formulas, and so can the Formula property.

3   Type **Let ActiveCell.Formula = 0** and press ENTER.

Only cell B2 changes to zero because you changed the formula of only the active cell.

	A	B	C	D
1				
2		0		
3		100		
4		100		
5		100		
6		100		
7				

Suppose you want to enter a value the first cell above the active cell and you don't want to assume that the active cell is cell B2.

4   Type **Let ActiveCell.Offset(RowOffset:=-1, ColumnOffset:=0).Formula = 1** and press ENTER.

The cell B1 changes to the number 1.

	A	B	C	D
1		1		
2		0		
3		100		
4		100		
5		100		
6		100		
7				

You start with the active cell, use the Offset method to calculate a new cell one up from that starting cell, and then set the Formula property for the resulting cell.

5   Type **Let Selection.Formula = "=B1*5"** and press ENTER.

The value in each cell of the selection changes to five times that of the cell above it.

	A	B	C	D
1		1		
2		5		
3		25		
4		125		
5		625		
6		3125		
7				

Now the selected cells contain a real formula, not a constant. This formula works properly, but to create this formula you had to know that the selection started in cell B2. Otherwise the cell address B1 would not be appropriate to mean "one cell above." R1C1 notation allows you to specify a relative cell reference in a way that is independent of the current location of the formula.

Range objects in Excel have one property for entering and reading the formula in A1 notation and another property for entering and reading the formula in R1C1 notation.

6   Type **?ActiveCell.FormulaR1C1** and press ENTER.

The formula $=R[-1]C*5$ appears. This is the same formula as $=B1*5$, except that it is displayed using R1C1 notation. This formula means "multiply the value of the cell one row above me by 5." When you use R1C1 notation for relative references in a formula, you don't have to worry about the actual location of the cell that contains the formula.

All cells have both a Formula property and a FormulaR1C1 property. You can assign a formula to either one, and you can read the formula from a cell with either one. If you are assigning a constant or a formula that doesn't include cell addresses, the Formula and FormulaR1C1 properties are identical.

Format the contents of a range

Excel ranges offer a wide variety of formatting options. You can use the Object Browser and the Help system together to help you learn how to format cells.

Object Browser button

1   Click the Object Browser button, and select Range from the list of object names.

2   In the list of methods and properties, search for the NumberFormat property, and select it.

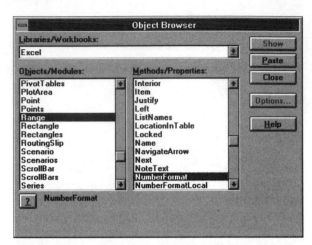

The Object Browser does not tell you what kind of value to assign to the NumberFormat property.

? button

3   Click the ? (question mark) button at the bottom of the Object Browser.

The NumberFormat Property topic appears. When you find an interesting property or method in the Object Browser but need more information, you can click the ? (question mark) button to go directly to Help for that topic. (The Help button takes you to the Help topic that explains the Object Browser dialog box.)

According to the Help topic, the NumberFormat property applies to several classes of objects, including Range objects. At the top of the topic is a hyperlink to an example. Each method and property topic in the Help system has one or more simple examples for you to look at or copy.

4   Click the Example hyperlink.

The Visual Basic Reference Example window appears. The third example shows how to format a column as currency. You can copy that example and paste it into your code.

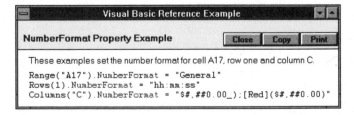

5   Click the Copy button. The Copy dialog box appears.

6   Select the entire last line of the example, and click Copy.

```
┌─────────────────────────────────────────────────────────────┐
│ ═                           Copy                              │
├─────────────────────────────────────────────────────────────┤
│ Select text to copy to the Clipboard.                        │
│ ┌─────────────────────────────────────────────┬─┐ ┌───────┐ │
│ │                                             │▲│ │ Copy  │ │
│ │ NumberFormat Property Example               │ │ └───────┘ │
│ │                                             │ │ ┌───────┐ │
│ │ These examples set the number format for cell A17, row one and column C. │ │ │Cancel │ │
│ │                                             │ │ └───────┘ │
│ │                                             │ │           │
│ │ Range("A17").NumberFormat = "General"       │ │           │
│ │ Rows(1).NumberFormat = "hh:mm:ss"           │ │           │
│ │ Columns("C").NumberFormat = "$#,##0.00_);[Red]($#,##0.00)" │▼│           │
│ └─────────────────────────────────────────────┴─┘           │
│  ◄                                              ►            │
└─────────────────────────────────────────────────────────────┘
```

Select the example you want, and click Copy.

7   Switch back to the Immediate pane in Excel, and choose Paste from the Edit menu to paste the example into the Immediate pane.

The example you copied from Help sets the number format for all of column C. Try it out in the Immediate pane.

8   Insert the word **Let** at the beginning of the pasted example, and insert **.Item** after the word *Columns*. The resulting formula should be
Let Columns.Item("C").NumberFormat = "$#,##0.00_);[Red]($#,##0.00).)
Then press ENTER to change the number format of column C.

Note   The words *Let* and *Item* are optional, and are not in the Help example, but you should use them at first to help clarify the distinctions between methods and properties, and between collections and items.

Since none of the cells in column C contain values, you don't see a change. The column has been formatted, however. Enter a value into column C.

9   Type **Let Cells.Item(2, 3) = 4**. The value appears in cell C2, formatted as $4.00.

Often in a macro, you don't want to put absolute column addresses into the code. Instead, you want to format the current selection or a calculated range.

10   Replace *Columns.Item("C")* from the example with **Selection** to produce the statement *Let Selection.Numberformat = "$#,##0.00_);[Red]($#,##0.00)"*. Then press ENTER.

The cells within the selection change to the new format, but the cell above the selection does not change.

	A	B	C	D
1			1	
2		$ 5.00	$ 4.00	
3		$ 25.00		
4		$ 125.00		
5		$ 625.00		
6		#######		
7				

11   Immediately after the word *Selection*, type **.EntireColumn** to create the statement
Let Selection.Entirecolumn.Numberformat = "$#,##0.00_);[Red]($#,##0.00)".
Then press ENTER to format all the cells in the column as currency.

	A	B	C	D
1		$ 1.00		
2		$ 5.00	$ 4.00	
3		$ 25.00		
4		$ 125.00		
5		$ 625.00		
6		########		
7				

With the new number formatting, some of the numbers probably no longer fit
within the cell width.

12   Type **Selection.EntireColumn.Autofit** and press ENTER.

	A	B	C	D
1		$ 1.00		
2		$ 5.00	$ 4.00	
3		$ 25.00		
4		$ 125.00		
5		$ 625.00		
6		$3,125.00		
7				

By looking around in the Object Browser and switching to Help for more information
and examples you can copy and use, you can quickly learn how to manipulate Excel
objects.

Retrieve the contents of a cell

In addition to putting values and formulas into cells, sometimes you will want to
retrieve the contents of cells. The contents of a cell, however, can be more than just its
value.

1   Type **?Range("B2").Formula** and press ENTER.

The formula for the cell, *=B1*5*, appears. If you want to see the formula with
references displayed in R1C1 notation, use the FormulaR1C1 property.

2   Type **?Range("B2").Value** and press ENTER.

The value from the cell, *5*, appears. The value is the result of the formula's
calculation. If the cell contains a constant, the value and the formula are the same.

3   Type **?Range("B2").Text** and press ENTER.

The formatted contents of the cell, *$5.00*, appears.

The Text property is read-only. To change the contents of the cell, you must use the Value or Formula property. To change the number formatting of the cell, you must use the NumberFormat property.

4   Type **?Range("B2")** and press ENTER.

The unformatted value from the cell, 5, appears, the same as when you used the Value property. If you do not specify a property for a Range object, you get the Value property as a default.

5   Type **Let Range("B1") = 10** and press ENTER.

	A	B	C	D
1		$ 10.00		
2		$ 50.00	$ 4.00	
3		$ 250.00		
4		$1,250.00		
5		$6,250.00		
6		#########		
7				

Since Value is the default property for a Range object, you can assign a new value to a range simply by assigning the value to the Range object. You don't need to specify which property.

6   Type **Let Selection.Formula = Selection.Value** and press ENTER.

See Lesson 2 for a macro that uses the PasteSpecial method.

This statement does not change the appearance of the worksheet, but it converts all the formulas in the selection to the values from those cells. This statement has the same effect as copying the cells and then using the PasteSpecial method to paste just the values.

The Range object is probably the most important single object in Excel. Ranges—with formulas, values, and formats—are what define a spreadsheet program. Excel's Range object has many properties and methods for you to utilize, and the Help system can help you learn how to use them.

Quit Excel

▶   In the Immediate pane, type **Application.Quit**, and click No when asked to save changes.

Lesson Summary

To	Do this
Select the fifth cell in the third row of the active worksheet	Use the statement *Cells(3,5).Select*.
Select the range B2:C5 on the active worksheet	Use the statement *Range("B2:C5").Select*.
Count the columns in the current selection	Use the expression *Selection.Columns.Count*
Select a new range one row down from the selection	Use the statement *Selection.Offset(1,0).Select*.
Fill the cells in the selection with the value 100	Use the statement *Let Selection.Formula = "100"*.
Enter a formula into only the active cell that calculates the value of the cell above	Use the statement *Let ActiveCell .FormulaR1C1="=R[-1]C"*.
Retrieve a value from the active cell	Use the expression *ActiveCell.Value*.
Retrieve a formula from the active cell	Use the expression *ActiveCell.Formula* or the expression *ActiveCell.FormulaR1C1*.
Retrieve the formatted value from the active cell	Use the expression *ActiveCell.Text*.
Open the Visual Basic Help reference file	With a worksheet active, press F1, and then choose the topic *Programming With Visual Basic*.
Go to Help on a particular method or property from the Object Browser	With the method or property selected in the Object Browser, click the ? (question mark) button.

For more information on	See
Using Visual Basic Help	"Introduction" in the *Microsoft Excel Visual Basic User's Guide*.

Preview of the Next Lesson

Excel is well known for exceptional graphical output. In the next lesson you explore graphical objects. Graphical objects include not only circles and rectangles on the worksheet, but also charts and textboxes. Even dialog box controls are graphical objects in Excel. As you learn to work with graphical objects, you will see how to use the macro recorder in an entirely new way: as a reference tool for learning about objects.

Explore Graphical Objects

On a warm summer day, nothing is grander than to lie on your back on a grassy field and watch clouds float across the sky. Trees and mountains and buildings just sit there; they are attached firmly to the ground. But clouds move. Clouds change shape. They change color. Clouds can come in layers, too, with closer clouds drifting in front of the clouds in back.

On a worksheet, ranges with their formulas and formats are attached firmly to the worksheet just as buildings are attached to the ground. Cell A1 will always be in the top left corner of the worksheet. Drawing objects, however, are like clouds. They float freely above the worksheet. They can disappear and reappear. They can change color and shape.

Drawing objects—including not only objects such as rectangles, ovals, and lines, but also including charts, and even list box controls and spinner controls—add interest, information, and functionality to a worksheet. In this lesson, you will learn how to work with drawing objects from a Visual Basic macro, and along the way you will find out more about how to use Microsoft Excel's reference tools to learn more about all objects, properties, and methods.

You will learn how to:

- Manipulate drawing objects on a worksheet.
- Manipulate chart objects.
- Use the macro recorder as a reference tool.

Estimated lesson time: 35 minutes

Start the lesson

▶ Open Microsoft Excel with a blank workbook.

Exploring Graphics Using the Macro Recorder

The Object Browser and the Help system are like a spelling dictionary: In the same way that you practically have to know how to spell a word before you can find it in the dictionary, you practically have to know the property or method before you can find it in the Object Browser or in Help. One of the most useful reference tools for learning how to use Excel objects may not seem to be a reference tool at all: the macro recorder.

Some people think of the macro recorder as a tool for beginners—and it is. In Part 1 of this book, you did use the macro recorder to build finished macros without having to understand very much about how Excel objects really work. But the macro recorder is also a powerful reference tool for advanced developers. In this lesson you will see how you can use the macro recorder as one more reference tool for learning how to work with Excel objects.

Record a rectangle

Graphical objects—such as rectangles, ovals, text boxes, and charts—can make your worksheets appealing and understandable. The macro recorder is a very good tool for learning how to work with graphical objects. Record creating a rectangle, and see how much you can learn from a simple recorded macro.

Drawing button

1   Open a new workbook, and click the Drawing button in the Standard toolbar to display the Drawing toolbar.

Record Macro button

2   Click the Record Macro button in the Visual Basic toolbar, type **MakeRectangle** as the name for the macro, and click OK.

Rectangle button

3   Click the Rectangle button in the Drawing toolbar (not the Filled Rectangle button), and then click the top left corner of cell B2 and drag to the bottom right corner of cell B3.

Color button

4   Click the arrow on the Color button in the Formatting toolbar, and then click the third box in the top row of the color palette: the red color.

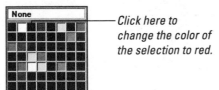

Click here to change the color of the selection to red.

The rectangle changes to red.

Stop Macro button

5   Click the Stop Macro button and switch to the Module1 sheet to look at the resulting macro.

```
Sub MakeRectangle()
    ActiveSheet.Rectangles.Add(48, 12.75, 48, 25.5).Select
    Selection.Interior.ColorIndex = xlNone
    Selection.Interior.ColorIndex = 3
End Sub
```

This macro is very short, but a lot happens in those three statements. The statement

```
ActiveSheet.Rectangles.Add(48, 12.75, 48, 25.5).Select
```

starts by pointing at the active sheet and ends by selecting something. The word *Rectangles* is a plural noun, and it's followed by the word *Add*, so it looks like Rectangles is a collection. The word *Add* is followed by a list of numbers in parentheses. You can probably guess that the numbers have something to do with the location and size of the rectangle since nothing else in the macro sets the location.

These recorded statements give you several clues about how to create a new rectangle. Now you can use Excel's other reference tools—the Object Browser, the Help system, and the Immediate pane—to fill in the details.

Note   The macro recorder typically does not record optional keywords such as *Let* and *Item*. As you become more comfortable with the language of Excel objects, you may choose to abbreviate more. Even some experienced macro developers, however, prefer to use optional keywords to make the code more readable. Macros created by the macro recorder can give you an idea of what abbreviated macro code looks like. You can then decide whether you prefer to use the extra keywords.

Create a rectangle

1   From the View menu, choose the Debug Window command and resize the Debug window as needed so that you can see the workbook behind it.

2   In the Immediate pane, type **Sheets.Item("Sheet1").Select** and press ENTER to activate the worksheet with the rectangle.

Your macro is in the Code pane, the bottom half of the Debug window.

3   Select the words *Activesheet.Rectangles.* (including both periods) from the Code pane, and choose the Copy command from the Edit menu.

You can copy code from the Code pane up into the Immediate pane to test specific statements. As long as you are not stepping through a macro, you can also copy code from the Immediate pane and paste it into the macro in the Code pane.

4   Click in the Immediate pane, and choose the Paste command from the Edit menu.

5   Click the Object Browser button in the Visual Basic toolbar, select Excel from the Libraries/Workbooks list, select Rectangles from the Objects/Modules list, and select Add from the Methods/Properties list.

Object Browser button

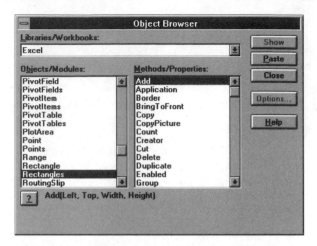

At the bottom of the Object Browser dialog box is a list of the arguments used by the Add method. The description, however, does not let you know whether to enter values for the arguments using inches or centimeters or something else. You can find more detailed information in Help.

? button

6   Click the ? (question mark) button next to the method description.

The Add Method topic in the Help system appears. The Add method applies to many different objects, and it works differently depending on the class of object, so the main Add Method topic has pointers to other Help topics.

7   Click the Rectangles hyperlink to jump to the Add Method topic for drawing objects.

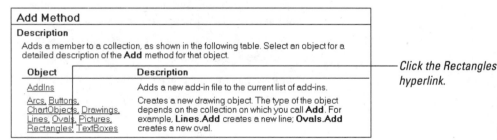

Click the Rectangles hyperlink.

The Add Method (Drawing Objects) topic appears.

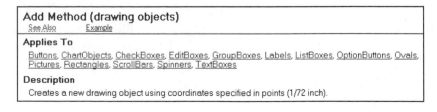

Points are the measurement traditionally used to lay out text for publishing.

In the first line of the description you see that the units of measurement are *points*, equal to 1/72 inch. That is what you needed to know.

8 Switch back to Excel—you should still be in the Object Browser dialog box with the Add method selected—and click Paste to paste the Add method and its arguments into the Immediate pane.

9 For the arguments, type **72** for Left, **36** for Top, **72** for Width, and **36** for Height. Then press END to get to the end of the statement, type **.Select**, and press ENTER.

```
ActiveSheet.Rectangles.Add(Left:=72, Top:=36, Width:=72, Height:=36).Select
```

A new rectangle appears on the worksheet, about ½ inch from the top and 1 inch from the left. The rectangle is ½ inch high and 1 inch wide. The rectangle also has selection handles around its border to show that it is the current selection, but you can't see the gridlines through the rectangle. The default rectangle is not transparent; it is filled with white.

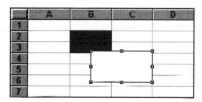

In this example, you were able to create a rectangle by following the pattern given by the recorder, but you also used the Object Browser and Help to find out how to modify and control the recorded statement.

Set the color of the rectangle

The macro recorder does not include the optional word Let for assignments.

The next two statements in the recorded macro set the color of the rectangle. The statement

```
Selection.Interior.ColorIndex = xlNone
```

changes the color of the selection from the default white color to transparent, and the statement

```
Selection.Interior.ColorIndex = 3
```

changes the color from transparent to that of the third color in the palette. You can execute similar statements in the Immediate pane.

1 Copy the statement *Selection.Interior.ColorIndex = xlNone* from the Code pane to the Immediate pane, and press ENTER.

The new rectangle you created now becomes transparent.

2 Replace the word *xlNone* with the number **1,** and reexecute the statement.

If you want to use a color that is not in the palette, search Help for the topic "RGB."

The rectangle changes to black. In Excel's default color palette, black is the first color. The color palette holds 56 different colors, so you can use any number from 1 through 56 for the ColorIndex property.

The macro's recorded statement did not set the color of the rectangle directly but rather changed the color of the interior of the rectangle. That might make you curious about the ColorIndex property.

3 Double click the word *ColorIndex* to select the entire word, and press F1 to display the Help topic for the ColorIndex property.

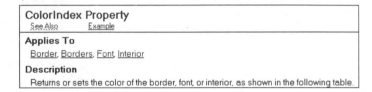

The ColorIndex property controls the color of the border, borders, and font as well as the color of the interior. To find the border of a Rectangle object, should you use the word *Border* or the word *Borders*?

4 Switch back to Excel. Double click the word *Interior* and click the Object Browser button. Select Rectangle from the list of object names.

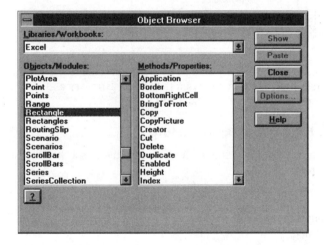

The word *Border* appears in the list of methods and properties, but the word *Borders* does not. So you should use the word *Border* to refer to the border of a rectangle.

5 Select Border from the Methods/Properties list, click the Paste button to replace the word *Interior* with the word *Border*, change the number at the end of the statement to 5, and press ENTER.

A thin blue border appears around the rectangle.

Since a rectangle has a border, perhaps a border has other attributes you can set.

6   Type **Let Selection.Border.**, click the Object Browser button, select Border from the list of object names, and look at the list of methods and properties.

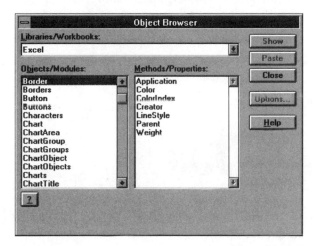

Aside from the standard properties and methods, the Border object lists only Color, ColorIndex, LineStyle, and Weight.

7   Select Weight from the list of methods and properties, click Paste to paste it into the Immediate pane, type = **4,** and press ENTER.

The thin blue border around the rectangle changes to a thick blue border.

You can find valid settings for the border's Weight property either by reading the Weight property topic in Help or by trial and error.

Once you have recorded a statement, you can use the Help system and the Object Browser to help you find related properties and methods that might be useful.

Create a rectangle without selecting it

The statement you used to add a new rectangle has the word *Select* at the end of it. After the Add method creates the rectangle, it returns a link to the newly created object. The Select method uses that link to select the object. All Add methods return a link to the objects they create. If you don't need to select the new drawing object, you can leave off the Select method.

Note   When you use the Add method for the Workbooks object to create a new workbook, you usually just discard the link that the Add method returns. Since the new workbook becomes the active workbook, you can establish a link with it at any time using the ActiveWorkbook property.

---

1   In the Immediate pane, type **ActiveSheet.Rectangles.Add Left:=144, Top:=36, Width:=72, Height:=36**. This is the same as the Add statement you used before, except that the value of the Left argument is 144, *.Select* is missing from the end, and the parentheses are gone.

Note If a method takes arguments and you use the return value of the method, you must include parentheses around the arguments; if you do not use the return value of the method, you must not include the parentheses.

A new rectangle appears on the worksheet, next to the rectangle you created earlier. The selection handles are still on the previous rectangle.

2 Type **Let Selection.Interior.ColorIndex = 6** and press ENTER.

The interior of the selected rectangle changes to yellow. The new rectangle is unchanged.

If you don't select the new object as you create it, you may wonder how to change its interior color now. The Rectangles object is a collection, and you can work with rectangles using the same techniques you use with other collections.

3 Type **?ActiveSheet.Rectangles.Count** and press ENTER.

The number of rectangles, probably 3, appears. You want the most recently created rectangle, so that is rectangle number 3.

4 Type **Let ActiveSheet.Rectangles.Item(3).Interior.ColorIndex = 3** and press ENTER.

The interior of the newest rectangle changes to red, but the selection handles indicate that the other rectangle is still the current selection.

Sometimes you want to create and manipulate objects without changing the selection. You can do that, but if you discard the link to the object that the Add method offers you, be sure you can establish a link some other way. In Lesson 11, you will learn how to save the link to the object so that you can use it later.

5   Double click the Control Menu box at the top left corner of the Debug window to close the window.

Control Menu box

Excel has several classes of drawing objects: rectangles, ovals, arcs, and so forth. All these drawing objects work very much the same as rectangles do. Even dialog controls such as check boxes, option buttons, and scroll bars are drawing objects, and they are very similar to rectangles. Embedded charts are also drawing objects in Excel. You add, manipulate, and delete Chart objects the same as you do Rectangle objects. Chart objects, of course, have additional properties that are unique to charts, and the macro recorder is an effective tool for finding out what they are.

Exploring Chart Objects

Charts and chart objects have hundreds of properties and methods. Many of the attributes of a chart are themselves separate objects. Learning how to create and manipulate charts by reading a reference manual is very difficult because charts have so many objects and properties. But creating and manipulating a chart is easy to record, and even though you may see many new methods, properties, and objects, the new objects work according to the same principles as other objects in Excel.

Record creating a chart object

1   Click the Sheet2 tab to activate a new worksheet, enter the sample values for the chart into the range A1:C5 as shown here, and select the range A1:C5.

	A	B	C	D
1	Student	Tests	Projects	
2	Aja	90	380	
3	Alan	50	450	
4	Alex	65	320	
5	Amy	35	400	
6				

Record Macro button

2   Click the Record Macro button in the Visual Basic toolbar, type **MakeChart** as the name for the macro, and click OK.

Chart Wizard button

3   Click the ChartWizard button in the Standard toolbar, and then, while holding down the ALT key, drag a rectangle from the top left corner of cell B7 through the bottom right corner of cell F13.

Tip   If you hold down the ALT key while you create or resize a drawing object, the corners of the object snap to the corners of cells on the worksheet.

Step 1 of the ChartWizard appears. Notice that the selected cells have a glittering marquee around them. The ChartWizard temporarily copies the selected range to the clipboard while it creates the chart.

4   Click the Finish button to create the default chart.

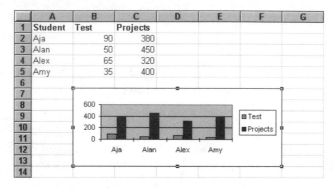

Stop Macro button

5   Click the Stop Macro button and activate the Module1 sheet to look at the recorded macro.

```
Sub MakeChart()
    ActiveSheet.ChartObjects.Add(48, 76.5, 240, 89.25).Select
    Application.CutCopyMode = False
    ActiveChart.ChartWizard Source:=Range("A1:C5"), Gallery:=xlColumn,_
        Format:=6, PlotBy:=xlColumns, CategoryLabels:=1, SeriesLabels _
        :=1, HasLegend:=1
End Sub
```

The macro creates an embedded chart in the same way that you create a rectangle or other drawing object: using the Add method.

The statement with the Add method produces an empty box—a container for the chart.

The statement that sets the CutCopyMode property to False is in the macro because the ChartWizard temporarily copies the selection. You can delete this statement without changing the result because the ChartWizard method in the next statement turns off the copy mode anyway.

The statement with the ChartWizard method is what really defines the chart that goes inside the box. The ChartWizard method has several arguments; these arguments correspond to various possible settings for the chart.

Now see how you can control the chart yourself from the Immediate pane.

Modify a chart object

1   From the View menu, choose the Debug Window command, and activate the Immediate pane.

2   Type **Worksheets.Item(2).Select** and press ENTER to activate the worksheet with the chart. The chart container should still be selected—you should see the selection handles on the edges. (If the chart container is not selected, type **ActiveSheet.ChartObjects.Item(1).Select** and press ENTER to select it.)

3   Type **ActiveChart.ChartWizard Gallery:=xlBar** and press ENTER.

The chart changes to a horizontal bar chart.

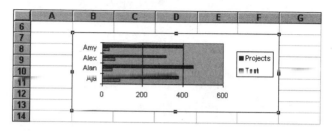

To see the list of possible Gallery settings in Help, select the word ChartWizard and press F1.

This statement is the same as the recorded ChartWizard statement from the Code pane, except that you left out all the arguments except Gallery and changed the value for the Gallery argument to *xlBar*.

Tip   When you use the ChartWizard method on an existing chart, omit the arguments for any attributes you don't want to change.

Because the chart's container is a drawing object—just like a rectangle—you can set its properties—and the properties of its interior and border—in the same way that you work with a rectangle.

4   Type **Let Selection.Interior.ColorIndex = 6** and press ENTER.

The color of the chart container box changes to yellow.

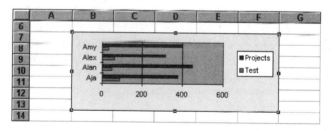

Notice that you use the word *ActiveChart* when you use the ChartWizard method and the word *Selection* when you use the ColorIndex property.

The word *Selection* refers to the container box for the chart. It is a drawing object on the worksheet, similar to a rectangle. You set the ColorIndex property of the interior of the container box. The word *ActiveChart* refers to the chart inside the box. You use the ChartWizard method to modify the chart inside the box.

The container box is a ChartObject object. The chart inside the box is a Chart object. Never confuse a ChartObject object with a Chart object. A ChartObject object can exist only on a worksheet as a drawing object. A Chart object can exist either inside a ChartObject container box or on its own separate sheet in the workbook.

Because the chart's container is a drawing object, you can manipulate other of its properties, such as its size and position.

5   Type **Let Selection.Left = 0** and press ENTER to shift the chart to the left side of the worksheet.

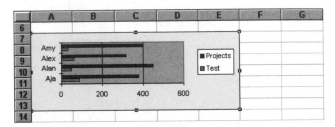

6   Type **Let Selection.Width = Columns("D:G").Width** and press ENTER to make the width of the chart the same as the width of columns D through G.

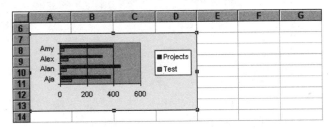

7   Double click the Control Menu box at the top left corner of the Debug window to close the window.

Control Menu box

You can change the attributes of a chart's container box by changing the ChartObject object, which you refer to by using the word *Selection*. You can also change some of the attributes of the chart itself using the ChartWizard method on the Chart object, which you refer to by using the word *ActiveChart*. But to change many of the attributes of a Chart object, you need to get down inside the Chart object itself.

Record modifying a chart

Interactively, you modify the internal attributes of a chart by double clicking the chart to *activate* the chart. Activating a chart is different from merely selecting it. When you select a chart, you select the chart's container box—the ChartObject object. When you activate a chart, you activate the chart inside the box—the Chart object. When you activate a chart, the border of the chart becomes thick and gray, and the menu bar changes to include commands specifically designed for working with charts.

Once you activate a Chart object, you can select and modify all the internal attributes of the chart. You can use the macro recorder to see how to modify the internal attributes of a chart.

Record Macro button

1 With the chart you created earlier selected, click the Record Macro button, type **EditChart** as the name for the macro, and click OK.

2 Double click the chart to activate the Chart object.

3 Click the legend box, and press DELETE to remove it.

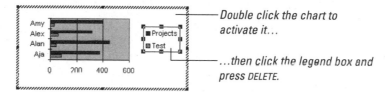

————*Double click the chart to activate it...*

...then click the legend box and press DELETE.

4 To enlarge the plot area, click the plot area to select it, and drag one of the sizing handles on the right side further to the right to fill the space left by the legend.

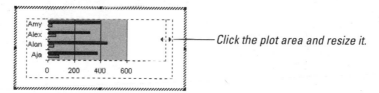

————*Click the plot area and resize it.*

5 From the Format menu, choose the AutoFormat command, select Combination from the Galleries list, select number 3 from the set of formats, and click OK.

The chart changes to a line chart with separate axes for each of the two series.

6 Double click one of the number labels on the left value axis to display the Format Axis dialog box, and select the Scale tab. Type **200** in the Maximum box, and click OK.

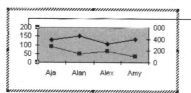

————*Double click this axis label, and change the maximum scale to 200.*

7 Click outside the chart to deactivate the Chart object. Now the ChartObject object is the selection again.

Stop Macro button

8 Click the Stop Macro button and activate the Module1 sheet to look at the recorded macro.

```
Sub EditChart()
    ActiveSheet.DrawingObjects("Chart 1").Select
    ActiveSheet.ChartObjects("Chart 1").Activate
    ActiveChart.Legend.Select
    Selection.Delete
    ActiveChart.PlotArea.Select
    Selection.Width = 176
    ActiveChart.AutoFormat Gallery:=xlCombination, Format:=3
    ActiveChart.Axes(xlValue).Select
    With ActiveChart.Axes(xlValue)
        .MinimumScaleIsAuto = True
        .MaximumScale = 200
        .MinorUnitIsAuto = True
        .MajorUnitIsAuto = True
        .Crosses = xlAutomatic
        .ReversePlotOrder = False
        .ScaleType = False
    End With
    ActiveWindow.Visible = False
    Windows("Book1").Activate
End Sub
```

In brief, this macro activates the embedded chart, deletes the legend, changes the width of the plot area, formats the chart as a combination chart, changes the maximum scale for the value axis to 200, and deactivates the chart.

The macro recorder does not always record the simplest way of accomplishing a task, but it does show you the names of the object classes, properties, and methods you will need to work with. Now you can go into the Immediate pane and see how to really control the chart.

Modify the chart

1   From the View menu, choose the Debug Window command, and activate the Immediate pane.

2   Type **Sheets.Item(2).Select** and press ENTER to activate the worksheet containing the chart. The chart's container object should still be selected—you should see the selection handles on the chart. If the chart's container object is not selected, type **ActiveSheet.ChartObjects.Item(1).Select** and press ENTER to select it.

The statement *ActiveSheet.ChartObjects("Chart 1").Activate* is what the macro produced when you activated the chart. But specifying the chart by name may make the macro difficult to use with a different chart. The chart container is already the current selection, so you can use the word *Selection* to refer to it.

3   Type **Selection.Activate** and press ENTER to activate the chart.

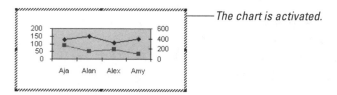

The chart is activated.

Now that the chart is activated, you can select various objects inside the chart.

4   Type **ActiveChart.PlotArea.Select** and press ENTER to select the plot area.

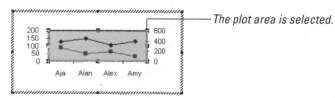

The plot area is selected.

5   Type **Let Selection.Width = 100** and press ENTER to make the plot area narrower.

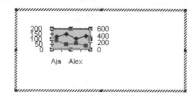

To make the plot area as wide as possible, use an oversize number for the width.

6   Type **Let Selection.Width = 500** and press ENTER to make the plot area as wide as possible.

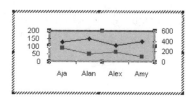

7   Type **ActiveChart.Axes(xlValue).Select** and press ENTER to select the value axis.

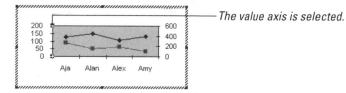

The value axis is selected.

8 Type **Let Selection.Minimumscale = -50** and press ENTER to change the range of the value axis.

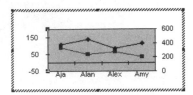

The recorded macro has the lines *With ActiveChart.Axes(xlValue)...End Selection* surrounding several statements that set the axis properties. The recorder did not know you changed only one setting. You can eliminate the statements for all the settings you did not change.

9 Type **ActiveWindow.Visible = False** and press ENTER.

The thick gray border around the chart disappears and the selection changes back to the chart container.

The recorded macro treats the activated chart as a separate window, even though it does not look like a typical window. (If you want, you can enter the statements *?Window.Count* and *?ActiveWindow.Caption* into the Immediate pane to see that the chart is in a separate window.) Normally, to close a window you use the Close method, but you close the special chart editing window by setting its Visible property to False.

The macro recorder included the statement *Windows("Book1").Activate* at the end of the macro. You do not need this statement since hiding the chart's editing window already activated the original workbook window. You should eliminate this statement from all the macros you create, because it will cause the macro to fail if you save the workbook with a new name.

If you simplify the recorded macro based on the exploring you've done in the Immediate pane—but without changing the functionality of the macro at all—this is what you get:

```
Sub EditChart()
    Selection.Activate
    ActiveChart.Legend.Select
    Selection.Delete
    ActiveChart.PlotArea.Select
    Selection.Width = 176
    ActiveChart.AutoFormat Gallery:=xlCombination, Format:=3
    ActiveChart.Axes(xlValue).Select
    ActiveChart.Axes(xlValue).MaximumScale = 200
    ActiveWindow.Visible = False
End Sub
```

Modify the chart remotely

When you modify a chart interactively, you must activate the chart in order to select or modify any of the objects inside the chart. From a macro, you can manipulate a chart's objects even if they are not selected, as long as you refer to the correct object.

1　Type **Range("A1").Select** and press ENTER to make cell A1 the selection. Now not even the chart container is selected.

2　Type **Let Activesheet.ChartObjects.Item(1).Chart.PlotArea.Width = 50** and press ENTER to make the plot area narrow.

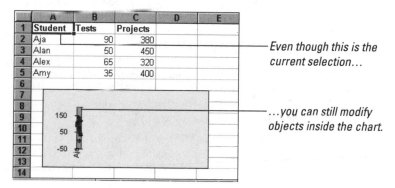

Even though this is the current selection...

...you can still modify objects inside the chart.

This means, "Start with the active sheet. Find its collection of chart container boxes. Find the first container box in the collection. Find the actual chart inside the container box. Find the plot area of that chart. Set that plot area's width to 50."

The entire statement may look long and intimidating, but if you break it into separate pieces, each piece simply returns the next object down the chain until you finally get to the object that has a property you want to change.

3　Type **Let Activesheet.ChartObjects.Item(1).Chart.PlotArea.Left = 100** and press ENTER to shift the plot area to the right.

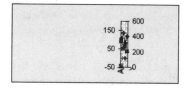

In the Immediate pane, each command must be on a single line, so you can't use With statements.

In a macro, when you use the same long chain of objects more than once, you can put the entire chain of objects into a With statement to make the macro easier to read and faster to run. Using a With statement, the two statements that change the plot area could be written like this:

```
With Activesheet.ChartObjects.Item(1).Chart.PlotArea
    Let .Width = 50
    Let .Left = 100
End With
```

Using a With statement is similar in some ways to selecting an object interactively. When you include an object in a With statement, you can think of the object as "virtually selected" until you use End With to deselect it. The object is not really selected, but any properties or methods that begin with a period apply to the object.

When you record actions, the resulting macro always selects each object before it changes it. That's because you must select an object before you can change it when you work interactively. You can use the recorder to help you find out the names of the object classes, properties, and methods you need to work with, and then you can change the recorded macro to manipulate objects without selecting them. Manipulating objects without selecting them makes a macro run much faster.

Exploring the Application Object

You have seen references to the Application object in passing a few times: For example, to find the Workbooks method in the Object Browser, you select Application from the list of object names. Also, every object class name listed on the left side of the Object Browser includes the Application property in the list on the right.

The Application object is Microsoft Excel itself. It is the ultimate parent object for every object in Excel. The application object is also the repository for all the workspace-wide settings and for all the actions that just don't fit anywhere else.

The Application object's properties and methods

If you select the Application object from the list of object names in the Object Browser, you will find about 400 entries in the list of properties and methods on the right. Don't panic, however; you don't have to learn very many of those 400 properties and methods to function effectively in Excel. The Application object's properties and methods fall into a few broad groups:

Globally known properties and methods About 40 properties and methods of the Application object can be used without including the word *Application*. These will be reviewed in more detail in the next section.

Worksheet functions Excel has more than 200 worksheet functions—functions like SUM and PMT. You can access any of these functions from a macro as methods of the Application object.

Recordable workspace settings Excel has about 60 properties and methods that you can set or run using standard commands, keyboard actions, and mouse movements. For example, you can use the mouse to set the size and location of Excel's window. You can use the Formula Bar command on the View menu to hide or display the formula bar. Or you can recalculate the current workbook by pressing F9. These attributes and actions are all properties and methods of the Application object. The easiest way to learn any of these properties and methods is to record changing the attribute or carrying out the command.

Workspace information Excel has about 30 properties that tell you about the working environment, such as whether you are operating in Windows or on a Macintosh and how much memory is available.

Macro settings About a dozen of the Application method's properties are properties that you can set to control Excel as your macros work. For example, you can keep Excel from updating the screen while your macro runs, or you can add a message to the status bar.

Miscellaneous methods The remaining approximately 30 methods cover a wide range of uses, from converting centimeter measurements to points, to managing mail, to starting the Help system.

Most of the Application object's properties and methods are either easily recorded or apply to advanced macro applications. When you are ready to learn more about the Application object, look in the Object Browser and the Help system.

Global properties and methods

When you refer to the first cell on the active worksheet, you use the expression *Cells.Item(1)*. But when you refer to the first rectangle on that same worksheet, you must use *ActiveSheet.Rectangles.Item(1)*. Similarly, the word *Workbooks* can stand alone, but the word *ChartObjects* must be preceded by the parent worksheet object— for example, *Worksheets.Item(1).ChartObjects*. Likewise, the words *Selection* and *Cells* can stand alone, but the words *Interior* and *Border* must be preceded by a parent object.

Why can some objects stand alone while others must be preceded by a parent object?

When you address a letter, you always need to include the recipient's name, street address, city, state, and ZIP code. If you are sending the letter to a different country, you also need to include the name of the country. If you were sending the letter to London, however, or to New York City, you could probably leave off the country name, and the letter would still arrive at its destination. Some cities are big enough to be globally known.

About 40 of the Application object's properties and methods are important enough to be globally known in Excel, and you don't need to specify an object for them. For example, the Workbooks method is globally known. Technically, you should use the expression *Application.Workbooks* instead of just *Workbooks*, but Excel "knows" what Workbooks is, just as most post offices "know" where Tokyo is.

For a property or method to be globally known, it must belong to the Application object. In Help, if a method or property does not need the object specified, the Help topic for the method or property includes the word *Optional* after the description of the object.

The globally known properties and methods fall into a few groups:

The ThisWorkbook property points to the workbook containing the macro, in case it's different from the active workbook.

Pointer properties The Selection property, the ThisWorkbook property, and all the "Active" properties: ActiveCell, ActiveChart, ActiveDialog, ActiveMenuBar, ActivePrinter, ActiveSheet, ActiveWindow, and ActiveWorkbook.

Range object methods The most common methods that return range objects: Range, Union, Intersect, Cells, Columns, and Rows.

Sheets collections Methods that return the different sheet collections that can occur in a workbook: Sheets, Worksheets, Charts, DialogSheets, Modules, Excel4MacroSheets, and Excel4IntlMacroSheets.

Other collections Methods that return other common collections: Addins, MenuBars, Names, ShortcutMenus, Toolbars, Windows, and Workbooks.

Commands Methods that perform common tasks: Calculate, Evaluate, Run, and SendKeys, along with seven commands for Dynamic Data Exchange (DDE), which is used in certain advanced applications.

Lesson Summary

To	Do this
Create a 1-inch rectangle in the top left corner of the active sheet	Use the statement *ActiveSheet.Rectangles.Add(0,0,72,72)*.
Change the color of the selected object to red	Use the statement *Selection.Interior.ColorIndex = 3*.
Create a chart	Use the ChartWizard method.
Modify specific items on an existing chart	Use the ChartWizard method, deleting all arguments except the ones you need to change.
Activate a chart so you can select objects inside the chart	Select the chart and use the statement *Selection.Activate*.
Deactivate a chart	Use the statement *ActiveWindow.Visible = False*.
Select the second chart on the active sheet	Use the statement *Activesheet.ChartObjects(2).Select*.

For more information on	See
Using charts	Part 3, "Creating Charts from Worksheet Data," in the *Microsoft Excel User's Guide*.

Preview of the Next Lesson

In Part 3, you have worked intensively with Excel objects. You have learned to control those objects, largely by executing single statements in the Immediate pane. To build applications that control Excel objects, you need to execute more than a single statement. Visual Basic is the tool that manages large numbers of statements. You have already worked with Visual Basic code as produced by the macro recorder. In Lesson 10 and Lesson 11, you will explore how to develop Visual Basic code to achieve results that cannot be done with only the macro recorder.

4 Exploring Visual Basic

Explore Visual Basic Procedures

Have you ever driven a radio remote controlled car? On the remote control, you use one lever to make the car go forward or reverse, another lever to make it turn left or right, and another lever to control the speed. You can stand on a table in your dining room and make that little car crash its way all around the room. Now imagine that, instead of a table, you're standing on an apartment building; instead of a miniature car, you're controlling a full-size sedan; and instead of being empty, the car has a real driver inside. Both you and the driver can control the car. You have levers on the remote control; the driver has a stick shift, a steering wheel, and a gas pedal. Inside the car, the driver uses one set of controls, and outside the car, you use a different set of controls.

Microsoft Excel is like a car that has two sets of controls. Excel has certain inherent capabilities which it *exposes* to the interactive user using one set of controls—menus, toolbar buttons, keyboard keys, and mouse clicks—and which it *exposes* to a Visual Basic program using a different set of controls. The set of controls that Excel exposes to Visual Basic are the objects you learned about in Part 3 of this book.

In this part, you will learn more about working with Visual Basic. Everything you learn about Visual Basic in Excel will apply to writing a stand-alone Visual Basic program, and to writing macros in Excel, Project, or other Microsoft applications that will eventually include Visual Basic for Applications.

You will start with a very small, simple macro—a *seed* macro—and then gradually modify and enhance the macro to make it more sophisticated, powerful, and error-resistant. Along the way, you will learn much about how to organize and control macros using Visual Basic.

You will learn how to:

- Use various conditional expressions in your procedures.
- Create subroutine procedures.
- Create function procedures.
- Create custom worksheet functions.
- Use named constants in your procedures.

Estimated lesson time: 35 minutes

Start the lesson

▶ Start Excel with a new workbook. Delete all but one of the worksheets in the workbook, and save the file as LESSON10.XLS.

Creating a Seed Macro

In this lesson you will practice Visual Basic skills by formatting selected cells in a block of data. The example is similar to the formatting task in Lesson 3, and the first few steps in building the macro are similar to the first few steps in that lesson. This time, however, you will format random numbers, and you will learn more powerful techniques for controlling Visual Basic programs.

Create sample data

1   Double click the tab for the current worksheet, and rename the worksheet **SampleData**.

2   Select the range A1:D8.

3   Type =**RAND**(), hold down the CTRL key, and press ENTER.

Random numbers ranging from 0 to 1 fill all the selected cells.

	A	B	C	D	E	F	G
1	0.678861	0.309862	0.362173	0.110884			
2	0.199959	0.010881	0.07151	0.513949			
3	0.707029	0.940068	0.618681	0.275026			
4	0.240814	0.248583	0.540546	0.911592			
5	0.954295	0.341195	0.086018	0.998141			
6	0.957416	0.993798	0.304669	0.367702			
7	0.413936	0.476899	0.835539	0.038563			
8	0.941018	0.953556	0.084282	0.949504			
9							

Percent Style button

4   Click the Percent Style button in the Formatting toolbar to make the random numbers more readable.

5   From the Tools menu, choose the Options command, and select the Calculation tab. Select the Manual option button, and click OK.

These numbers will now change to new random numbers whenever you press F9.

Your first task is to format all the cells that have values greater than 50%. Start by recording a macro to format a single cell, much as you did in Lesson 3.

Format a single cell

1   Select any cell within the block of random numbers that is greater than 50%.

Record Macro button

2   Click the Record Macro button in the Visual Basic toolbar, type **FormatExceptions** as the name for the macro, type **Format a single cell** as the description, click the Options button, clear the Shortcut Key check box, and click OK.

Using the macro recorder is an easy way to create the shell for a new macro.

Color button

3   Click the arrow at the side of the Color button in the Formatting toolbar, click the red box in the color palette, and then click the Stop Macro button.

Create Button button

4   Create a button that extends from the top left corner of cell F2 to the bottom right corner of cell H7 and assign the FormatExceptions macro to it. (Use the Create Button button in the Drawing toolbar.)

5   Type **Format Exceptions** as the label for the button, and press ESC twice to deselect the button.

6   Select another cell that's greater than 50%, and click the Format Exceptions button to turn the cell red.

7   Activate the new Module1 sheet, rename the sheet **FormatModule**, and look at the macro.

The macro recorder does not put the optional keyword Let *at the beginning of an assignment.*

```
Sub FormatExceptions
    With Selection.Interior
        .ColorIndex = 3
        .Pattern = xlSolid
    End With
End Sub
```

This macro changes the interior pattern color of the selected cell. This macro will be the seed for developing more sophisticated procedures for formatting the exception cells.

Note   The terms *macro* and *procedure* are often used interchangably. In the Visual Basic environment, the word *procedure* has historically been used to refer to programmed code, whereas in the Excel environment, the word *macro* has historically been used. In general, I will use the word *procedure* to refer to an individual Visual Basic routine, and I will use the word *macro* to refer to code as it is run from Excel, whether that code consists of one or more procedures.

Making Decisions

FormatExceptions is a perfectly fine simple procedure. It makes the current selection red. But you want a procedure that will format the active cell only if its value is greater than 50%, and will then move down to the next cell. Rather than add the new statements to your current perfectly fine procedure as you did in Lesson 3, make a separate master procedure that uses the current FormatExceptions procedure when necessary. Treat the procedure you have now as a subordinate, or servant, procedure. When a master wants a servant to do something, the master *calls* the servant. When a Visual Basic procedure wants a subroutine to do something, it *calls* the subroutine.

Add a master procedure

1   Activate the FormatModule sheet, and change the name of the FormatExceptions procedure to **FormatColor**. You will reserve the name FormatExceptions for the master procedure since that is the name linked to the button on the worksheet.

2   Move the insertion point above the FormatColor procedure, and type the following:

```
Sub FormatExceptions()
    If ActiveCell > .5 Then FormatColor
    ActiveCell.Offset(1,0).Select
End Sub
```

You can put the master procedure above or below the subordinate procedure, but if you always put subordinates below master procedures, you will be able to find them easily, even as your projects get larger and you have more layers of master and subordinate procedures.

> **Note** A subordinate procedure is typically called a *subroutine*, which accounts for the word *Sub* used to define the name of a procedure. Since master procedures can also be subordinate to other, higher masters, you use the word *Sub* when defining both master and subordinate procedures.

3   Switch back to the SampleData worksheet, select the top cell in one of the columns, and click the Format Exceptions button several times.

A master procedure can delegate a task to a subordinate procedure, or subroutine. Using a subroutine has several advantages over putting all the statements into the master procedure: the master procedure usually becomes simpler and easier to read, and you often find that other procedures can utilize the subroutine. The subroutine becomes a specialist at a single task, serving many masters.

Watch the procedures work

The macro formats the cells nicely, but you may want to watch the macro at work. In Lesson 2 you learned how to use the Step button in the Macro dialog box to step through a macro. In order to use the Step button, however, you must choose the Macros, Run command from the Tools menu and select the macro name. You probably much prefer using this very nice Format Exceptions button to run the macro. You can tell the macro to start proceeding one statement at a time, starting with any statement in the macro you want.

1   Activate the FormatModule sheet and put the insertion point anywhere on the statement *Sub FormatExceptions()*.

2   Click the Toggle Breakpoint button in the Visual Basic toolbar.

Toggle Breakpoint button

The color of the statement changes to red. This statement is now a *breakpoint* because everytime the macro gets to this point, it will break into a walk, stepping through all subsequent statements.

3   Activate the SampleData worksheet, select a cell that is less than 50%, and click the Format Exceptions button.

The Debug window appears, showing the FormatExceptions procedure in the Code pane. The breakpoint statement has a box around it indicating that this is the next statement that will execute.

Step Into button

4 Resize the Debug window so that you can see the worksheet behind it, and click the Step Into button to step through the procedure.

The statement

```
If ActiveCell > .5 Then FormatColor
```

calls the FormatColor subroutine if the value of the active cell is greater than .5. The whole If statement fits on a single line, so you don't need to put the words *End If* at the end. An If statement that fits on a single line is sometimes called an *inline* or *single-line* If. You could also write this statement as

```
If ActiveCell > .5 Then
    FormatColor
End If
```

which you may find easier to recognize as an If structure. An If structure that is made up of several statements and ends with End If is called a block If. The statement

```
ActiveCell.Offset(1,0).Select
```

starts with the active cell, calculates a new cell reference one cell down, and selects the new cell. You can record moving the active cell down with the macro recorder, but once you are comfortable with manipulating a Range object, you may prefer to type the statement directly into the procedure.

After the macro finishes, select a cell with a large value and click the Format Exceptions button again. The macro starts stepping in the same place.

Step Into button

Toggle Breakpoint button

5 Click the Step Into button repeatedly and watch how the FormatExceptions procedure calls the FormatColor subroutine.

6 To turn off the breakpoint, activate the FormatModule sheet, put the insertion point on the breakpoint statement, and click the Toggle Breakpoint button.

Add an argument to the subroutine

What if you want to change the color you format the cells from red to yellow? Rather than create one subroutine that makes a cell red and a second subroutine that makes a cell yellow, the master procedure should be able to give the subroutine instructions on how to do its job. When you use an Excel method, you give it instructions on how to do its job by giving it arguments. You can make the FormatColor subroutine capable of accepting arguments when it is called.

Imagine a human master who needs to give secret instructions to a servant. The master calls the servant, writes the instructions on a note, puts a code on the outside of the note so that the servant can identify the instructions, and *passes* the note to the servant. Compare the human situation to that of a Visual Basic procedure that needs to give an instruction to a subroutine. The master procedure calls the subroutine and *passes* an argument to the subroutine, using an argument name as a code to clarify the type of instruction.

1   In the FormatColor line of the subroutine, put the insertion point between the open and close parentheses and type **NewColor**.

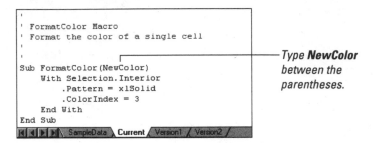

Type **NewColor** between the parentheses.

Putting a word inside the parentheses after the name of a procedure adds that word as the name of an argument for the procedure. The argument name is the subroutine's way of telling any procedures that want to call it what argument it will accept. You can invent whatever you wish for the name of an argument, but avoid any names that are already used by Excel or Visual Basic. When a master procedure calls the FormatColor subroutine, it passes a number as the value of the NewColor argument.

2   Replace the number 3 after the word *ColorIndex* with the word **NewColor**.

The subroutine uses the argument name the same as it would use any variable.

3   In the FormatExceptions procedure, change the word *FormatColor* to **FormatColor NewColor:=6**.

The number 6 is the color index number of the color yellow in the default color palette.

When a statement in a master procedure calls a subroutine with an argument, you put the argument name, then a colon and an equal sign (:=), and then the value of the argument. Calling a subroutine using an argument is exactly the same as calling an object method with an argument.

Here's what the resulting macro looks like. You can now easily switch the formatting color without having to modify the FormatColor procedure at all.

```
Sub FormatExceptions()
    If ActiveCell > 0.5 Then FormatColor NewColor:=6
    ActiveCell.Offset(1, 0).Select
End Sub

Sub FormatColor(NewColor)
    With Selection.Interior
        .Pattern = xlSolid
        .ColorIndex = NewColor
    End With
End Sub
```

Color button

4   Activate the SampleData worksheet, select the top cell in one of the columns, and try the macro.

5   To clear all the color formatting for the random number cells, select the range of random numbers, click the arrow at the side of the Color button in the Formatting toolbar, and click the word *None* in the palette.

6   To change to a new set of sample random numbers, press F9.

Using arguments makes a subroutine flexible and easy to use more than once. Instead of having four different subroutines to format cells with four different colors, you can use a single subroutine and pass it an argument for the color.

Add more conditions

Suppose you don't want to format just the cells that are greater than 50%. Suppose you want to make cells greater than 80% red, cells greater than 50% yellow, cells greater than 30% green, and all other cells white. Now that the FormatColor procedure can handle any color, enhancing the macro will be simple.

1   In the FormatExceptions macro, replace the statement beginning with the word *If* with these lines:

```
If ActiveCell > 0.8 Then
    FormatColor NewColor:=4
ElseIf ActiveCell > 0.5 Then
    FormatColor NewColor:=6
ElseIf ActiveCell > 0.3 Then
    FormatColor NewColor:=3
Else
    FormatColor NewColor:=2
End If
```

Because you pass the color as an argument to FormatColor, you can handle multiple colors without making any changes at all to the FormatColor subroutine.

2   Switch back to the SampleData worksheet, select the top cell in a column of random numbers, and try out the macro.

When you use the block form of the If statement, you can add new conditions with new results by preceding each condition with the word *ElseIf*. Notice that *ElseIf* is all one word, with no space. When you have one or more statements you want to run if none of the preceding conditions is true, put them after the word *Else*.

Watch the value of the argument change

An expression is any combination of words and symbols that returns a value.

Sometimes while you are developing procedures, you need to know the value of a variable or argument. Visual Basic provides a tool that allows you to *watch* the value of an expression in your procedures.

Toggle Breakpoint button

1   Activate the FormatModule sheet, put the insertion point anywhere on the *Sub FormatColor(NewColor)* statement, and click the Toggle Breakpoint button.

2   Activate the SampleData worksheet, select a cell with a number, and click the Format Exceptions button.

When the FormatColor procedure starts to run, the Debug window appears for you to start stepping through the statements.

Instant Watch button

3   Select the word *NewColor* inside the parentheses and click the Instant Watch button in the Visual Basic toolbar.

The Instant Watch dialog box appears, showing you the current value of the expression *NewColor*. Depending on the value in the active cell, the number is 2, 3, 4, or 6.

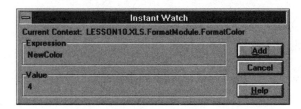

4   Click the Add button.

The Instant Watch dialog box disappears, but nothing else seems to happen.

5   Click the Watch tab toward the top of the Debug window.

The Watch pane appears, replacing the Immediate pane. The expression *NewColor* is in the left column, and its current value appears next to it.

Note   The Instant Watch button shows you the value of an expression *instantly*, but only for as long as the dialog box is displayed. Adding an expression to the Watch pane allows you to watch the value of the expression over time.

Resume Macro button

6   Click the Resume Macro button to let the macro finish, and then click the Format Exceptions button again. When the Debug window appears, notice the new value of the *NewColor* expression.

Toggle Breakpoint button

7   In the Code pane, select the breakpoint statement and click the Toggle Breakpoint button. Then click the Resume Macro button to let the macro finish.

Make constants easier to read

When you recorded setting the color of a cell, the macro recorder set both the color and the pattern of the cell. This is the statement the macro recorder generated to give the cell a solid pattern: *.Pattern = xlSolid*.

The word *xlSolid* represents the number 1. You could give a cell a solid pattern with the statement *.Pattern = 1*. But the word *xlSolid* is easier to interpret than the number 1. Excel supplies a long list of constants you can use when setting Excel object properties. (To see the list of constants you can use in Excel, open the Object Browser, select Excel from the Libraries/Workbooks list, select Constants in the Objects/Modules list, and look at the entries in the Methods/Properties list.)

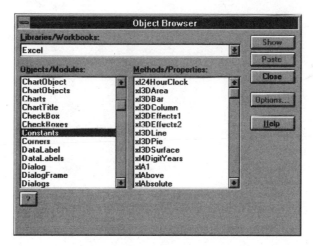

When the FormatExceptions procedure calls FormatColor, it passes the new color as a number. You may forget that the number 3 corresponds to the color red. Excel does not have built in constants for the color index numbers. You can make your color index numbers readable the same way that Excel made the pattern number readable.

1 Activate the FormatModule sheet, and put the insertion point at the end of the *Sub FormatExceptions()* statement.

2 Press ENTER and then TAB.

3 Enter these new lines:

```
Const myWhite = 2
Const myRed = 3
Const myGreen = 4
Const myYellow = 6
```

To define a constant in Visual Basic, you use the word *Const* followed by the name you want to use for the constant, an equal sign, and the value for the constant. A constant is like a variable, except that you cannot change it later in the procedure. The only time you can assign a value to a constant is when you first define it. The difference between a constant and a variable is that a variable can change values, and a constant cannot.

Note You can use any name you want for the constant, but as with argument names, you should avoid names already used by Excel or Visual Basic. Visual Basic constants all have the prefix *vb* (in lowercase). Excel constants all have the prefix *xl*. You might want to decide upon a similar prefix for constants you define.

Once you have defined constants equal to the color index numbers you want to use, you can replace the numbers in the FormatExceptions procedure with constants that are easier to interpret.

4 In the statements that call FormatColor, change the constant 2 to **myGreen**, 6 to **myYellow**, 3 to **myRed**, and 2 to **myWhite**.

When you're finished, FormatExceptions should look like this:

```
Sub FormatExceptions()
    Const myWhite = 2
    Const myRed = 3
    Const myGreen = 4
    Const myYellow = 6
    If ActiveCell > 0.8 Then
        FormatColor myGreen
    ElseIf ActiveCell > 0.5 Then
        FormatColor myYellow
    ElseIf ActiveCell > 0.3 Then
        FormatColor myRed
    Else
        FormatColor myWhite
    End If
    ActiveCell.Offset(1, 0).Select
End Sub
```

5 Activate the SampleData worksheet and try the revised macro. It should work exactly the same as before.

Simplify lists of conditions

The FormatExceptions macro distinguishes four conditions for formatting a cell. The conditions are all parallel—they all compare ActiveCell to various values.

When you have several ElseIf conditions in a row, you might be able to write the conditions in a more easily understandable form using the *Select Case* statement.

1 In the FormatExceptions macro, select the lines from the If statement through the End If statement.

```
Sub FormatExceptions()
    Const myWhite = 2
    Const myRed = 3
    Const myGreen = 4
    Const myYellow = 6
    If ActiveCell > 0.8 Then
        FormatColor myGreen
    ElseIf ActiveCell > 0.5 Then
        FormatColor myYellow
    ElseIf ActiveCell > 0.3 Then
        FormatColor myRed
    Else
        FormatColor myWhite
    End If
    ActiveCell.Offset(1, 0).Select
End Sub
```

Select these lines...

2   Type the following new lines.

```
Select Case ActiveCell
Case Is > 0.8
    FormatColor NewColor:=myGreen
Case Is > 0.5
    FormatColor NewColor:=myYellow
Case Is > 0.3
    FormatColor NewColor:=myRed
Case Else
    FormatColor NewColor:=myWhite
End Select
```

...and replace them with these lines.

The Select Case structure begins with the words *Select Case*, which are followed by the expression you are comparing. You can use Select Case only when you are comparing a single base expression (such as ActiveCell) against multiple possible values (such as the various percentages). Each part of the structure compares the base expression to a new value. You could read the first comparison section in this example as "In case the active cell is greater than 80%...." As with the If statement, you can use the word *Else* to catch all the other options: "In case the active cell is anything else."

3   Activate the SampleData sheet and try out the macro. It should work the same as before, and you might find the Select Case structure easier to understand.

Making decisions is an important task in almost all macro applications. In Visual Basic you can choose between an inline If statement, a block If statement—possibly with several ElseIf clauses—and a Select Case statement.

Returning Values from Procedures

A master procedure delegates tasks to subordinate procedures. Often the master procedure wants to get a job done: "Take care of formatting that cell." Sometimes the master procedure wants some research done: "Please figure out what the formatting of that cell should be." When the subordinate procedure carries out an action, you call the procedure a subroutine, and you use the word *Sub* to define it. When the subordinate procedure does research to return a value, you call the procedure a function, and you use the word *Function* to define it.

Create a research assistant

Creating a function is like creating a research assistant. The assistant does a lot of work and returns information to the supervisor.

1   Between the end of the FormatExceptions macro and the beginning of the FormatColor macro, enter these two statements:

```
Function ChooseColor()
End Function
```

You use the word *Function* along with the name of the function to begin a function, and you use the words *End Function* to end it.

2   In the FormatExceptions procedure, select all the lines from the first Const line through the End Select line, and choose Cut from the Edit menu.

3   Paste the lines in front of the End Function statement of the ChooseColor function.

The ChooseColor function should now look like this:

```
Function ChooseColor()
    Const myWhite = 2
    Const myRed = 3
    Const myGreen = 4
    Const myYellow = 6
    Select Case ActiveCell
    Case Is > 0.8
        FormatColor NewColor:=myGreen
    Case Is > 0.5
        FormatColor NewColor:=myYellow
    Case Is > 0.3
        FormatColor NewColor:=myRed
    Case Else
        FormatColor NewColor:=myWhite
    End Select
End Function
```

The ChooseColor function calculates the color for the active cell, but it should not call the FormatColor subroutine directly. Keep the subprocedures independent, to make them easy for other procedures to call.

Note The word *procedure* applies to both subroutines and functions. I will use the term *procedure* when the distinction between a subroutine and a function is not important. A procedure can be either a subordinate procedure, a master procedure, or both at the same time. I will use the term *subprocedure* to refer to a procedure that is being called by another procedure.

In a function, you pass a value back to the calling procedure by assigning the value to the name of the function. In the new ChooseColor function, you need to replace the phrase *FormatColor NewColor:=* with *ChooseColor =*.

4 Drag through any occurrence of the phrase *FormatColor NewColor:=* in the ChooseColor function, and then choose Replace from the Edit menu.

The Replace dialog box appears, with the phrase *FormatColor NewColor:=* already entered in the Find What box. (If you have one or more words selected when you choose Replace, the selected words become the default find value.)

To undo the changes made by Replace All, press CTRL+Z.

5 Type **ChooseColor =** in the Replace With box, select Procedure from the Look In list, and click Replace All. (If you are cautious, you can click the Replace button four times and then close the dialog box.)

To change words quickly, type the old words here...

...and the new words here.

The ChooseColor function is now finished. It should look like this:

```
Function ChooseColor()
    Const myWhite = 2
    Const myRed = 3
    Const myGreen = 4
    Const myYellow = 6
    Select Case ActiveCell
    Case Is > 0.8
        ChooseColor = myGreen
    Case Is > 0.5
        ChooseColor = myYellow
    Case Is > 0.3
        ChooseColor = myRed
    Case Else
        ChooseColor = myWhite
    End Select
End Function
```

The ChooseColor function looks at the value in the active cell and calculates which color that cell should be.

The ChooseColor function should return the value to the FormatExceptions procedure. In a function, you return a value for the function by assigning the value to the name of the function. For example, the following function returns the value 5.

```
Function ThisFunction()
    ThisFunction = 5
End Function
```

The function uses the name of the function as if it were a variable.

Use the research assistant

The FormatExceptions procedure can now delegate the task of finding out the correct color to the ChooseColor function and then turn around and give that value to the FormatColor subroutine to implement.

1 In the FormatExceptions procedure, insert a new line right before the *ActiveCell.Offset(1, 0).Select* statement.

2 On the new line, type **FormatColor NewColor:=**.

At this point, you would normally type 4, or myGreen, or some other color number. Instead, you want to use the value returned by the ChooseColor function.

3 Type **ChooseColor**. The finished statement should be *FormatColor NewColor:=ChooseColor*.

The finished FormatExceptions macro should look like this:

```
Sub FormatExceptions()
    FormatColor NewColor:=ChooseColor
    ActiveCell.Offset(1, 0).Select
End Sub
```

4 Activate the SampleData worksheet and test the macro. It should work the same as before.

Save the result from the function

When you click the Format Exceptions button, the FormatExceptions procedure delegates the task of calculating the appropriate color for the active cell to the ChooseColor function. It then turns around and delegates the task of formatting the cell to the FormatColor subroutine in the same statement. You might find delegating to only one subprocedure per statement less confusing. You can save the value returned by the ChooseColor function until you are ready to use it.

1 Insert a new line before the *FormatColor* statement in the Format Exceptions procedure.

2 In the new line, type **Let myColor = ChooseColor**.

The Let statement accepts the result of the ChooseColor function and assigns that value to a name, myColor. A word you assign a value to is called a *variable*. In the statement on the previous page, the variable is myColor. You can use any name you want for the variable, but as with argument names and constants, you should avoid names already used by Excel or Visual Basic.

3   In the statement *FormatColor NewColor:=ChooseColor* (the next line down), replace the word *ChooseColor* with **myColor**.

When you assign a value to a variable, you can then use the value later in the macro. Once you assign a value to myColor, you can use myColor as the argument value for the FormatColor subroutine.

The revised FormatExceptions procedure should look like this:

```
Sub FormatExceptions()
    Let myColor = ChooseColor
    FormatColor NewColor:=myColor
    ActiveCell.Offset(1, 0).Select
End Sub
```

4   Activate the SampleData worksheet and test the macro. It should work the same as before.

Note Most experienced writers of Visual Basic omit the keyword *Let* when assigning a value to a variable. Using the keyword *Let* for now, however, will help you in Lesson 11 when you learn about the keyword *Set*, which assigns an object to a variable.

Make the subprocedures independent

All three procedures in the macro know that you are working with the active cell. The FormatExceptions procedure moves down one cell from the active cell. The ChooseColor function analyzes the value of the active cell. The FormatColor subroutine formats the active cell. You can make subprocedures much more flexible and reusable if you make them get all the information they need from the master procedure. You use arguments to communicate from the master procedure to the subprocedures.

1   Between the parentheses in the *Function ChooseColor()* statement, type **TestValue**.

The word *TestValue* is the name that the ChooseColor function will use for the test value the master procedure will pass it.

2   In the statement *Select Case ActiveCell* of the same procedure, replace the word *ActiveCell* with the word **TestValue**.

Once you change the word *ActiveCell* to *TestValue*, the ChooseColor function no longer knows anything about how the value it is to test was obtained.

3   In the FormatExceptions procedure, after the word *ChooseColor*, type **(TestValue:=ActiveCell)**.

When you pass arguments to the ChooseColor function, you must put parentheses around the arguments, because you use the value returned by the function.

4   In the statement *Sub FormatColor(NewColor)*, immediately before the word *NewColor*, type **NewCell,** (with the comma).

The word *NewCell* is the name that the FormatColor subroutine will use for the cell address the master procedure will pass it. You don't need to use the same name for FormatColor's argument as for ChooseColor's argument because these two subprocedures are completely independent of each other.

5   In the statement *With Selection.Interior* in the same procedure, change the word *Selection* to **NewCell**.

6   In the FormatExceptions procedure, after the statement *FormatColor NewColor:=myColor*, type **, NewCell:=ActiveCell**.

When you pass one or more arguments to a subroutine, you must *not* put parentheses around the arguments, because you do not use a return value from the subroutine. (A subroutine does not return a value.)

When you include the names of the arguments in the master procedure, you can put the arguments in any order you like. If you put the arguments in the same order as they are defined in the subprocedure, you can leave out the names.

7   Activate the SampleData worksheet and test the macro. It should work the same as before.

The revised macro should look like this:

```
Sub FormatExceptions()
    Let myColor = ChooseColor(TestValue:=ActiveCell)
    FormatColor NewColor:=myColor, NewCell:=ActiveCell
    ActiveCell.Offset(1, 0).Select
End Sub

Function ChooseColor(TestValue)
    Const myWhite = 2
    Const myRed = 3
    Const myGreen = 4
    Const myYellow = 6
    Select Case TestValue
    Case Is > 0.8
        ChooseColor = myGreen
    Case Is > 0.5
        ChooseColor = myYellow
    Case Is > 0.3
        ChooseColor = myRed
    Case Else
        ChooseColor = myWhite
    End Select
End Function
```

```
Sub FormatColor(NewCell, NewColor)
    With NewCell.Interior
        .Pattern = xlSolid
        .ColorIndex = NewColor
    End With
End Sub
```

Use a function from a worksheet

One of the benefits of making a subprocedure work completely through the master procedure is that the subprocedure then becomes usable in a wide variety of contexts. Suppose, for example, that you want to call the ChooseColor function from a cell on the worksheet. Because the ChooseColor function gets information only from the procedure that calls it, and passes information back only as a return value, you can put the ChooseColor function directly into a worksheet cell, the same as you do with Excel's standard functions such as SUM and PMT.

Excel's Function Wizard helps you enter built-in functions into cells on the worksheet. You can use the Function Wizard with the ChooseColor function as well.

1   Select cell A11 on the SampleData worksheet.

You will enter a formula here to calculate the color for cell A1, and then you can fill that formula into a rectangle of cells.

Function Wizard button

2   Click the Function Wizard button in the Standard toolbar.

3   In Step1, select User Defined from the Function Category list.

4   Select ChooseColor from the Function Name list, and click Next.

5   In Step 2, type A1 in the box labeled TestValue, and click Finish.

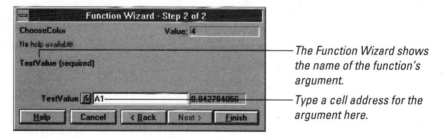

— *The Function Wizard shows the name of the function's argument.*

— *Type a cell address for the argument here.*

The color index number appropriate for the value in cell A1 appears in the cell. The worksheet cell is taking the place of the master procedure and is calling the ChooseColor function.

6   Select the range A11:D18 on the SampleData worksheet. This is a range the same size and shape as the range of random numbers. This is where you want the color numbers for the sample values.

7   Press F2 to edit the cell with the formula, and then press CTRL+ENTER to fill the entire range with the formula.

8   Press F9 to calculate new random numbers.

As Excel recalculates the worksheet and creates new random numbers, it calls your function for each cell that changes. The color numbers change to match the values of the new random numbers.

Tip When you have long, complex formulas on a worksheet, you can create custom functions so that you don't have to squeeze all the computations into a single worksheet cell.

Creating a function that you can use from a worksheet is exactly the same as creating a function that you can use from a master procedure in a macro. As long as you ensure that the function gets all the information it needs through arguments, and returns a value only as its result, you can call the function from a worksheet cell.

Prevent spelling errors

When you need to use a name in Visual Basic—whether as a variable, an argument, or a constant—you just start using the name and Visual Basic takes care of all the housekeeping involved with setting up a storage location for the value in the variable and so forth. Because Visual Basic allows you to use new names at anytime, starting to use names is easy. But creating new names any time you like is also dangerous—if you ever misspell a name. Now you'll see what happens when you misspell a name, and you'll also see how to fix it.

1   Activate the FormatModule sheet.

2   In the FormatExceptions procedure, in the statement *FormatColor NewColor:=myColor, NewCell:=ActiveCell*, change the word *myColor* to **myColorr**, a simple enough typographical error.

3   Activate the SampleData worksheet, select the range containing the random numbers, click the arrow on the Color button, and choose None as the fill color.

4   Click cell A1, and try out the Format Exceptions button on several sample cells.

The macro turns every cell white.

The macro turns the cells white because Visual Basic assumed you meant to use a new variable when you used the word *myColorr*, and it put the initial value zero into the variable for you. Every time the FormatExceptions procedure calls the FormatColor subroutine, it passes the value zero as the color.

In this case, Visual Basic assumed you wanted to create a new variable. As far as Visual Basic was concerned, the procedure performed exactly as you intended.

5   Activate the FormatModule sheet and, at the very top of the module, enter the statement **Option Explicit**.

The Option Explicit statement tells Visual Basic that you want to explicitly tell it the name of every variable you will use so that it can warn you if you misspell one of them. The Option Explicit statement applies only to the current module sheet.

6 Insert a new line below the *Sub FormatExceptions( )* statement, and enter the statement **Dim myColor**.

The word *Dim* tells Visual Basic that you want to *dimension* the word following it as a variable. When put a word after the the keyword *Dim*, you *declare* to Visual Basic that you intend to use that word as a variable. This is called *declaring a variable*, and the Dim statement is sometimes called a *variable declaration*.

The variable *myColor* is the only variable you need to declare. Both NewColor and NewCell are variables also, but since you used them as argument names for a function or subroutine, Visual Basic counts that as a declaration,

7 Activate the SampleData worksheet and try running the macro.

An error message appears informing you that there is a variable that is not defined. The word *myColorr* is not defined, and the Option Explicit statement requires you to explicitly declare all variables.

8 Click the OK button to go to the offending line in the procedure, correct the spelling, switch back to the worksheet, and try the macro again.

Spelling and typographical errors are so dangerous that you may want to always put Option Explicit at the top of every module you create. You can tell Visual Basic to do that for you.

9 From the Tools menu, choose the Options command, and select the Module General tab. Select the Require Variable Declaration check box, and press ENTER.

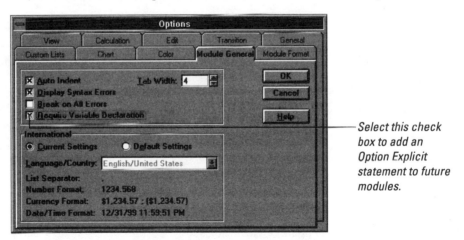

Select this check box to add an Option Explicit statement to future modules.

Setting the Require Variable Declaration check box does not put the Option Explit statement into any existing modules, but it adds the statement to any modules you create in the future.

The top part of the module now looks like this:

```
Option Explicit
Sub FormatExceptions()
    Dim myColor
    Let myColor = ChooseColor(TestValue:=ActiveCell)
    FormatColor NewColor:=myColor, NewCell:=ActiveCell
    ActiveCell.Offset(1, 0).Select
End Sub
```

You have now learned how to delegate tasks from a master procedure to both functions and subroutines. Functions are very similar to subroutines. The only difference is that a function can return a value. The only real advantage to creating subroutines instead of functions is that the word *Sub* is shorter than the word *Function*, so you have fewer characters to type.

Lesson Summary

To	Do this
Execute statements only if a condition is true	Insert the statements between If and End If statements.
Test for different values of a single variable	Use a Select Case structure.
Create a custom worksheet function.	Create a function procedure that gets information from arguments and returns a value.
Set a breakpoint	Select a statement and click the Set Breakpoint button.

For more information on	See
Creating procedures	Lesson 6, "Working with Visual Basic Code in Procedures," in the *Microsoft Excel Visual Basic User's Guide*.
Making decisions	Lesson 7, "Controlling How Your Code Runs," in the *Microsoft Excel Visual Basic User's Guide*.
Stepping through code and watching expressions	Lesson 8, "Testing and Debugging Your Code," in the *Microsoft Excel Visual Basic User's Guide*.

Preview of the Next Lesson

This lesson was the first part of your exploration of Visual Basic tools. In the next lesson you will explore additional capabilities of Visual Basic, including creating different kinds of loops and watching for errors.

Explore Visual Basic Control Structures

Single-cell organisms are all small. Bacteria, amoebas, paramecia—none are even large enough to see with the naked eye. Large, sophisticated organisms require multiple cells. Cells give structure and add specialization to living things.

Recorded macros are like single-cell organisms. The macro recorder puts everything you do into a single procedure. Like single-cell organisms, single-procedure macros should be small. Large, sophisticated applications, however, require multiple procedures and control structures such as conditional statements and loops. Large, sophisticated applications require mechanisms for dealing with error conditions. In this lesson, you will learn more about Visual Basic control structures—the tools you need to make more sophisticated applications.

You will learn how to:

- Use various loops in your procedures.
- Assign objects to variables.
- Handle run-time errors.
- Communicate with Microsoft Excel 4 macros.

Estimated lesson time: 40 minutes

Start the lesson

▶   Start Microsoft Excel, open the workbook LESSON10.XLS that you created in Lesson 10, and save a new copy of it as LESSON11.XLS.

Repeating Tasks

In Lesson 10, you learned how to delegate tasks from a master procedure to a subprocedure. To format all the cells in a block, however, you still needed to click the Format Exceptions button once for each cell.

In Lesson 3, you learned how to format exception cells for an entire range. In that lesson, you used a Do Loop structure to repeat statements in the macro until the active cell was blank. Visual Basic has tools specially designed for repeating statements in a loop. These tools are particularly useful when you repeat an action for each item in a collection such as a range of cells.

Process all the cells in a range

When you instruct another human to format cells in a rectangular range, you don't say, "Look at the first cell in the first column, look at the second cell in the first column, look at the first cell in the second column," and so forth. You just say, "Look at each cell in the range." You can also tell Visual Basic to look at each cell in the range.

1   Activate the FormatModule sheet, create a new line after the *Dim myColor* statement, and type **Dim myCell**.

This declares the word *myCell* as a variable. You will use myCell to store the address of the current cell as you work through the range.

You can use For Each with any collection, not just ranges.

2   Create another new line, and enter the statement **For Each myCell in Selection**.

The For Each statement tells Visual Basic to put the first item in the collection into the variable myCell. In this case, the collection is the selected range. After the For Each statement runs, the variable myCell contains a single cell Range object.

3   Change the word *ActiveCell* to **myCell** in the statements that call ChooseColor and FormatColor.

Instead of using the ActiveCell property to refer to the active cell, the statements will now use the myCell variable, which contains a link to the first cell in the selection as provided by the For Each statement.

4   Replace *ActiveCell.Offset(1, 0).Select* with **Next myCell**.

This statement tells Visual Basic to go back to the For Each statement and assign the next item (the next cell) from the collection (the selection) to the variable myCell and reexecute the statements inside the loop.

5   Indent the two statements between the For Each statement and the Next statement so that you can tell they are controlled by the loop.

6   Activate the SampleData worksheet, select the entire range of random numbers, and click the Format Exceptions button to test the macro.

The revised FormatExceptions procedure should look like this:

```
Sub FormatExceptions()
    Dim myColor
    Dim myCell
```

```
        For Each myCell in Selection
            Let myColor = ChooseColor(TestValue:=myCell)
            FormatColor NewColor:=myColor, NewCell:=myCell
        Next myCell
End Sub
```

Process the cells in a named range

Formatting all the exceptions in the range at once is much more convenient than formatting one cell at a time. But for the Format Exceptions button to work, you have to preselect the range of cells. If you give a name to the range you want to test, you can make the macro work even if you don't remember to preselect the range.

1   On the SampleData worksheet, select the range of random numbers, and type **NewValues** in the Reference area to name the range.

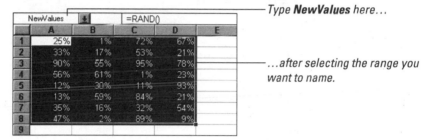

*Type **NewValues** here...*

...after selecting the range you want to name.

2   Activate the FormatModule sheet, and replace the word *Selection* with **Range("NewValues")**.

You can use a named range as the argument to the Range method.

3   Activate the SampleData worksheet, and press F9 to calculate new random numbers.

4   Select any cell—do not select the range of random numbers—and click the Format Exceptions button to test the macro.

When you create a macro using the macro recorder, the resulting code makes extensive use of the current selection. When you write procedures directly in Visual Basic, you can make the macro work independently of the current selection. The revised FormatExceptions procedure should look like this:

```
Sub FormatExceptions()
    Dim myColor
    Dim myCell
    For Each myCell in Range("NewValues")
        Let myColor = ChooseColor(TestValue:=myCell)
        FormatColor NewColor:=myColor, NewCell:=myCell
    Next myCell
End Sub
```

Compare cells from two ranges

A For Each loop is perfect for working through all the cells in a range. Sometimes, however, you need to work through two parallel ranges. For example, suppose you have an old copy of the range of values and you want to compare the old values with the new ones. You need to work through both ranges simultaneously. A For Each loop cannot do that.

Visual Basic has a different kind of loop, a For loop, that uses a counter to work through the loop. The loop counter allows you to look at the corresponding values of two ranges.

1   Choose the Insert Worksheet command from the Edit menu, and rename the new worksheet **Archive**.

2   Activate the SampleData worksheet, select the NewValues range, and press CTRL+C to copy the range.

Percent Style button

3   Activate the Archive worksheet, choose the Paste Special command from the Edit menu, select the Values option, and click OK. Then click the Percent Style button in the Formatting toolbar to format the numbers.

4   Click in the Reference area and type **OldValues** to name the current range.

The OldValues range is a frozen copy of the NewValues range.

5   Activate the SampleData worksheet, and press F9 to calculate new random numbers.

After you recalculate, the numbers in the NewValues range are different from the numbers in the OldValues range. You can write a macro to highlight any new values that are greater than the corresponding old values.

Create a macro to compare two ranges

1   Insert a couple of blank line lines above the FormatExceptions procedure, and then type in this new FormatDifferences procedure:

```
Sub FormatDifferences()
    Dim myCellPtr
    For myCellPtr = 1 To Range("NewValues").Count
        If Range("NewValues").Cells(myCellPtr) _
                > Range("OldValues").Cells(myCellPtr) Then
            FormatColor _
                NewCell:=Range("NewValues").Cells(myCellPtr) _
                , NewColor:=3
        Else
            FormatColor _
                NewCell:=Range("NewValues").Cells(myCellPtr) _
                , NewColor:=2
        End If
    Next myCellPtr
End Sub
```

Here is an explanation of each line in the macro:

```
Sub FormatDifferences()
```

defines the new procedure.

```
Dim myCellPtr
```

tells Visual Basic that you will be using a variable named *myCellPtr* (my cell pointer). This variable will act as a loop counter.

```
For myCellPtr = 1 To Range("NewValues").Count
```

begins the For loop. You give the For loop the name of a variable (myCellPtr), a number to store in the variable as the initial value (1), and the highest value you ever want in the variable (the number of cells in the NewValues range). Each time this line runs it increases the value of the variable by one until the value of the variable is greater than the limit.

```
If Range("NewValues").Cells(myCellPtr) _
```

is the first part of the If statement. This statement is too long to print on a single line. The underscore at the end of the line tells Visual Basic to treat this line and the next as a single statement, as if the statement were typed on a single line.

```
> Range("OldValues").Cells(myCellPtr) Then
```

is the second part of the If statement. This statement compares a single cell in the NewValues range with the corresponding cell in the OldValues range. When the value of myCellPtr is 5, for example, this statement compares the fifth item from the first collection with the fifth item from the second collection.

```
FormatColor _
    NewCell:=Range("NewValues").Cells(myCellPtr) _
        ,NewColor:= 3
```

is the statement you want to execute if the new value is greater than the old value. You want to tell the FormatColor subroutine to format the current cell in the NewValues range with a red color (color index number 3). Even though you originally wrote FormatColor as a subroutine for the FormatExceptions macro, you can call it from FormatDifferences as well because you made it able to run independently.

```
Else
```

means that any statements that follow should be executed only if the new value is *not* greater than the old value.

```
FormatColor _
  NewCell:=Range("NewValues").Cells(myCellPtr) _
  , NewColor:=2
```

tells the FormatColor subroutine to format the cell as white (color index 2).

```
End If
```

turns off the earlier If statement for any statements that follow.

```
Next myCellPtr
```

adds one to the loop counter variable (myCellPtr) and then tells Visual Basic to go back up to the For statement. The For statement then compares the variable to the limit (the count of cells in the range). If the variable is greater than the limit, the procedure continues with the statement following the Next statement.

```
End Sub
```

ends the procedure.

Run Macro button

2   With the insertion point anywhere within the FormatDifferences procedure, click the Run Macro button in the Visual Basic toolbar.

Nothing in the macro assumes that any particular cell is selected, so you can run the macro from anywhere.

When the insertion point is not in a procedure, clicking the Run Macro button displays a list of macros. When the insertion point is in a procedure, clicking the Run Macro button runs the current procedure.

3   Activate the SampleData worksheet. The numbers are formatted according to whether they are greater than the original values.

4   Hold down the CTRL key and drag the Format Exceptions button down a little to make a copy of the button.

5   From the Tools menu, choose the Assign Macro command, select FormatDifferences from the list of macro names, and click OK.

6   Type **Format Differences** as the label for the new button, and click a cell to deselect the button.

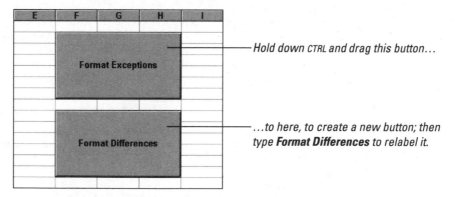

Hold down CTRL and drag this button...

*...to here, to create a new button; then type **Format Differences** to relabel it.*

7   Press F9 to calculate new random numbers, and then click the Format Differences button so that you can watch the macro work.

Remember cell ranges

The FormatDifferences procedure accomplishes the desired task of comparing the old and new ranges, but it is more complicated than it needs to be. You use the expression *Range("NewValues")* four times. Each time you use *Range("NewValues")*, Excel has to go find the name *NewValues*, figure out which range it refers to, and establish a link to that Range object. Since the expression is inside a loop, Excel ends up establishing a new link to the Range object dozens of times. You can let Excel establish the link to the Range object once and then store that link in a variable to use for the rest of the procedure.

1 Activate the FormatModule sheet.

2 After the statement *Dim myCellPtr*, enter the line **Dim myNew**, press ENTER, and then enter the line **Dim myOld**.

These statements declare these two names as variables.

3 Press ENTER to get a new line, and type **Set myNew = Range("NewValues")**.

This statement assigns the Range object for the range named NewValues to the variable myNew. When you assign an ordinary value, such as a text string or a number, to a variable, you use the word *Let*. When you assign an object to a variable, you use the word *Set*. If you want, you can omit the word *Let* when you assign a value to a variable, but you must always use the word *Set* when you assign an object to a variable.

4 Press ENTER to get a new line, and type **Set myOld = Range("OldValues")**.

5 Without moving the insertion point, choose Replace from the Edit menu.

6 Type **Range("NewValues")** in the Find What box, type **myNew** in the Replace With box, select the word *Down* in the Search list, select the word *Procedure* in the Look In list, and click Replace All. This replaces the four subsequent occurrences of the expression *Range("NewValues")* in the procedure with the new variable name.

Click No when asked if you want to start searching from the beginning.

7 In the line *> Range("OldValues").Cells(myCellPtr)*, select the expression *Range("OldValues")* and replace it with **myOld**.

A Range object can be a collection of cells, of columns, or of rows. If you don't use the Columns method or the Rows method to specify which type of collection, a Range object behaves like a collection of cells. So you can also eliminate the use of the Cells method after the Range objects.

8 From the Edit menu, choose Replace. Type **.Cells** in the Find What box, clear the Replace With box, select All from the Search list, select Procedure from the Look In list, and click Replace All.

The statement comparing the two cells is now short enough to fit on a single line.

9 Put the insertion point immediately in front of the greater than character (>), and press the BACKSPACE key until you have deleted the underscore character (_). It should take approximately five backspaces. (If you start at the end of the first line and delete forwards, you remove one space at a time. If you start at the beginning of the second line and delete backwards, you remove one tab stop at a time.)

10 Activate the SampleData worksheet, recalculate the random numbers, and test the revised macro.

The simplified macro should look like this:

```
Sub FormatDifferences()
    Dim myCellPtr
    Dim myNew
    Dim myOld
    Set myNew = Range("NewValues")
    Set myOld = Range("OldValues")
    For myCellPtr = 1 To myNew.Count
        If myNew(myCellPtr) > myOld(myCellPtr) Then
            FormatColor NewCell:=myNew(myCellPtr), NewColor:=3
        Else
            FormatColor NewCell:=myNew(myCellPtr), NewColor:=2
        End If
    Next myCellPtr
End Sub
```

Share the constants

The FormatDifferences procedure uses the number constants 3 and 2 to tell FormatColor which colors to use. The ChooseColor function has constants named for these colors, but FormatDifferences cannot use them because those constants apply only within the ChooseColor procedure. You can make the constants available to all the procedures in the current module.

1 Activate the FormatModule sheet.

2 In the ChooseColor function, select the block of Const lines, and press CTRL+X to cut them.

3 Move the insertion point to the beginning of the line following *Option Explicit*, and press CTRL+V to paste the constants.

4 Change the numbers in the FormatDifferences procedure to the color constant names, and test the macro.

When you use Const or Dim inside a procedure—that is, after the procedure's name—the constants or variables you declare are valid only within that one procedure. When you put declarations outside of any procedures, the constants and variables become available to every procedure in the module.

Handling Errors

Believe it or not, computer programs do not always work perfectly. Every now and then you may actually write a macro that doesn't do quite exactly what you want. Errors come in several different types:

Syntax errors   These are mistakes such as using an opening quotation mark and leaving off the closing quotation mark. When you type a statement into a procedure, the Visual Basic editor checks the statement for syntax errors as soon as you leave the statement.

Compiler errors   Some mistakes cannot be detected on a single-line basis. For example, you might start a For Each loop but forget to put a Next statement at the end. The first time you try to run a procedure, Visual Basic translates that procedure (along with all the other procedures in the module) into internal computer language. Translating to computer language is called *compiling*, and errors that Visual Basic detects while translating are called *compiler errors*. Syntax errors and compiler errors are usually easy to find and fix.

Logic errors   The computer can never detect some mistakes. For example, if you mean to change a workbook caption to "My Workbook", and you accidentally spell the caption "My Werkbook", the computer will never complain. Or if you compare the new values with the wrong copy of the old values, the computer won't find the error for you. You can toggle breakpoints, step through the procedures, and watch values, but you still have to find the problem.

Run-time errors   Sometimes a statement in a procedure works most of the time but fails under certain conditions. For example, you might refer to a named range on a worksheet. As long as the name exists, the statement works. If, however, you delete the range name, Visual Basic doesn't know what else to do but quit with an error message. These errors cannot be detected until you run the procedure, so they are called *run-time* errors. This section will show you how to handle run-time errors gracefully.

Cause an error

1   In the statement *Set myNew = Range("NewValues")*, change *"NewValues"* to **"NweValues"**, which is an error.

Run Macro button

2   Click the Run Macro button to run the macro.

An error message appears, informing you that the Range method did not work. You would prefer to have the macro give you a descriptive warning and quit without offering potentially confusing options.

3   Click the End button to dismiss the error message.

Respond to the error

You can tell Visual Basic not to halt when it discovers a run-time error. Instead, when an error occurs, Visual Basic will set a special variable, named Err, to a nonzero number. Your procedure can then check to see if Err contains a nonzero number.

1 Insert a line after the statement *Dim myOld*, and enter the statement **On Error Resume Next**. Put a blank line above and below the new statement so that you can see it better.

This statement tells Visual Basic that if it encounters a run-time error, it should just set the Err value and continue with the next statement.

2 Insert a new line after the *Set myNew = Range("NweValues")* statement, and enter these four new lines:

```
If Err <> 0 Then
    MsgBox Prompt:="Undefined range name"
    End
End If
```

If no error has occurred, the built-in Err variable is equal to zero. If an error has occurred, Err will be a nonzero value. MsgBox is a built-in Visual Basic function that displays a message; you use the Prompt argument to tell MsgBox what to display. The keyword End means to stop the macro.

3 Copy the four new lines and insert them below the statement *Set myOld = Range("OldValues")* because this statement could fail as well if someone deleted the OldValues range name.

Run Macro button

4 Click the Run Macro button.

The macro still quits, but this time it displays your descriptive message rather than the standard error message.

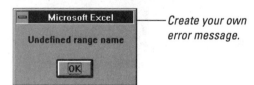

— *Create your own error message.*

The FormatDifferences procedure should now look like this:

```
Sub FormatDifferences()
    Dim myCellPtr
    Dim myNew
    Dim myOld
```

```
    On Error Resume Next

    Set myNew = Range("NweValues")
    If Err Then
        MsgBox Prompt:="Undefined range name"
        End
    End If
    Set myOld = Range("OldValues")
    If Err Then
        MsgBox Prompt:="Undefined range name"
        End
    End If
    For myCellPtr = 1 To myNew.Count
        If myNew(myCellPtr) > myOld(myCellPtr) Then
            FormatColor NewCell:=myNew(myCellPtr), NewColor:=myRed
        Else
            FormatColor NewCell:=myNew(myCellPtr), NewColor:=myWhite
        End If
    Next myCellPtr
End Sub
```

Note If you don't check the Err value after a statement, the procedure continues with the next statement. Sometimes you don't care whether a statement had an error. For example, your procedure may delete a file from the hard disk to make sure the file is not there. You don't care if the delete fails. The Err variable, however, remembers the error. The next time you check for an error, you may think an error has occurred because of the previous statement. If you intentionally ignore a possible error, reset the Err variable to zero by adding the statement *Let Err = 0*.

Trap an error

You can usually create more meaningful error messages than the standard Visual Basic dialog box. If you need to put in only a few checks for common problems, adding a few error-checking statements here and there is not a bad solution. But you may not be happy with the prospect of adding four or more error-checking statements after every working statement in a procedure.

One solution is to write one subroutine named *CheckError* that checks the Err value and, if it is not zero, displays a message along with the error value, and then quits. Then you would need to enter *CheckError* only after each statement you want to check. Visual Basic gives you an even better solution, however. You can tell Visual Basic to check the error value after each statement and go to your display error message procedure only if the error value is not zero.

1 Replace the statement *On Error Resume Next* with **On Error Goto HandleError**.

This tells Visual Basic to check the Err value after each statement and to go to a special place in the procedure that you will name *HandleError*. (You can use any name you want for the name of the error handler.)

2   Immediately above the *End Sub* statement at the bottom of the FormatDifferences procedure, insert a new line and type **Exit Sub**.

You have to put the instructions for handling errors inside the same procedure as the On Error Goto statement, but you must also stop the regular procedure before it gets to those instructions. The statement *Exit Sub* is the way to quit a subroutine before reaching the End Sub statement.

3   On the next line, type **HandleError:**.

This must be the same name you used in the On Error Goto statement above, and it must be followed by a colon (:). This name is called a label. The only time you should ever need to use a label in a procedure is when creating error handling instructions.

4   On the next line, press TAB, and then type **Dim Msg** to let Visual Basic know you intend to use a variable named *Msg*.

5   On the next line, type **Let Msg = "Error: " & Err**.

This puts the text string *Error:* into the variable Msg and then tacks the error number that Visual Basic will supply to the variable Err onto the end.

6   On the next line, type **Let Msg = Msg & " - " & Error()**.

This takes the current value of the variable Msg, adds a hyphen, and then adds a descriptive message for the most recent error, which is supplied by the Visual Basic function named *Error*. The variable Msg is then redefined using this new composite text string.

7   On the next line, type **MsgBox Prompt:=Msg**.

This displays the message you pieced together. If you want, you can also add other information to the message, such as "Please contact Tex Miller for assistance," by using the ampersand (&) again.

8   On the next line, type **End**. This quits the macro, which is what you want to do in case of a run-time error.

9   Remove the error-checking lines you inserted earlier after assigning the two ranges to variables.

Run Macro button

10   Click the Run Macro button to see if the error handler takes care of the error properly.

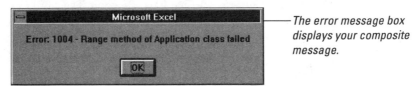

The error message box displays your composite message.

11   Change the misspelled *"NweValues"* to the correct **"NewValues"**, and click the Run Macro button again. The macro should run without a complaint.

The revised FormatDifferences procedure should now look like this:

```
Sub FormatDifferences()
    Dim myCellPtr
    Dim myNew
    Dim myOld

    On Error Goto HandleError

    Set myNew = Range("NewValues")
    Set myOld = Range("OldValues")
    For myCellPtr = 1 To myNew.Count
        If myNew(myCellPtr) > myOld(myCellPtr) Then
            FormatColor NewCell:=myNew(myCellPtr), NewColor:=myRed
        Else
            FormatColor NewCell:=myNew(myCellPtr), NewColor:=myWhite
        End If
    Next myCellPtr
Exit Sub
HandleError:
    Dim Msg
    Let Msg = "Error: " & Err
    Let Msg = Msg & " - " & Error()
    MsgBox Prompt:=Msg
    End
End Sub
```

Dealing with run-time errors is always a difficult part of a programming task. The error trapping facilities of Visual Basic are a little tricky to first set up, but having Visual Basic watch for errors for you is much better than adding a block of error-checking code after each statement.

Exploring Visual Basic Reference Tools

The word *MsgBox* is a Visual Basic function. The word *Error()* is a Visual Basic function. What are Visual Basic functions? In addition to the methods and properties that are available for Excel objects, Visual Basic has its own set of procedures that you can utilize in your macros. How can you learn about them? How can you use them?

In Part 3 of this book, you learned about how to use the Object Browser and the Help reference to find out about Excel objects. You can also use these reference tools to find out about built-in Visual Basic procedures you can call from your macros.

Find Visual Basic procedures in the Object Browser

*Object Browser
button*

1   Activate the FormatModule sheet and click the Object Browser button.

2   Select VBA in the Libraries/Workbooks list.

The Objects/Modules list changes to show categories of common tasks. These are categories of tasks for which Visual Basic has built-in procedures you can use.

The first category in the list is Constants. When you select the Constants category, the list on the right does not actually include procedures. Rather, this is a list of names you can use as arguments with Visual Basic procedures to make your code easier to read. The list of Visual Basic constants is included in the Object Browser for your convenience, just as the list of Excel constants is included in the Object Browser.

At the bottom of the Object Browser dialog box is a brief description of the selected item.

3   Select the Interaction category in the Objects/Modules list.

The list in the Methods/Properties list changes, and the text at the bottom of the dialog box describes the type of procedures in this category.

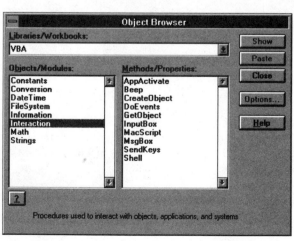

The MsgBox function you used in this lesson and the InputBox function you used in Lesson 2 are in the list of procedures for the Interaction category.

4   Select MsgBox in the Methods/Properties list.

The description at the bottom of the dialog box explains what the MsgBox function does, and above that is a list of the arguments you may want to use with the MsgBox function. You can paste a Visual Basic procedure from the Object Browser into your module the same as you can paste an Excel object method or property.

Find Visual Basic procedures in the Help reference

The Object Browser gives only a brief description of each Visual Basic procedure, along with a list of the procedure's arguments. You can get more detailed information about the procedure in the Help Reference system.

? button

1   With the MsgBox function selected in the Object Browser, click the ? (question mark) button at the bottom of the dialog box.

The Visual Basic Reference appears in Help showing the MsgBox Function topic.

The topics for Visual Basic procedures in Help are very similar to the topics for Excel methods and properties except that they do not link to any objects.

2   Click the Contents button to jump to the Visual Basic Reference contents screen.

Under the Programming Language Summary heading are six hyperlinks. Three of the hyperlinks—Methods, Objects, and Properties—pertain to Excel objects and their methods and properties. The remaining three hyperlinks—Functions, Statements, and Keywords By Task—pertain to Visual Basic.

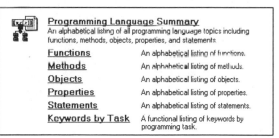

3   Click the Functions hyperlink.

A Visual Basic Reference Index window appears, displaying an alphabetical list of all the topics for Visual Basic functions.

This list is very similar to the lists of topics for Excel objects, methods, and properties.

4   Click the See Also hyperlink to display a list with six hyperlinks that seems remarkably similar to the list of six hyperlinks on the Visual Basic Reference contents page. Click the Statements hyperlink.

See Also
　Keywords by Task
　Methods
　Objects
　Programming Language Summary
　Properties
　Statements

The Visual Basic Reference Index window changes to display the list of Visual Basic statements.

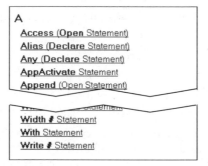

Note When you create a Visual Basic procedure, you make it either a subroutine or a function. A subroutine is like a function except that it never returns a value. In the Visual Basic Help system, the word *Statement* essentially refers to what you would write as a subroutine: a procedure that never returns a value.

All the keywords in Visual Basic appear in Help as either functions or statements. The keywords MsgBox, InputBox, and Error are functions. The keywords Sub, If, End If, Do, Loop, For Each, and Next are all listed as statements.

Visual Basic also includes some tools you can utilize that are neither statements nor functions. For example, the ampersand (&) that joins two text strings is neither a statement nor a function; it is an operator. You can find information about operators in Help also.

5 Click the See Also hyperlink and choose Keywords By Task to display the Keywords By Task summary.

Category	Description
Arrays	Creating, defining, and using arrays.
Control Flow	Looping and controlling procedure flow.

This list shows several categories of tasks you may want to perform using Visual Basic. This list is similar to the list of categories you saw in the Object Browser, except this list contains additional categories. One of the categories is Operators.

6 Click the Operators hyperlink to display the list of Visual Basic operators.

Action	Keywords
Arithmetic.	^ - * / \ Mod, +, &
Comparison.	=, <>, <, >, <=, >=, Like, Is
Logical operations.	Not, And, Or, Xor, Eqv, Imp

7 Click the ampersand (&) hyperlink to display the & Operator topic.

& Operator
See Also   Example

Description
Used to force string concatenation of two expressions.

Syntax
result = *expression1* **&** *expression2*

8 Double click the Control Menu box to close each Help window until you return to the Object Browser.

Control Menu box

9 Click the Cancel button to close the Object Browser.

In Lesson 13 you will learn how to control Microsoft Word from Visual Basic.

Excel and Visual Basic are two separate tools. Excel is like a home entertainment system. You can operate the system interactively or with remote controls. Visual Basic procedures run the remote controls to operate Excel. You can use Visual Basic to control Excel or to control other applications that can respond to the kinds of commands Visual Basic can give.

Excel exposes its capabilities to Visual Basic through objects, with their methods and properties. Visual Basic also has its own collection of procedures—statements, functions, and other keywords. You can use the Object Browser and the Help system to learn about objects, properties, and methods for Excel, and to learn about statements, functions, and other keywords for Visual Basic.

Communicating with Old-Style Macros

If you have existing applications written in Microsoft Excel 4 macros, you may need to integrate the Excel 4 macros with Visual Basic procedures.

Call an old-style command macro

The sample macros in this section are in the LESSON11.XLS file in the FINISHED directory on the disk that comes with this book.

Here is a simple Excel 4 command macro. It takes an argument and displays the value of the argument in an alert box, but it does not return a value.

```
Excel4Command
Call this command from Visual Basic
=ARGUMENT("Prompt")
=ALERT(Prompt)
=RETURN()
```

Here is a Visual Basic procedure that calls the Excel4Command macro, passing "Hello, Excel" as an argument:

```
'Call Excel4 Style Command Macro
Sub RunExcel4Command()
    Run "Excel4Command", "Hello Excel"
End Sub
```

Use the Run method to call an Excel 4 command macro. Pass the name of the macro as the first argument, and pass any arguments for the macro as additional arguments.

Call an old-style function macro

Here is a simple Excel 4 function macro. It prompts you for your name and then returns your name to the calling procedure.

```
Excel4Function
Call this function from Visual Basic
=RETURN(INPUT("What is your name?",2))
```

Here is a Visual Basic procedure that can call the Excel4Function macro, displaying in a message box the name passed back from the function:

```
'Call Excel4 Style Function Macro
Sub RunExcel4Function()
    Dim Answer
    Let Answer = Run("Excel4Function")
    MsgBox Answer
End Sub
```

You use the Run method to run an Excel 4 function macro the same as you run an Excel 4 command macro. The return value from the Excel 4 macro becomes the return value of the Run method. When you use the return value from the Run method, enclose all the arguments in parentheses.

Call a Visual Basic subroutine from an old-style macro

Here is a simple Visual Basic subroutine. Like the Excel4Command macro, it takes an argument and displays that argument in a message box:

```
'Call this Command from Excel4 Style Macro
Sub BasicCommand(Prompt)
    MsgBox Prompt
End Sub
```

Here is an Excel 4 macro that can run the BasicCommand subroutine, passing "Hello, Visual Basic" as an argument:

RunBasicCommand
This calls Visual Basic Command
=BasicCommand("Hello, Visual Basic")
=RETURN()

To call a Visual Basic subroutine from an Excel 4 macro, you enter the name of the subroutine as a function, and you include any arguments in parentheses.

Call a Visual Basic function from an old-style macro

Here is a simple Visual Basic function. Like the Excel4Function macro, it prompts you for your name and then returns that name as its return value.

```
'Call this Function from Excel4 Style Macro
Function BasicFunction()
    BasicFunction = InputBox("What is your name?")
End Function
```

Here is an Excel 4 macro that can run the BasicFunction function, displaying the result of the function in an alert box:

RunBasicFunction
This calls Visual Basic Function
=ALERT(BasicFunction())
=RETURN()

To call a Visual Basic function from an Excel 4 macro, you enter the name of the function as a function. The Visual Basic function is indistinguishable from a built-in function.

The fact that Excel 4 macros and Visual Basic procedures can communicate directly with each other makes it possible for you to gradually transition old applications to Visual Basic. If you are already comfortable writing Excel 4 macros, you can continue to be productive developing and supporting Excel 4 macros as you build expertise with Visual Basic.

Lesson Summary

To	Do this
Execute statements for each item in a collection	Insert the statements between a For Each statement and a Next statement.
Create a loop that uses a counter variable to keep track of the position in the loop	Use a For statement with a Next statement.
Assign an object to a variable	Use the Set keyword to make the assigment, rather than the Let keyword.
Cause Visual Basic to ignore errors so that you can check for an error after each statement	Use the statement *On Error Resume Next*.
Cause Visual Basic to run the statements starting a line labeled ErrorHandler	Use the statement *On Error Goto ErrorHandler*.
Call an Excel 4 macro from a Visual Basic procedure	Use the Run statement.
Call a Visual Basic procedure from an Excel 4 macro	Use the procedure name as if it were a built-in function.

For more information on	See
Using loops	Chapter 7, "Controlling How Your Code Runs," in the *Microsoft Excel Visual Basic User's Guide*.
Handling errors	Chapter 9, "Handling Errors and Error Values," in the *Microsoft Excel Visual Basic User's Guide*.

Preview of the Next Lesson

You now have had a broad overview of Excel objects and Visual Basic procedures. In the next three lessons, you will put these skills to work building an application that solves a practical business problem, using the skills you have learned in Parts 3 and 4. In Lesson 12, you will write procedures that automate the production of some standard reports.

5 Building an Application

Build a Report Generator

It's spring cleaning time. The shelves in your bedroom closet have been accumulating various treasures for some time now. You just hope you never have to find anything. Or remove anything.

But now it's time to clean it up. At first, as you remove item after item, placing them all in various piles on the floor and on the bed, the mess just gets worse. Occasionally you find a delightful surprise, such as the wide angle lens for your camera that you needed last month at the reunion, or the letter from your sister that has her new address so that you can return the book you borrowed last year. Finally, as you find boxes and files and new shelves for all the piles, the room returns to normal.

Everything is much as it was before you started. The room is clean and the treasures are in the closet. But now you are not afraid to open the closet door.

When you first create macros using the macro recorder, as you did in Parts 1 and 2 of this book, you may look at the recorded macro as you would a cluttered closet: You don't dare touch anything inside. When you first explore Microsoft Excel objects and Visual Basic structures, as you did in Parts 3 and 4 of this book, you may feel as if you are in the middle of spring cleaning: You find occasional treasures, but the piles around the room are unusable. Now you're ready to organize the closet, to put the concepts to work, to solve real-world problems, to modify recorded macros and write new procedures with confidence.

In this lesson you will create a macro that automates creating reports, in Lesson 13 you will add macros to communicate with Microsoft Word for Windows and a database, and in Lesson 14 you will package the macros into an easy-to-use application.

You will learn how to:

- Use variables to store objects.
- Control pivot tables, charts, and printer setup from procedures.
- Ask charts and pivot tables for their locations on a worksheet.

Estimated lesson time: 40 minutes

Start the lesson

▶   Start Microsoft Excel and open the workbook LISTS.XLS. Save the workbook as LESSON12.XLS.

Creating Reports from a Database

Miller Textiles has a planning meeting at the beginning of every month to discuss the previous month's orders. You are responsible for bringing printed order information for key market segments to the meeting. After the meeting, your manager usually asks you to put together a document with tables and charts, along with comments and explanations of unusual order activity.

You want to build a macro that will allow you to easily select and print the order information you want. You also want the macro to put selected charts and tables directly into a word processing file so that you can easily add explanatory text. Eventually, you want to refine the macro so that others in the company can use it even if you are not around.

Creating the Report by Hand

The reports you create for the planning meeting all look basically the same: order units and dollars summarized in a table illustrated with a chart. If you create the report once, by hand, you can then create a macro to modify the report for the different market segments you need to analyze. For the first report, you will extract the most recent month's orders from the database, create a pivot table, and then create a chart.

Create a database extract

1   Insert a new worksheet and rename it **Extract**.

To activate Program Manager, press CTRL+ESC and select Program Manager from the task list.

2   From the Microsoft Office group in the Windows Program Manager, double click the icon for Microsoft Query, and close the Cue Card window if it is visible.

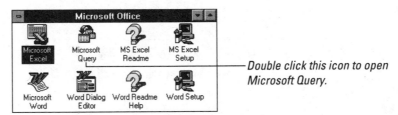

Double click this icon to open Microsoft Query.

Microsoft Query is a separate program that comes bundled with Excel. Query can retrieve data from any external database that has an Open Database Connectivity (ODBC) driver available. In Lesson 4, you accessed the Query program directly from the PivotTable Wizard. In this lesson, use Query to retrieve selected records from the database, which you will then copy to a worksheet in Excel.

New Query button

3   In Query, click the New Query button, double click Miller Textiles in the list of data sources, double click the ORDERS.DBF table, and click Close.

Note   If Miller Textiles is not in the list of data sources, follow the instructions in the section "Set up the database as a data source" at the beginning of Lesson 5.

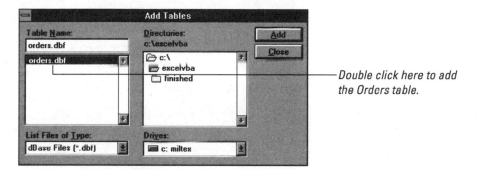

Double click here to add the Orders table.

4   In the list of fields from the Orders table, double click the asterisk (*) to add all the fields to the query, and then delete the columns labeled List and Gross. (Click each column heading and press DELETE.)

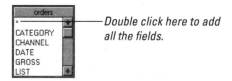

Double click here to add all the fields.

5   Click the heading for the Date column, and choose the Add Criteria command from the Criteria menu. Type **1994-02-01** in the Value box, click the Add button, and then click the Close button.

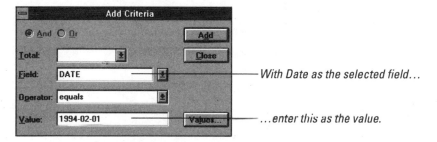

With Date as the selected field...

...enter this as the value.

The query now contains the Date, State, Channel, Price, Category, Units, and Net columns for the records from February 1994.

6   Click the box to the left of the Date column label to select the entire query result.

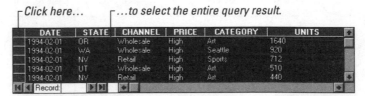

7   From the Edit menu, choose the Copy Special command, select the Include Column Headings check box, and click OK.

8   Activate Microsoft Excel, select cell A1 of the Extract worksheet, and choose Paste from the Edit menu to paste the result of the query. This range will be an intermediate extract range from which you will supply data to a pivot table.

9   While the entire query is still selected, enter **Database** in the Reference area to name the range. Then select cell A1.

The Database range on the Extract worksheet now contains the order information you want to analyze.

Note In Lesson 5, you imported data from a database directly into a pivot table, without creating an intermediate extract range on a worksheet. This lesson shows an alternate way of getting data from a database into a pivot table. In some situations, you may want to use Excel functions to add calculated fields to the pivot table. (For example, you might want to calculate return on investment values.) To add calculated columns to a pivot table, you must create an intermediate extract range in Excel.

Create a tabular report

The PivotTable Wizard is the easiest way make a summary table from the database extract.

1   From the Data menu, choose the PivotTable command, and in the first two steps of the PivotTable Wizard, click Next, accepting the default options.

2   In Step 3 of the PivotTable Wizard, drag the Category field tile and the Date field tile to the Page area, drag the State field tile to the Row area, and drag the Units field tile and the Net field tile to the Data area. Then click Next.

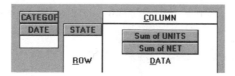

3   In Step 4, clear the PivotTable Starting Cell box, type **ReportTable** as the name for the pivot table, clear both Grand Totals check boxes, clear the AutoFormat Table check box, and click Finish.

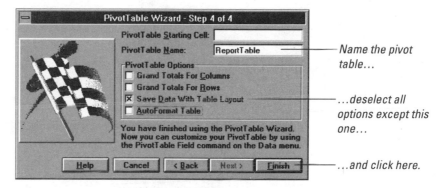

If you leave the AutoFormat Table check box selected, the PivotTable Wizard will adjust the column widths of the table each time you refresh or modify the pivot table. You don't want that to happen for this report.

4   Drag the Data field tile below the word *Total* to display the unit and net dollar columns side by side.

	A	B	C	D
1	CATEGOR	(All)		
2	DATE	(All)		
3				
4	STATE	Data	Total	
5	AZ	Sum of UN	273	
6		Sum of NE	6813.52	
7	CA	Sum of UN	2745	
8		Sum of NE	7506.84	
9	ID	Sum of UN	917	

Drag the Data tile...

...under the Total heading to rearrange the pivot table.

5   Change the name of the worksheet with the pivot table to **Report**.

This is essentially the tabular report you will present at the planning meeting. You can make the table easier to understand by enhancing its formatting.

Format the report table

1   Select columns A:C. From the Format menu, choose the Column, Width command, type **12** as the width, and click OK.

2   Select the cell with the Data field tile, and choose the Row, Hide command from the Format menu.

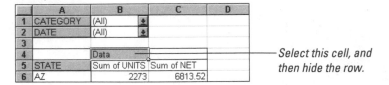

Select this cell, and then hide the row.

PivotTable Wizard button

3   Select any cell within the pivot table, click the PivotTable Wizard button (or choose the PivotTable command from the Data menu), and double click the field labeled Sum Of Net in the PivotTable Wizard dialog box.

4   Replace the name *Sum of Net* with **Net $**, and click the Number button.

5   Select the first currency format, click OK to return to the PivotTable Field dialog box, and then click OK again to return to the PivotTable Wizard.

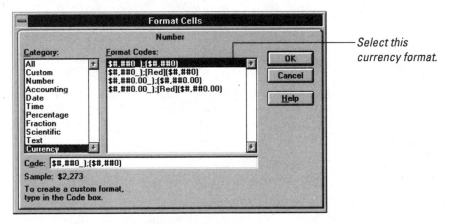

Select this currency format.

You can format the cells of a pivot table on the worksheet using standard cell formatting tools, but if you do, the PivotTable Wizard will clear the formatting each time you modify or refresh the pivot table. If you define the number format within the PivotTable Wizard, the cells will retain the correct formatting.

6   Double click the field labeled Sum Of Units, and replace the name with **Units**, followed by a space.

You cannot use a field name from the database as the name for a data field. Adding a space to the end of the field name, however, satisfies the ReportWizard's requirement for a unique name.

7   Click the Number button, select the #,##0 format, click OK, and click OK again to get back to the PivotTable Wizard. Click Finish to recalculate the pivot table.

8   In the Category list, select Dinosaurs, and in the Date list, select 2/1/94.

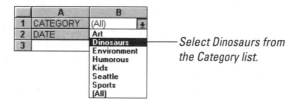

Select Dinosaurs from the Category list.

The pivot table is now easier to understand.

Note   The Date field shows the month for the current report. Since the database extract contains only values for February, the report displays the same values whether you choose 2/1/94 or (All). Explicitly showing the date, however, eliminates the need to put a separate date heading on the report.

Chart the information

Tables of numbers are almost always easier to understand if the numbers can also be seen in chart form.

1   Drag from cell C5 through cell A12. This range contains the values you want to chart.

ChartWizard button

2   Click the ChartWizard button, drag a rectangle in the range D1:H12, and click Next in the first step of the ChartWizard.

3   In Step 2 of the ChartWizard, select the 3-D Column option, and click Next.

3-D Column option

4   In Step 3 of the ChartWizard, select option 5, and click Finish to create the chart.

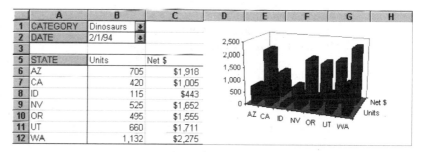

When you view different market segments with the pivot table, the chart will change to reflect the new table information.

Create reports for market segments

Change the definitions in the pivot table to create reports for different market segments.

1   Select Seattle from the Category list box in cell B1.

This changes the page item in the pivot table. The values in the table and the chart change appropriately. With a pivot table, changing from one page to another is very easy. But what if you want to change which field is in the Page area?

2   Select any cell in the pivot table.

PivotTable Wizard button

3   Click the PivotTable Wizard button, drag the Category field tile away from the Page area, drag the State field tile from the Rows area to the Page area (above the Date field tile), drag the Price field tile to the Rows area, and click Finish to create the report.

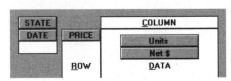

4   From the State list, select OR.

In a pivot table, changing which field tile is in which position is not difficult, but it does entail several steps.

The basic structure of the report is in place. You have the data from the database, a pivot table to summarize it, and a chart. You have set up all this by hand, without any macros. Now you can create a macro that changes the pivot table for you.

Creating a Report Generating Tool

Each time you specify a market segment, you change three items on the pivot table: the database field name you use as the page field (currently State), the specific item for that page field (currently OR), and the database field name you use as the rows field (currently Price). You can make a macro that will switch the pivot table for you when you specify those three items.

Create a control worksheet

1   Activate the **Control** worksheet.

This worksheet was provided for you in the original LISTS.XLS workbook, which you renamed as LESSON12.XLS. The Control worksheet contains a list of the key fields from the database, along with the lists of possible values for each of the key fields.

2   Enter **PageField** in cell A11, **PageItem** in cell A12, and **RowField** in cell A13.

You can also press
CTRL+SHIFT+F3 to
display the Create
Names dialog box.

3   Select the range A11:B13. From the Insert menu, choose the Name, Create command, select the Left Column check box, and click OK.

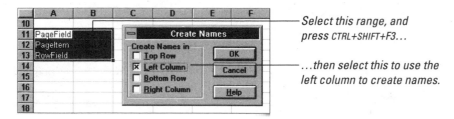

— Select this range, and press CTRL+SHIFT+F3...

...then select this to use the left column to create names.

Cells B11, B12, and B13 now have the names **PageField**, **PageItem**, and **RowField**, respectively.

4   Enter **Channel** in cell B11, **Retail** in cell B12, and **State** in cell B13.

Now if you select cell B11, the Formula bar displays Channel as the cell's value, and the Reference area displays PageField as the cell's name.

You can enter any value from the list of keys in the PageField cell, and you can enter any other value from the list of keys in the RowField cell. The value of the PageItem cell must be one of the entries from the list appropriate to the current PageField name. Channel is the current value in the PageField cell, so in the PageItem cell, you can use either of the two values from the list of channels (Wholesale or Retail).

Record a macro to change the pivot table

Now you need a macro that can put the value of the PageField cell into the Page area of the pivot table, the value of the RowField cell into the Rows area, and the value of the PageItem cell as the specific page item for the page field. Start by recording a sample macro:

1   Activate the Report worksheet.

2   Select (All) from the list of dates so that you will be able to set the date with the macro recorder turned on. Then select any cell within the pivot table.

Record Macro button

3   Click the Record Macro button in the Visual Basic toolbar, type **AdjustTable** as the name for the macro, and click OK.

4   Click the PivotTable Wizard button.

PivotTable Wizard button

5   Drag the State field tile from the Page area to the Rows area, drag the Price field tile away from the Rows area, drag the Channel field tile into the Page area (above the Date field tile), and click Finish.

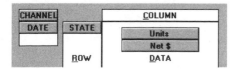

6 Select Retail from the list of channels in cell B1.

7 Select 2/1/94 from the list of dates in cell B2.

8 Click the Stop Macro button to stop the recorder.

Stop Macro button

9 Rename the Module1 sheet as **ReportModule** and look at the recorded macro.

```
Sub AdjustTable()
    ActiveSheet.PivotTables("ReportTable").AddFields RowFields:="STATE",_
        ColumnFields:="Data", PageFields:=Array("DATE", "CHANNEL")
    ActiveSheet.PivotTables("ReportTable").PivotFields("CHANNEL"). _
        CurrentPage = "Retail"
    ActiveSheet.PivotTables("ReportTable").PivotFields("DATE"). _
        CurrentPage = "2/1/94"
End Sub
```

The body of this macro consists of three long statements. The first statement specifies which fields to use as rows, columns, and pages. The second statement sets the item for the current Channel page field, and the third statement sets the item for the current Date page field.

Simplify the macro

The macro uses the expression *ActiveSheet.PivotTables("ReportTable")* three times. That expression establishes a link to the current pivot table. You can establish that link once and use it over and over by assigning the pivot table object to a variable. Rather than assume that the pivot table is on the active sheet, set up a variable to point explicitly at the Report worksheet. Then you can run the macro regardless of which sheet in the workbook is active.

1 Insert these statements after the *Sub AdjustTable()* statement:

```
Dim myReport
Dim myPivot

Set myReport = Worksheets("Report")
Set myPivot = myReport.PivotTables("ReportTable")
```

The Dim statements tell Visual Basic that you will be using the words *myReport* and *myPivot* as variables. The first Set statement establishes a link to the worksheet named Report and assigns that link to the myReport variable. The second Set statement assigns the pivot table named ReportTable, found on the worksheet pointed to by the myReport variable, to the myPivot variable. Now you can use the word *myPivot* in the macro instead of using the longer expression *ActiveSheet.PivotTables("ReportTable")*.

2   Insert a blank line between the Dim statements and the Set statements, and between the Set statements and the pivot table statements, to clarify the three parts of the procedure.

3   Change all three original occurrences of *ActiveSheet.PivotTables("ReportTable")* to **myPivot**. (You may want to use the Replace command from the Edit menu.)

4   Delete the argument *ColumnFields:="Data"*, from the statement with the AddFields method since you will always leave the Units and Net $ fields as the column headings in the report.

5   Delete the underscores in the last two statements and then shorten them to a single line each.

The revised macro should look like this:

```
Sub AdjustTable()
    Dim myReport
    Dim myPivot

    Set myReport = Worksheets("Report")
    Set myPivot = myReport.PivotTables("ReportTable")

    myPivot.AddFields RowFields:="STATE", _
        PageFields:=Array("DATE", "CHANNEL")
    myPivot.PivotFields("CHANNEL").CurrentPage = "Retail"
    myPivot.PivotFields("DATE").CurrentPage = "2/1/94"
End Sub
```

Link the macro to the control values

The next step is to replace the words in quotation marks—*"STATE"*, *"CHANNEL"*, and *"Retail"*—with links to the named cells on the Control worksheet. Then, by simply changing the control values and running the macro, you can change the pivot table. First create variables inside your procedure to hold the control values, and then substitute these variable names for the constants in the statements. Since you will refer to the Control worksheet multiple times, you can create a variable to hold it.

1   After the statement *Dim myPivot*, enter these statements to let Visual Basic know the names you will use for the variables:

```
Dim myControl
Dim myRowField
Dim myPageField
Dim myPageItem
```

2 After the statement that begins with the words *Set myPivot*, enter these statements to make the variables point to the cells on the Control worksheet:

```
Set myControl = Worksheets("Control")
Set myRowField = myControl.Range("RowField")
Set myPageField = myControl.Range("PageField")
Set myPageItem = myControl.Range("PageItem")
```

Note If you use Set to assign a cell to a variable, you assign a single-cell Range object; when the value in the cell changes, the value in the variable changes as well. If you use Let to assign a cell to a variable, you assign the current value of the cell; when the value in the cell changes, the variable does not change with it.

3 Replace the word *"STATE"* with **myRowField.Value**. State was the field tile you used for row headings. You want the macro to set the row heading field to the current value in the cell named RowField on the Control worksheet.

4 Replace both occurrences of the word *"CHANNEL"* with **myPageField.Value**. Channel was the field tile you assigned to the Page area. You want the macro to set the page field to the current value in the cell named PageField on the Control worksheet.

5 Replace the word *"Retail"* with **myPageItem.Value**. Retail was the specific Channel you assigned as the page item. You want the macro to set the page item to the current value in the cell named PageItem on the Control worksheet.

The revised procedure should look like this:

```
Sub AdjustTable()
    Dim myReport
    Dim myPivot
    Dim myControl
    Dim myRowField
    Dim myPageField
    Dim myPageItem

    Set myReport = Worksheets("Report")
    Set myPivot = myReport.PivotTables("ReportTable")
    Set myControl = Worksheets("Control")
    Set myRowField = myControl.Range("RowField")
    Set myPageField = myControl.Range("PageField")
    Set myPageItem = myControl.Range("PageItem")

    myPivot.AddFields RowFields:=myRowField.Value, _
        PageFields:=Array("DATE", myPageField.Value)
    myPivot.PivotFields(myPageField.Value).CurrentPage = myPageItem.Value
    myPivot.PivotFields("DATE").CurrentPage = "2/1/94"
End Sub
```

Change control values to change the pivot table

Now you're ready to put the procedure to work. You need a button on the Control worksheet to make the macro easy to run. But first, if you add a second window to the workbook, you can see what is happening on the Report worksheet while you make changes on the Control worksheet.

Restore button

Create Button button

1   Activate the Report worksheet and choose the New Window command from the Window menu. If the window is maximized, click the window's Restore button.

2   In the new window, activate the Control worksheet, and create a button to the right of the control variables. (Use the Create Button button in the Drawing toolbar.) Assign the AdjustTable macro to the button, and type **Change** as the label for the button.

3   Reduce the size of the active window so that you can see the Report worksheet behind it.

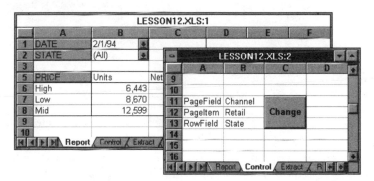

4   Enter **State** in cell B11, **OR** in cell B12, and **Price** in cell B13. Then click the Change button.

If the macro fails, set a breakpoint and watch the values of expressions as you learned in Lesson 10.

The table changes to reflect the new specifications from the Control worksheet, and the chart changes to reflect the table values.

5   Enter **Category** in cell B13, and click the Change button to change the row headings in the pivot table.

6   Close the Control worksheet window, and save the LESSON12.XLS workbook.

You now have a simple macro for quickly manipulating the pivot table. Much of the work in setting up this macro was setting up the report in the first place. The Visual Basic procedures make only relatively few changes to produce the result you want.

Controlling the Printer

Now that you can easily make different tables and charts, you are ready to print each report. Sometimes you want to print the chart beside the table, with a landscape orientation. Other times you want to print the chart below the table, with a portrait orientation. Either way, you want the report to look as good as possible.

Set up the printed page layout

You can change most of the settings for the printer one time, before using a macro. Then you can create a macro to change only the settings that will vary from report to report.

Print Preview button

1   Activate the Report worksheet and click the Print Preview button.

The report does not look very good. It is small and in the corner of the page, it shows gridlines from the worksheet, and it includes a header and footer that you do not need.

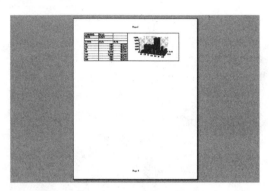

2   Click the Setup button and select the Page tab. Select the Landscape option, and set the Scaling to 130% normal size.

3   Select the Margins tab, and in the Center On Page group, select both the Horizontally and the Vertically check boxes.

4   Select the Header/Footer tab, and select (none) from both the Header and the Footer lists.

5   Select the Sheet tab, clear the Gridlines check box, and click OK.

The preview should look much better.

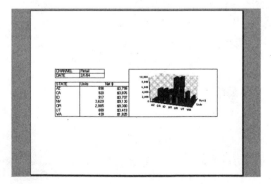

6   Click Close.

Add a macro to print the report

Instead of having the button on the Control worksheet simply update the report and display the report worksheet, you can make the button print the report as well.

1   Activate the ReportModule sheet and insert the following procedure above the AdjustTable procedure:

```
Sub PrintReport()
    AdjustTable
    Worksheets("Report").PrintPreview
End Sub
```

The PrintReport procedure runs the AdjustTable procedure and then displays the Report worksheet in print preview mode. While you are developing macros, you can use PrintPreview to see how the report will print without wasting paper.

Note   To make the macro actually print the report, change the word *PrintPreview* to **PrintOut**.

---

2   Activate the Control worksheet.

3   Use the right mouse button to click the Change button. Then choose the Assign Macro command, select PrintReport as the new macro name, and click OK.

4   Type **Print** as a new label for the button.

5   Enter **WA** in cell B12, and click the Print button.

6   After the Print Preview screen appears, click Close.

Prepare to switch the report orientation

To switch the report from landscape to portrait orientation, you must move the chart below the table. If you give a name to the chart, you will be able to refer to it easily from the procedure. You also need to add an input cell on the Control worksheet for the Orientation setting so that you can use that value from the procedure.

1   Activate the Report worksheet and select the chart.

2   In the Reference area (to the left of the formula bar), the chart's name appears. It is probably something like Chart 3.

3   Type **ReportChart** in the Reference area, and press ENTER to rename the chart.

If you give a name to a chart or other drawing object, you can be sure a procedure will always refer to the chart you want.

4   Activate the Control worksheet, enter **Orientation** in cell A14, and give cell A15 the name Orientation. (Select the range A14:B14, press CTRL+SHIFT+F3 to display the Create Names dialog box, and click OK.)

5   Enter **Landscape** in cell B14.

Use the Immediate pane to move the chart

When you put the chart below the pivot table, you want about ¼ inch between the table and the chart. The pivot table varies in height, however. When you use the Category field (with seven values) for the row labels, the pivot table is tall. When you use the Price field (with three values) for the row labels, the pivot table is short. You need a way to find out the height of the pivot table so that you can put the chart the proper distance below it. Use the Immediate pane to see how to move the chart to the right place.

1   Activate the ReportModule sheet, and display the Immediate pane. (Choose the Debug Window command from the View menu. Resize the Debug window so that you can see the workbook behind it.)

2   Type **Set myReport = Worksheets("Report")** and press ENTER to create a convenient variable that points at the Report worksheet.

3   Type **myReport.Select,** and press ENTER to show the Report worksheet.

You will need to manipulate both the chart and the pivot table. Rather than typing repeatedly the long expressions needed to refer to these objects, assign these objects to variables also.

4   Type **Set myPivot = myReport.PivotTables("ReportTable")**, and press ENTER.

5   Type **Set myChart = myReport.ChartObjects("ReportChart")**, and press ENTER.

6   Type **myChart.Left = 0**, and press ENTER to shift the chart to the left side of the worksheet.

You need to find the height of the pivot table so that you can set the Top property of the chart to slightly greater than that height.

The PivotTable object has several properties that return the locations of different parts of the pivot table. The property TableRange1 returns the range containing the body of the pivot table (not including the page fields). The property TableRange2 returns the range containing the entire pivot table.

7   Type **?myPivot.TableRange2.Height**, and press ENTER.

72 points equals 1 inch.

A number appears, probably something like 140.25. This is the height, in points, of the range containing the entire pivot table. This number will vary depending on which database field you use for the row headings. You want the chart to be about ¼ inch (18 points) below the table.

8   Type **myChart.Top = myPivot.TableRange2.Height + 18**, and press ENTER.

The chart moves below the pivot table.

You may want to give a name to the worksheet range that encompasses the pivot table and the chart. The range begins in cell A1, and it ends at the bottom right corner of the chart. A ChartObject object has a BottomRightCell property that returns the cell under the bottom right corner of the chart.

You can give the name ReportRange to this range of cells. A Range object has a Name property. Assigning a text string to the Name property of a Range object assigns that name to the range on the worksheet.

9   Type **Range("A1",myChart.BottomRightCell).Name = "ReportRange"**, and press ENTER.

The name is now defined. Select the named range.

10   Type **Range("ReportRange").Select**, and press ENTER.

Note A worksheet name is different from a Visual Basic variable. You use the Set statement to assign a cell to a variable, which you can then use in a procedure but not in an Excel worksheet formula. You use the Name property (or the Add method of the Names collection) to assign a worksheet name to a cell, and you can then use that name in a worksheet formula but not in a Visual Basic procedure. To refer to a worksheet name from a procedure, you must use the Range method.

Use a procedure to move the chart

Now that you have seen in the Immediate pane how to manipulate pivot tables, charts, and ranges, you can transfer useful statements back to the Code pane to help you write a procedure.

1   Activate the Code pane of the Debug window (the bottom half), scroll to the bottom, and enter this procedure.

Since some of the statements are identical to what you typed in the Immediate pane, you may want to copy those statements from the Immediate pane down into the Code pane. In the Immediate pane, each statement must be entered on a single line, but in a procedure you can split long statements into multiple lines.

```
Sub AdjustChart()
    Dim myReport
    Dim myChart
    Dim myPivot
    Dim myControl
    Dim myOrientation

    Set myReport = Worksheets("Report")
    Set myChart = myReport.ChartObjects("ReportChart")
    Set myPivot = myReport.PivotTables("ReportTable")
    Set myControl = Worksheets("Control")
    Set myOrientation = myControl.Range("Orientation")

    If myOrientation = "Portrait" Then
        myChart.Top = myPivot.TableRange2.Height + 18
        myChart.Left = 0
        myReport.PageSetup.Orientation = xlPortrait
    Else
```

```
                    myChart.Left = myPivot.TableRange2.Width + 18
                    myChart.Top = 0
                    myReport.PageSetup.Orientation = xlLandscape
                End If
                myReport.Range("A1", myChart.BottomRightCell) _
                    .Name = "ReportRange"
            End Sub
```

Note As long as a procedure is not currently running, you can enter and edit code in the Code pane, the same as if you were working in the module sheet itself. If you develop statements in the Immediate pane that you want to use in a procedure, you may want to edit that procedure in the Code pane so that you can copy the statements directly from the Immediate pane.

Almost everything in the procedure is something you already did in the Immediate pane. One new statement deserves mention:

The statement *myReport.PageSetup.Orientation = xlPortrait* sets the Orientation property of the PageSetup object of the Report worksheet to portrait mode. You set the same property to landscape mode using the built-in constant *xlLandscape*.

2   Close the Debug window, and activate the ReportModule sheet.

3   In the PrintReport procedure, immediately following the *AdjustTable* statement, insert the statement **AdjustChart.** Then click the Toggle Breakpoint button to make the AdjustChart statement into a breakpoint, and save the workbook.

Toggle Breakpoint button

4   Activate the Control worksheet, change the Orientation setting to **Portrait**, click the Print button, and step through the macro.

Simplify the variables in the module

The ReportModule sheet contains three procedures: The PrintReport procedure is the master procedure. It runs the two subprocedures and then prints the report. The AdjustTable subroutine uses settings from the Control worksheet to adjust the pivot table. The AdjustChart subroutine uses the Orientation setting from the Control worksheet to place the chart properly on the report.

Both the subroutine procedures, AdjustTable and AdjustChart, set variables to make the code easier to read. When you declare a variable inside a procedure, that variable can be used only inside that one procedure, and the value of the variable is discarded when that procedure ends. When you declare a variable outside (above) all the procedures in a module, the variable can be used by any procedure in the module.

Since you use the variables from the Control worksheet in several places in the module, you may want to assign the objects once so that you can use the variables anywhere inside the module.

1   In the ReportModule sheet, move all the variable declaration statements to the top of the module, just above the *Sub PrintReport( )* statement. Delete any duplicate declarations.

The list of variable declarations should look like this:

The order of the declarations is not important. Use any order that makes sense to you.

```
Dim myReport
Dim myChart
Dim myPivot
Dim myControl
Dim myOrientation
Dim myRowField
Dim myPageField
Dim myPageItem
```

? Move all the assignment statements to a new procedure named InitializeVariables below the PrintReport procedure, and delete any duplicate assignments. The new procedure should look something like this:

The order of the assignments is not important, except that you must assign a variable before you use it.

```
Sub InitializeVariables()
    Set myReport = Worksheets("Report")
    Set myPivot = myReport.PivotTables("ReportTable")
    Set myChart = myReport.ChartObjects("ReportChart")
    Set myControl = Worksheets("Control")
    Set myOrientation = myControl.Range("Orientation")
    Set myRowField = myControl.Range("RowField")
    Set myPageField = myControl.Range("PageField")
    Set myPageItem = myControl.Range("PageItem")
End Sub
```

Toggle Breakpoint button

3 As the first statement in the body of the PrintReport procedure, enter the statement **InitializeVariables**. Then click the Toggle Breakpoint button to make the InitializeVariables statement into a breakpoint, and clear any other breakpoints in the module. You learned about toggling breakpoints in Lesson 10.

Every time you run the PrintReport procedure, it will run the InitializeVariables procedure, which will assign the objects to variables that can be used anywhere inside the module.

4 In the PrintReport procedure, change the statement *Worksheets("Report").PrintPreview* to **myReport.PrintPreview**.

5 Save the workbook, activate the Control worksheet, click the Print button, and step through the finished macro.

The complete module reads the values you enter on the Control worksheet, adjusts the pivot table to reflect the desired market segment, adjusts the chart position and the printer orientation to reflect the desired page layout, and prints the report.

Exit Microsoft Excel

1 Close Microsoft Excel by choosing the Exit command from the File menu.

2 Close the Query application by choosing the Exit command from the File menu. Do not save the query.

Lesson Summary

To	Do this
Copy records from Query into Excel, including column headings	In Query, select the records, use Copy Special from the Edit menu to copy the records, switch to Excel, and use Paste from the Edit menu.
Store a pointer to a cell named ThisCell into a variable named myCell	Use the statement *Set myCell = Range("ThisCell").*
Store the value from a cell named ThisCell into a variable named myValue	Use the statement *Let myCell = Range("ThisCell").Value.*
Find out the size of a pivot table (excluding page fields)	Use the TableRange1 property.
Find out the size of a pivot table (including page fields)	Use the TableRange2 property.
Find out the cells under the corners of a chart	Use the TopLeftCell and BottomRightCell properties.
Use a variable in all procedures of a module	Declare the variable outside of any procedure and assign a value to the variable in the first procedure that runs.

Preview of the Next Lesson

In this lesson, you built a macro for creating order status reports for various market segments. In the next lesson, you will extend the macro to work with other applications. You will learn how to send copies of the report to Microsoft Word for Windows, using Visual Basic for Applications' ability to remotely control other applications. You will also learn how to extract information directly from the database system using powerful database connectivity tools available to Visual Basic.

Interact with the World

In 1616, the ruler of Japan, Shogun Ieyasu, closed the doors of his country to foreign traders and missionaries. For nearly a quarter of a millenium, during which time the rest of the world was caught up in burgeoning international commerce, Japan was effectively isolated from the outside world. On July 8, 1853, Commodore Matthew C, Perry sailed with four American ships into Tokyo harbor, ending Japan's isolation.

The rest of the world was shocked by how quickly Japan imitated, assimilated, and adapted Western ideas and technology. During its years of isolation, Japan had a sophisticated and effective society, but its impact was limited. Once Japan began to interact with other nations, it became first a powerful military force and subsequently an even more powerful economic force in the world.

For years, computer applications have each functioned in isolation. Each one has been sophisticated and effective on its own, but still limited in solving complete business problems. New tools are now becoming available to allow major applications and databases to communicate freely with one another. In this lesson you will learn how to communicate directly with other applications from Microsoft Excel using Visual Basic.

You will learn how to:

- Execute commands in Word for Windows from Microsoft Excel.

- Attach additional code libraries to a workbook.

- Request data from a database directly into Microsoft Excel.

Estimated lesson time: 50 minutes

Start the lesson

▶ Start Microsoft Excel, open the LESSON12.XLS workbook, and save a copy as LESSON13.XLS.

Note If you do not have Word for Window version 6 or later, you will not be able to do the exercises in the first part of this lesson. You can continue with the "Retrieving Data from a Database" section of the lesson.

Controlling Word for Windows Immediately

In Lesson 12, you developed a macro for creating the market segment order status reports you need for your monthly review meetings at Miller Textiles. Usually, after the meeting, you are asked to prepare a document that contains discussions of the reports along with the reports themselves. You use Microsoft Word for Windows as your word processor, and you would like to enhance your macros so that they can optionally put the report directly into a Word document.

Microsoft Word for Windows version 6 can receive commands directly from Visual Basic. With earlier versions of Word for Windows, you could send commands from Microsoft Excel, but the procedures necessary to set up and use the connection were difficult. Word for Windows version 6 does not yet include Visual Basic for Applications, and you cannot yet work directly with objects in Word, but you can now easily control Word documents using Word's internal programming language: WordBasic.

To build a procedure that can communicate with Word for Windows, first carry out the commands in the Immediate pane so that you can see the effect of each statement, and then transfer the useful statements to the Code pane.

Open communication with WordBasic

1   Make sure that Word for Windows is closed. Restore Microsoft Excel's window if it is maximized, and resize the window so that it fills the right half of your monitor screen.

2   Maximize the LESSON13.XLS workbook window, activate the ReportModule sheet, choose the Debug Window command from the View menu, and activate the Immediate pane.

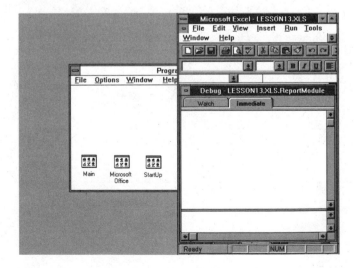

3   In the Immediate pane, type **Set myWord = CreateObject("Word.Basic")**, and press ENTER.

The Word for Windows application loads. The word *CreateObject* is a Visual Basic function that establishes a link with objects that can accept commands from Visual Basic but do not appear in the Object Browser. The WordBasic language used by Word can accept commands from Visual Basic.

To establish a connection with an object, you must find out the name that the object responds to. Word's programming language responds to the name *Word.Basic*.

The CreateObject function launches Word and returns a link to the Word.Basic object, which you assign to the variable *myWord*.

4   Activate Word for Windows, restore the window if it is maximized, and resize the window so that it fills the left half of your monitor screen.

5   Activate the Excel window, in the Immediate pane type **myWord.FileNew**, and press ENTER.

A new document appears in Word.

You can control the Word application in interesting ways.

6   Type **myWord.AppMinimize 1**, and press ENTER.

The Word application changes to an icon at the bottom of the screen. You can still issue commands to the minimized application.

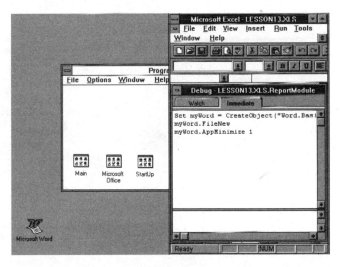

7   Type **myWord.AppRestore**, and press ENTER to make Word reappear.

Word for Windows version 6 can accept commands from Visual Basic, but you cannot manipulate objects inside Word the way you can manipulate objects inside Excel. You must use WordBasic statements.

Find WordBasic commands

Most WordBasic statements that correspond to menu commands consist of the menu name followed by the command name, with all spaces removed. For example, the New command from the File menu becomes the FileNew statement. You can use Word's Help facility to find other statements and to find arguments you can use with statements.

Use Excel to change the Word document so that you can see the whole page.

1   Activate Word, and choose Contents from the Help menu.

2   On the Word Help Contents screen, click the Programming With Microsoft Word hyperlink to open WordBasic Help.

All the WordBasic statements you can use from Visual Basic are in this WordBasic Help file.

3   Click the Search button, type **ViewZoomWholePage**, and press ENTER twice to display the Help topic for the ViewZoomWholePage statement.

The Help topic describes the statement and any arguments you may need to use with it. For the ViewZoomWholePage command, you just use the word *ViewZoomWholePage*.

4   Minimize the WordBasic Help window, and activate Excel.

5   In the Immediate pane, type **myWord.ViewZoomWholePage**, and press ENTER.

If the Word document page was not already completely visible, this statement changes it.

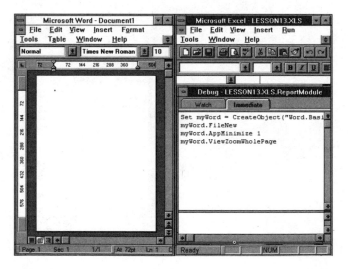

Note This is an Excel Visual Basic book, not a WordBasic book. To help you see how to use Visual Basic to control other applications, you will use a few of the most common WordBasic commands in the course of this lesson. The WordBasic commands, however, are not explained in depth. As you use the WordBasic commands, you may want to read the corresponding topics in WordBasic Help.

Copy the report range to Word

You want to copy the range containing the report into the Word document. The report is in the range named ReportRange on the worksheet named Report.

1   Type **Worksheets("Report").Range("ReportRange").Copy** in the Immediate pane, and press ENTER.

The message in the status bar at the bottom of Excel's window changes to *Select destination and press ENTER or choose Paste*. This message confirms that the range is ready to paste.

You can paste into Word using any of several formats. In this case, you want to paste the table range and the chart together, so pasting as a picture is a good choice.

For details about the
EditPasteSpecial
statement, search
WordBasic Help.

2   Type **myWord.EditPasteSpecial DataType:="PICT"**, and press ENTER.

Use a colon and an equal sign (:=) to separate the argument name from the argument value for WordBasic commands, the same as for Excel object methods.

A picture of the report appears in the Word document.

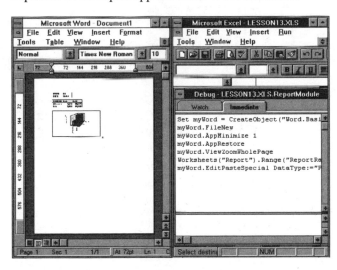

3   Type **Application.CutCopyMode = False**, and press ENTER to change the message in the status bar back to *Ready*.

4   Type **myWord.InsertPara**, and press ENTER to add a paragraph after the report.

Change the orientation of the page in Word

When you print the reports directly from Excel, sometimes you print them with a portrait orientation and sometimes you print them with a landscape orientation. You want to be able to switch the page orientation in Word to match the orientation of the report. Word requires a section break to change orientation within a document.

1   Type **myWord.InsertSectionBreak**, and press ENTER.

A new page appears in the Word document. The new page is a new section. Now you can change the page orientation of the new section to landscape.

Use whatever measurement you set in Word. For example, if you set Word to use points, pass the page width and height values in points.

2   Type **myWord.FilePageSetup Orientation:=1, PageWidth:="11", PageHeight:="8.5"**, and press ENTER.

The orientation of the new page changes to landscape.

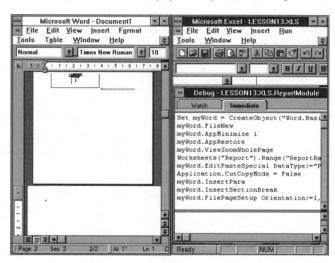

In Excel, the number values for the portrait and landscape orientations are 1 and 2 respectively. In Word, the number values are 0 and 1. When you change the page orientation, you must also give the new page width and height values, as text strings, in the measurement system currently set in Word.

3   Type **myWord.InsertPara**, and press ENTER.

4   Type **myWord.InsertSectionBreak**, and press ENTER.

5   Type **myWord.FilePageSetup Orientation:=0, PageWidth:="8.5", PageHeight:="11"**, and press ENTER to change the orientation for the new page to portrait.

Save and close the Word document

After you add various reports to the Word document, your procedure will need to save the document and give it a name. Use the name of the month as the name for the file.

1   Type **myWord.FileSaveAs Name:="FEB.DOC"**, and press ENTER.

The caption of the file changes from Document1 to FEB.DOC to show that the file has been saved.

2   Type **myWord.FileClose**, and press ENTER to close the document.

Close the connection to Word

When you establish a link to an object using the CreateObject function, you must always be sure to release the object when you have finished using it. Otherwise you may lose operating system resources. You can look at the variable where the WordBasic object is stored and see whether or not the object is released.

1   In the Immediate pane, type **?TypeName(myWord)**, and press ENTER.

The word *wordbasic* (in all lowercase letters) appears. The word *TypeName* is a Visual Basic function that returns the data type of a variable. The word *wordbasic* is the name WordBasic uses for the object you can give commands to from Visual Basic.

2   Type **Set myWord = Nothing**, and press ENTER.

The Word for Windows application closes. The word *Nothing* is a special keyword in Visual Basic that releases all the resources of an object.

3   Close the Debug window.

> **Note**   If you use the function *CreateObject("Word.Basic")* when Word is already running, the function returns a link to the currently running instance of the application. In that case, when you release the object, the Word application does not close. On the other hand, if Word is not running when you use CreateObject, creating the object launches the application and releasing the object closes it.

Controlling Word for Windows from a Procedure

Now you have all the pieces necessary to create a procedure to communicate with WordBasic. You can enhance your report creation macro to optionally send the report to Word. First add new options to the Control worksheet, and then enhance the PrintReport procedure to handle the new options, create a subroutine to copy the report to Word, and create another subroutine to close the connection to Word when you finish creating reports.

Control the report output location

You want your macro to send the report only to the printer, only to Word, or both to the printer and to Word.

1   Activate the Control worksheet. Type **SendToPrint** in cell A15, and enter **SendToWord** in cell A16.

2   Use the labels to name the adjacent cells. (Select the range A15:B16, press CTRL+SHIFT+F3 to display the Create Names dialog box, and click OK.)

3   Enter **FALSE** in cell B15 and **TRUE** in cell B16.

4   Activate the ReportModule sheet. After the last variable declaration at the top of the module, insert these two statements:

```
Dim mySendToPrint
Dim mySendToWord
```

5   In the InitializeVariables procedure, before the *End Sub* statement, insert the following two statements:

```
Set mySendToPrint = myControl.Range("SendToPrint")
Set mySendToWord = myControl.Range("SendToWord")
```

6   In the PrintReport procedure, replace the statement *myReport.PrintPreview* with this set of statements:

```
If mySendToPrint = True Then
    myReport.PrintPreview
End If
If mySendToWord = True Then
    DoSendToWord
End If
```

These statements form two separate If structures. You don't want to use *Else* because you want to be able to treat each part of the request separately.

The word *DoSendToWord* is the name of a subroutine you will write to send the report to Word. You can use the name of a subroutine even before you create the subroutine.

Create a procedure to control WordBasic

Now you can write the actual procedure to send the report to Word. You will use many statements that you tried out in the Immediate pane. You may want to activate the Debug window and copy usable statements from the Immediate pane to the Code pane.

1   At the top of the module, as the first variable declaration, insert the statement **Dim myWord**.

2 At the bottom of the module, insert this procedure:

```
Sub DoSendToWord()
    If TypeName(myWord) = "wordbasic" Then
        myWord.InsertSectionBreak
    Else
        Set myWord = CreateObject("Word.Basic")
        myWord.FileNew
        myWord.FileSaveAs Name:= "FEB.DOC"
    End If

    myReport.Range("ReportRange").Copy
    myWord.EditPasteSpecial DataType:="PICT"
    myWord.InsertPara
    Application.CutCopyMode = False

    If myOrientation = "Portrait" Then
        myWord.FilePageSetup _
            Orientation:=0, _
            PageWidth:="8.5", _
            PageHeight:="11"
    Else
        myWord.FilePageSetup _
            Orientation:=1, _
            PageWidth:="11", _
            PageHeight:="8.5"
    End If
    myWord.FileSave
End Sub
```

You will run this procedure only on those occasions when you choose to send the report to Word. You don't want to create the WordBasic object until you actually use it for the first time, in case you never use it at all. The procedure checks to see if the WordBasic object has already been created, and if not, the procedure creates it. If the WordBasic object does exist, the document must already have at least one report in it, so the procedure adds a section break to separate the new report from the previous report.

Once the WordBasic object is created and the file is ready, the procedure copies the report range and pastes the picture into Word. Next the procedure sets the page orientation in Word, based on the orientation setting on the Control worksheet. Finally, the procedure saves each revision to the file so that you won't have to re-create the reports in case of a power failure, fire, or flood.

3 Select the *Sub DoSendToWord()* statement and click the Toggle Breakpoint button. If you opened the Debug window to add the procedure, close it now.

Toggle Breakpoint button

4 Activate the Control worksheet, click the Print button, and step through the macro.

5   Enter a new database field in the RowField cell, change the print orientation setting, click the Print button, and step through the macro again.

6   Activate Word, and then close it by choosing Exit from the File menu.

Create a procedure to close Word

Your macro should release the object that links to Word, but you don't want to close Word after each report. You want to create several reports, store them all in the same Word document, and then close Word once when you are finished.

1   At the bottom of the ReportModule sheet, enter this procedure:

```
Sub CloseReport()
    If TypeName(myWord) = "wordbasic" Then
        myWord.FileClose
        Set myWord = Nothing
    End If
End Sub
```

Toggle Breakpoint button

2   Use the Toggle Breakpoint button to make the *Sub CloseReport()* statement into a breakpoint. Turn off any other breakpoints in the module.

3   Activate the Control worksheet, and create a new button. Assign the button to the CloseReport macro, and give it the label **Close**.

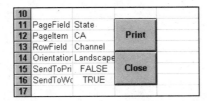

10		
11	PageField	State
12	PageItem	CA
13	RowField	Channel
14	Orientatior	Landscape
15	SendToPri	FALSE
16	SendToWc	TRUE
17		

With buttons labeled **Print** and **Close**.

4   Save the workbook, and then print several reports.

5   Click the Close button, and step through the CloseReport macro.

Word closes, and your document containing the various reports is ready for you to add annotations.

Retrieving Data from a Database

Your report generating macro can now create any of the market segment reports you want, and it can either print each report or export it to a Word document. You can run the entire tool from the Control worksheet. So far, however, you have used your tool only with February data. In Lesson 12, you copied the February data from the database into the Extract worksheet manually. When March, April, and May come, you would like to be able to create reports without manually copying the new data from the database.

The Microsoft Query program that comes bundled with Microsoft Excel is capable of retrieving data from a variety of data sources: dBASE files, Oracle databases, SQL Server databases, Microsoft Access databases, Paradox databases, and many others. Microsoft Query can retrieve data from any database program that has an ODBC driver. The letters *ODBC* stand for Open Database Connectivity. You communicate with Query, Query communicates with the ODBC driver, and the ODBC driver communicates with the database.

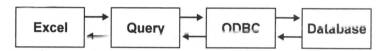

Using Visual Basic, you can communicate directly with the ODBC driver, eliminating the need for the Query program. You connect to the driver, make a request for data, and then retrieve the data into Excel.

A request for data is called a *query*. You make the request using *Structured Query Language*, or SQL (often pronounced "sequel"). SQL is an industry standard way of making queries. SQL is a powerful query language, and some SQL queries can become very complex. You can, however, also make very simple queries using SQL. In this lesson, you will make simple SQL queries of the Miller Textiles order database.

First you will ask the database for the most recent month for which data is available; then you will retrieve the order history information for that month.

Establish a connection to the database

Communicating with ODBC drivers can be complicated. Fortunately, Excel comes with an add-in that takes care of most of the complicated work for you. (An add-in is a file that adds functionality to Excel.) All you have to do is tell Excel to use that add-in.

Object Browser button

1 Maximize Excel, activate the ReportModule sheet, and click the Object Browser button in the Visual Basic toolbar. Click the arrow next to the box labeled Libraries/Workbooks.

The list contains *LESSON13.XLS*, *VBA*, *Excel*, and possibly others depending on which add-ins you have installed. LESSON13.XLS is, of course, the current workbook. VBA and Excel have libraries of procedures you can browse. You need to add the procedures for communicating with the ODBC driver to this list.

2 Click Close, and from the Tools menu, choose the References command.

A list labeled Available References appears, containing the items *Visual Basic For Applications* and *Microsoft Excel 5.0 Object Library.* These are the two libraries that appear in the Object Browser. You add the ODBC library here, and then its procedures will appear in the Object Browser.

3   Click the Browse button, find the directory where the Excel program is installed, double click the Library subdirectory, and then double click the MSQuery subdirectory.

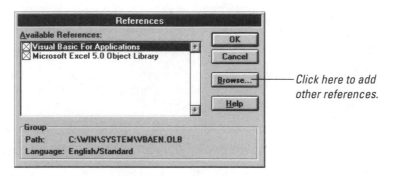

— *Click here to add other references.*

If the add-in files are not in the MSQuery directory, run Excel setup and add the Data Access options.

The add-in files QE.XLA, XLODBC.XLA, and XLQUERY.XLA appear.

4   Select XLODBC.XLA and click OK.

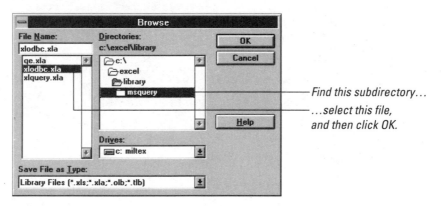

— *Find this subdirectory...*

— *...select this file, and then click OK.*

The XLODBC add-in appears in the list of available references.

5   Make sure that the check box next to the XLODBC add-in is selected, close the References dialog box, open the Object Browser, and select XLODBC from the list of libraries.

The entry *VBA Functions* is alone in the list of modules, but the list of procedures on the right contains several functions that all begin with the letters *SQL*. You will use four of these procedures for the simple queries you will make at this time.

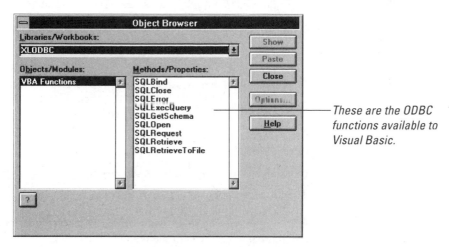

— *These are the ODBC functions available to Visual Basic.*

6   Close the Object Browser.

Retrieve a date from the database

You can make the queries first using the Immediate pane and then transfer the useful statements to a procedure. First create a place to put the date, and then query the database to retrieve the most recent date in the database.

1   Activate the Control worksheet, enter **MatchDate** into cell A17, and give the name MatchDate to cell B17.

2   Activate the ReportModule sheet, and display the Immediate pane. (Choose the Debug Window command from the View menu, resize the Debug window, and activate the Immediate pane.)

3   Type **Set myControl = Worksheets("Control")** and press ENTER.

4   Type **myControl.Select**, and press ENTER so that you can see the cell where the date will go.

5   In the Immediate pane, type **?**, and then open the Object Browser and paste the SQLOpen function.

6   As the value for the ConnectionStr argument, type **"DSN=Miller Textiles"** (including the quotation marks), and delete the other two arguments. Since you will be using the return value, leave parentheses around the argument.

The letters *DSN* stand for *Data Source Name*. You are telling the SQLOpen function to make a connection to the data source named *Miller Textiles*.

The statement should be *?SQLOpen(ConnectionStr:="DSN=Miller Textiles")*.

7   Press ENTER to run the SQLOpen function and display its return value.

The number 1 appears. When the SQLOpen function opens a new channel to a database, it assigns a channel number to it. The XLODBC add-in is capable of carrying on several conversations with different databases at the same time. For example, you might retrieve values from one database on channel 1, find related information from a second database on channel 2, and write values to a third database on channel 3, all at the same time. The channel number allows you and the ODBC add-in to keep straight which database you are talking with.

8 Type **?**, open the Object Browser, and paste the SQLExecQuery function. Type **1** (the channel number returned by SQLOpen) as the value of the ConnectionNum argument. Type **"SELECT Max(Date) from Orders"** (including the quotation marks) as the value of the QueryText argument.

The statement should be *?SQLExecQuery(ConnectionNum:=1, QueryText:="SELECT Max(Date) from Orders").*

9 Press ENTER to run the SQLExecQuery function and display its return value.

The number 1 appears. The SQLExecQuery function submits a request to the database. In this case, you told it to select the largest value from the Date column in the database. The return value of the SQLExecQuery function always tells you the number of *columns* in the result of the query.

Since you requested a single value, the query result has a single column, and the SQLExecQuery function returns the number 1. You can request multiple values in the same query. If you had requested two values—for example, the maximum date and the maximum units—the result would have had two columns and the return value of the function would have been the number 2. You will request multiple columns of values later in this lesson.

The SQLExecQuery function does not bring any data from the database back to Excel; it only gets the data ready to bring back. You need a different function to retrieve the data.

10 Type **?**, open the Object Browser, and paste the SQLRetrieve function. Then type **1** as the value of the ConnectionNum argument, type **myControl.Range("MatchDate")** as the value of the DestinationRef argument, and delete the remaining arguments.

The statement should be *?SQLRetrieve(ConnectionNum:=1, DestinationRef:=myControl.Range("MatchDate")).*

11 Press ENTER to run the SQLRetrieve function and display its return value.

The date appears in the MatchDate cell, and the number 1 appears in the Immediate pane. The *effect* of the SQLRetrieve function is to retrieve the data you select using the SQLExecQuery function and put it into the destination range you specify in Excel. The *return value* of the function tells you how many rows of values were returned.

Since you requested a single value, one row of values was retrieved into Excel, and the SQLRetrieve function returns the number 1. If you had retrieved 500 records from the database, the return value of the function would have been the number 500. You will request multiple records in the next section.

Retrieve one month's orders from the database

Now that you know the maximum date in the database, you can use that date to request all the order records for the most recent month. Since you will be requesting the records from the same database, you can keep using the same channel, or connection, number.

1 In the Immediate pane, type **Set myExtract = Worksheets("Extract")**.

2 Type **myExtract.Select**, and press ENTER to display the Extract worksheet. Then type **myExtract.Cells.Clear** to clear the entire current contents of the worksheet.

The SQL query command to retrieve all the orders for the month will require more words than the query to retrieve a single date did. If you assign the first part of the query statement to a variable and then append additional parts, the SQL query can become quite manageable. In a SQL query statement, first you specify the fields you want to *select*, then you specify the data file to get the fields *from*, and finally you specify the rule for deciding *where* to select the records.

3 Type **mySQL = "SELECT Date, State, Category, Channel, Price, Units, Net "**, leaving a space after the word *Net*, and press ENTER.

This is the list of fields you want to select from the database.

4 Type **mySQL = mySQL & "FROM Orders "**, and press ENTER.

This appends the data source to the list of fields.

5 Type **mySQL = mySQL & "WHERE Date = '1994-02-01'"**, and press ENTER.

This appends the decision criterion for which rows to accept. You must include the date comparison value in apostrophes and use the format yyyy-mm-dd.

You now have a complete SQL query request ready.

6 Type **?mySQL**, and press ENTER to display the entire SQL query: *SELECT Date, State, Category, Channel, Price, Units, Net FROM Orders WHERE Date = '1994-02-01'*. Make sure that the query statement has spaces before the words *FROM* and *WHERE*.

Note Capitalization is not important in a SQL statement, but traditionally the keywords *SELECT*, *FROM*, and *WHERE* are capitalized to make the SQL statement easier to read.

---

7 Type **?SQLExecQuery(ConnectionNum:=1, QueryText:=mySQL)**, and press ENTER.

The number 7 appears because the SQL query statement requested seven columns from the database. Do not type quotation marks around the word *mySQL* because this is a variable that contains the query, not the query itself.

8 Type **?SQLRetrieve(ConnectionNum:=1, DestinationRef:= myExtract.Cells(1), ColNamesLogical:=True)**, and press ENTER.

The worksheet fills with new values from the database, and the number 178 appears in the Immediate pane. You retrieved 178 rows of values from the database, plus the 1 row of column names.

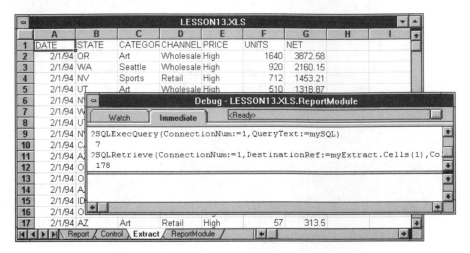

Because you specified a single cell as the destination range, the SQLRetrieve function filled from that cell down and to the right. When you retrieve data, be sure cells below and to the right of the destination range are expendable.

The *ColNamesLogical* argument is optional for the SQLRetrieve function. If you use True for the ColNamesLogical argument, the function pastes the column names along with the values. The row of column names is not included in the row count returned by the function.

9   Type **myExtract.Cells(1).CurrentRegion.Name = "Database"**, and press ENTER to give the name *Database* to the entire retrieved region of data.

When you created the pivot table, you told it to look for values in a range named Database. If you rename the Database range every time you retrieve the data from the database, the pivot table will always include the correct number of records.

10   Type **?SQLClose(ConnectionNum:=1)**, and press ENTER to close the connection to the database driver.

The number *0* appears. The SQLClose function returns 0 if the connection closes successfully.

11   Type **Worksheets("Report").PivotTables("ReportTable").RefreshTable** and press ENTER.

The pivot table always makes its own internal copy of the data in the table. After you retrieve new data into the Extract worksheet, you need to refresh the pivot table so that it will use the new data. A PivotTable object has a method named RefreshTable that refreshes the data in the pivot table.

Calculate the current date for the query

In the first query, you retrieved the date of the most recent month in the database. In the second query, you retrieved the values for that specific month. Your procedure will need to use the date retrieved by the first query in the Where clause of the second query.

1   Type **Set myMatchDate = myControl.Range("MatchDate")**, and press ENTER.

The myMatchDate variable now contains a pointer to the cell that contains the most recent date.

2   Type **?myMatchDate .Value**, and press ENTER.

The date *2/1/94* appears, but it is not in the correct format for the SQL query statement.

3   Type **?Format(myMatchDate.Value,"yyyy-mm-dd")**, and press ENTER.

The date *1994-02-01* appears. This is in the format needed by the SQL query statement. The Format function formats a number using essentially the same formatting codes as the Format Number dialog box in Excel.

4   Reexecute the statements that assign the first two parts of the SQL statement to the mySQL variable. (Perform steps 3 and 4 from the preceding section.)

5   Type **mySQL = mySQL & "WHERE Date = '"**, and press ENTER to add the first part of the date clause to the statement.

6   Type **mySQL = mySQL & Format(myMatchDate.Value,"yyyy-mm-dd")**, and press ENTER to add the formatted date to the statement.

7   Type **mySQL = mySQL & "'"**, and press ENTER to add the closing single quotation mark after the date.

These statements insert the formatted date from the MatchDate cell into the middle of the SQL statement.

8   Type **?mySQL**, and press ENTER to see the value of the SQL query statement. It should be the same as when you entered the date directly into the statement: *SELECT Date, State, Category, Channel, Price, Units, Net FROM Orders WHERE Date = '1994-02-01'.*

9   Close the Debug window.

Now you have all the pieces necessary to build a procedure to retrieve the current month's orders from the database.

Write a procedure to retrieve the current orders

You will write a new procedure named *InitializeData*. Then, since you need to run this procedure only once each month, you will create a button just for this procedure.

1 Activate the ReportModule sheet, and add these declarations at the top:

```
Dim myExtract
Dim myMatchDate
```

2 Add these statements to the end of the InitializeVariables procedure:

```
Set MyExtract = Worksheets("Extract")
Set myMatchDate = myControl.Range("MatchDate")
```

3 Add this new procedure at the bottom of the module:

```
Sub InitializeData()
    Dim myChannel
    Dim mySQL
    InitializeVariables
    Application.StatusBar = "Retrieving data. Please wait."

    myChannel = SQLOpen(ConnectionStr:="DSN=Miller Textiles")
    SQLExecQuery _
        ConnectionNum:=myChannel, _
        QueryText:="SELECT Max(Date) from Orders"
    SQLRetrieve _
        ConnectionNum:=myChannel, _
        DestinationRef:=myMatchDate

    myExtract.Cells.Clear
    mySQL = "SELECT Date, State, Category, Channel, Price, Units, Net "
    mySQL = mySQL & "FROM Orders "
    mySQL = mySQL & "WHERE Date = '"
    mySQL = mySQL & Format(myMatchDate, "yyyy-mm-dd")
    mySQL = mySQL & "'"
    SQLExecQuery _
        ConnectionNum:=myChannel, _
        QueryText:=mySQL
    SQLRetrieve _
        ConnectionNum:=myChannel, _
        DestinationRef:=myExtract.Cells(1), _
        ColNamesLogical:=True
    myExtract.Cells(1).CurrentRegion.Name = "Database"

    SQLClose ConnectionNum:=myChannel
    myPivot.RefreshTable
    Application.StatusBar = False
End Sub
```

If you do not use the return value of a function, do not put parentheses around the arguments.

The ODBC procedures all use the channel number returned by the SQLOpen statement. That value is assigned to the variable *myChannel*.

The procedure displays a status bar message by assigning the message to the Application object's StatusBar property. Setting the StatusBar property to False restores the default status bar message.

Instead of setting a breakpoint, you can run the macro, press CTRL+BREAK, and click the Debug button.

4   Set the InitializeVariables statement at the top of the procedure as a breakpoint, and clear any other breakpoints in the module.

5   Close the Debug window if it is open, activate the Control worksheet, create a new button, assign the InitializeData macro to it, and give it the label **Initialize**

6   Save the workbook, click the Initialize button to test the data retrieval macro, and step through the macro.

The procedure seems to work properly, but if you try to click the Print button, the pivot table commands will fail. The text values you retrieved from the database all have extra spaces after them.

Write a procedure to trim spaces from the data

In many databases, fields have a fixed width. For example, the width of the Category field in the order history database is 13 characters. The category names, however, vary in length—from Art to Environment. In the database, the extra characters are filled with blank spaces.

Some databases do not store extra spaces, so you don't need to trim the imported data.

Usually, when you import data from a database into Excel, you do not want the extra spaces. For example, extra spaces cause comparisons to fail, so the pivot table will not work properly. When you import the data from the Query tool, the Query tool trims the extra spaces for you. When you use an ODBC driver to import the data directly into Excel, you may have to trim the extra spaces after the data is in Excel.

1   In the InitializeData procedure, before the *myPivot.RefreshTable* statement, insert the statement **TrimData**.

2   Below the InitializeData procedure, add the TrimData procedure:

```
Sub TrimData()
    Dim myCell
    For Each myCell In myExtract.Range("Database")
        myCell.Value = Trim(myCell.Value)
    Next myCell
End Sub
```

The word *Trim* is a Visual Basic function. It returns the same value as the argument you pass it, but without any leading or trailing spaces. This procedure loops through all the cells in the range named Database, trimming the contents of each cell.

3   Turn off any breapoints, save the workbook, activate the Control worksheet and click the Initialize button.

4   Click the Restore button so that Excel is on only the right side of the screen, and click the Print button several times with different control settings.

5   When you finish, click the Close button, save the workbook, and close Excel.

Now your report generator tool can communicate with the outside world. It can retrieve the most recent orders from the database at the click of a button, and it can send the final reports to Word, ready for your analysis.

Lesson Summary

To	Do this
Assign a link to WordBasic commands to the myWord variable	Use the statement *Set myWord = CreateObject("Word.Basic")*.
Find out if a link to WordBasic is in the myWord variable	Use the expression *Typename(myWord) = "wordbasic"*.
Close the link to WordBasic	Use the expression *Set myWord = Nothing*.
Open a connection to an ODBC data source	Use the SQLOpen function.
Send a SQL query to an open ODBC channel	Use the SQLExecQuery function.
Retrieve values from a query	Use the SQLRequest function.
Close an ODBC channel	Use the SQLClose function.

For more information on	See
Controlling other applications	Chapter 10, "Controlling and Communicating with Other Applications," in the *Microsoft Excel Visual Basic User's Guide*.
Communicating with external databases	Chapter 23, "Retrieving Data with Microsoft Query," in the *Microsoft Excel User's Guide*.

Preview of the Next Lesson

The report generator macros are ready for you to use each month. Entering valid control settings, however, is still tricky. Since you created the macros, you can probably remember how to use them to produce reports. But if you make the macros easier to use, you can let others use them to create reports. If you make the macros foolproof, you can even let your boss use them. In the next lesson you will learn how to turn the report generator into a foolproof application.

Create a Packaged Application

Take a 3 foot by 4 foot piece of plywood and cans of blue, yellow, and orange paint. Drip, dribble, splash, and spread the paint on the plywood. You now have—a mess. But put a $500 frame around the painted plywood. You now have—a work of art! Even serious art does not look serious without a good frame. The best diamond brooch does not seem to be a precious gift if given in a paper bag.

You can write macros that are practical, convenient, and useful, but until you put a frame around them, until you tighten up the edges and make them easy to use, until you *package* them, you do not have a true application.

In this lesson you will enhance the macros you built in Lessons 12 and 13. You will add a powerful and appealing dialog box interface, start and stop the application automatically, and prevent unexpected error messages. You will create a packaged application.

You will learn how to:

- Create a custom dialog box.
- Link controls on a dialog box to cells in a worksheet.
- Change the dialog box while it is displayed.
- Start a macro automatically when the workbook is opened.

Estimated lesson time: 50 minutes

Start the lesson

▶ Start Microsoft Excel, and open the workbook LESSON13.XLS. Save a new copy of the workbook as LESSON14.XLS.

Making Dynamic List Boxes

In Lessons 12 and 13, you built macros to help you create reports for different market segments. Those macros may be convenient for you, but if you type a value from the wrong list in the PageItem cell, or if you misspell the word *Portrait* in the Orientation cell, the macros will not work properly.

Your ultimate goal is to make the application simple enough and foolproof enough that others in the company could produce the charts on their own. If you create a dialog box—with list boxes, option buttons, and check boxes—you can prevent the user of the application from making invalid choices and misspelling words.

Create a dialog box sheet

On the Control worksheet, you specify three values that control the pivot table: PageField, PageItem, and RowField. You can use list boxes to make sure the user enters only correct values into these cells. First, assume that State is the value of the PageField cell. You will create a dialog box with two list boxes: one to choose which state and another to choose the database field for row headings.

Dialog boxes in Excel have their own sheet type. To create a new dialog box, insert a dialog sheet.

1   From the Insert menu, choose the Macro, Dialog command to create a new dialog sheet in your workbook.

2   Rename the dialog sheet as **ReportDialog** and drag it to the right of the other worksheets in the workbook.

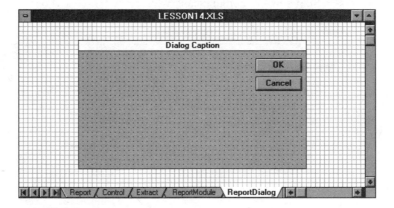

The default dialog box includes an OK button and a Cancel button. The Forms toolbar also appears when you activate a dialog sheet.

 *Use the Forms toolbar to add controls to the dialog box.*

To add additional controls to the dialog box, use the buttons in the Forms toolbar. You want to add two list boxes: one to select the state and one to select the field for the pivot table rows.

List Box button

3   Click the List Box button, and drag on the dialog box to create a list box. Then click the List Box button again, and drag to create another list box next to it.

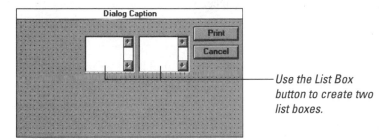

Use the List Box button to create two list boxes.

See Lesson 4 for information about using dialog box controls on a worksheet.

When you click a control button on the Forms toolbar, the mouse pointer changes to a small black cross, and you can drag on the dialog box to create a control of the type you chose. After you create the control, the mouse pointer changes back to an arrow, and you must click the control button again if you want to create another control of the same type. If you double click the control button, however, you can create multiple controls of the same type.

Label button

4   Double click the Label button, and drag on the dialog box to create two label controls, one above each list box.

5   Click the Label button to change the mouse pointer back to an arrow.

6   Click the label above the first list box, type **Item**, click the second label, and type **Row**. Do not press ENTER or you will get a second line in the label.

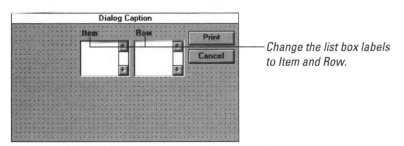

Change the list box labels to Item and Row.

You will select a state in the Item list, and you will select a field for row headings in the Row list.

Creating controls and labels on a dialog box is as easy as dragging, pointing, and typing.

Run the dialog box

On the ReportDialog sheet, you see the design view of the dialog box. To see what the dialog box really looks like, you run it.

1 Click the Run Dialog button in the Forms toolbar.

The dialog box appears, looking like a real dialog box.

Run Dialog button

2 Click OK to close the dialog box.

You can also create a macro to run the dialog box.

3 Click the Record Macro button in the Visual Basic toolbar, type **RunDialog** as the name of the macro, and click Options.

Record Macro button

4 Change the shortcut key to CTRL+SHIFT+D, and click OK.

5 Click the Run Dialog button, and then click OK to close the dialog box.

6 Click the Stop Macro button.

The macro recorder created a new module sheet.

Stop Macro button

7 Activate the new module sheet, and rename it **DialogModule**.

Macros related to the dialog box will be on the DialogModule sheet; macros related to creating the report are on the ReportModule sheet. You can use multiple modules in a workbook to keep large projects organized. Here is the macro that the recorder created:

```
Sub RunDialog()
    DialogSheets("ReportDialog").Show
End Sub
```

The word *DialogSheets* is a method that returns the collection of all dialog sheets in the active workbook. The word *Show* is a method for a DialogSheet object that displays the dialog box.

8 Activate the ReportDialog sheet.

Link the list boxes to a worksheet

The list boxes are empty. The values you want in the list boxes are on the Control worksheet. You can connect the list boxes on the dialog box directly to the lists on the worksheet. Each of the lists at the top of the Control worksheet has already been given the name at the top of the column. The range containing the list of state abbreviations, for example, is named StateList.

1 Double click the list box labeled Item to display the Format Object dialog box, and select the Control tab.

2 In the box labeled Input Range, type **StateList** and press ENTER.

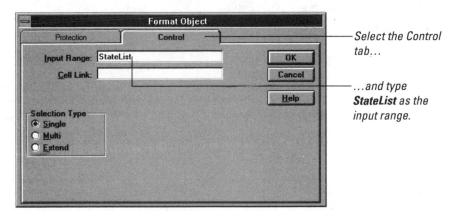

Select the Control tab...

...and type **StateList** as the input range.

The abbreviations for the states appear immediately in the list box.

3 Double click the Row list box, type **KeyList** in the Input Range box, and press ENTER to see the list of database fields.

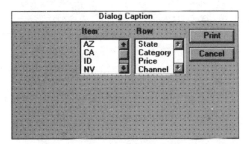

4 Press CTRL+SHIFT+D to display the dialog box.

5 Select CA in the Item list and Channel in the Row list, and then click OK to close the dialog box.

You can see the selected items in the dialog box.

You need a way to get the selected item name from the dialog box back onto the Control worksheet. The PrintReport macro you created in Lesson 12 uses the values from cells on the Control worksheet to control a pivot table.

Link the list box results to a worksheet

When you select an entry from a list box, the list box can tell you the *position number* of the entry in the list. You really need the label for the entry. You can put the position number into a cell on the worksheet and then use an Excel formula to calculate the value of the label.

1 Activate the Control worksheet, and enter **ItemNumber** in cell A18 and **RowNumber** in cell A19.

2   Use the labels in cells A18 and A19 to create names for cells B18 and B19.

3   Activate the ReportDialog sheet, double click the Item list box, type **ItemNumber** in the Cell Link box, and click OK.

4   Double click the Row list box, type **RowNumber** in the Cell Link box, and then click OK.

5   Activate the Control worksheet. The number 2 (for CA) is in the ItemNumber cell, and the number 4 (for Channel) is in the RowNumber cell.

You still need to convert the position numbers into readable words.

The INDEX function works well to interpret the value of a list box.

6   In cell B12, the PageItem cell, type **=INDEX(StateList,ItemNumber)**, and press ENTER to change the value of the cell to CA.

7   In cell B13, the RowField cell, type **=INDEX(KeyList,RowNumber)**, and press ENTER to change the value of the cell to Channel.

The ItemNumber and RowNumber cells are linked to the list boxes on the dialog box. The PageItem and RowField cells use the INDEX function to find the corresponding descriptive words from the StateList and KeyList ranges.

8   Press CTRL+SHIFT+D to run the dialog box. Click various entries in the Item and Row list boxes and watch the values change on the Control worksheet. Then click Cancel when you are finished.

Make the dialog box print the report

Now that the dialog box changes the PageItem and RowField cells on the Control worksheet, you can use the dialog box to select and print reports.

1   On the Control worksheet, enter **TRUE** in the SendToPrint cell (B15), and enter **FALSE** in the SendToWord cell (B16).

2   Activate the ReportDialog sheet, select the OK button, and change the caption of the button to **Print**.

You can also paste the name of the PrintReport procedure from the Object Browser.

3   Activate the DialogModule sheet, and insert the statement **PrintReport** after the statement *DialogSheets("ReportDialog").Show*.

The word *PrintReport* is the name of the procedure on the ReportModule sheet that prints the report.

4   Press CTRL+SHIFT+D to run the dialog box, select any state in the Item list box, select any field (except State) in the Row list box, and click Print.

The dialog box closes, and the PrintReport macro runs, displaying the report in print preview mode. The Print button on the dialog box does not run the PrintReport macro directly; it just closes the dialog box so that the RunDialog macro can continue, and the RunDialog macro runs the PrintReport macro.

The Cancel button, however, also dismisses the dialog box, so clicking the Cancel button has the same effect as clicking the Print button. You need to change the RunDialog macro so that it prints the report only if you click the Print button.

5   Close the print preview display, and activate the DialogModule sheet.

6   Change the RunDialog procedure to look like this:

```
Sub RunDialog()
    If DialogSheets("ReportDialog").Show = True Then
        PrintReport
    End If
End Sub
```

The Show method of a dialog box returns the value True when you click a button to dismiss the dialog box—unless the button is marked as a Cancel button, in which case the Show method returns the value False.

7   Save the LESSON14.XLS workbook before continuing.

Make a list box change lists

The current dialog box allows you to select orders by state. The value of the PageField cell never changes. You want to be able to change the page field in the dialog box. If you change the page field, the list of items for that page must change as well. For example, if you choose Channel as the page field, you want the Item list to display Retail and Wholesale.

You will create a new list box for choosing the page field: First, you will make a place on the Control worksheet to put the result from the list box. Then you will create the list box on the ReportDialog sheet. Finally, you will create a macro to switch the list of items to the appropriate range for the selected page field.

1   On the Control worksheet, enter **PageNumber** into cell A20, and use that label to give a name to cell B20.

2   Enter the number **4** in the PageNumber cell (B20), and enter the formula **=INDEX(KeyList,PageNumber)** in the PageField cell (B11).

The name Channel appears because Channel is the fourth entry in the list of keys.

List Box button

3   Activate the ReportDialog sheet, click the List Box button, and create a new list box to the left of the Item list box. If you need to make more room for the new list box, click the border of the dialog box and stretch the dialog box to the left. If you need to move controls and want to move more than one control at a time, drag a rectangle that encloses the controls. Then you can move them as a group.

4   Double click the new list box, type **KeyList** in the Input Range box, type **PageNumber** in the Cell link box, and click OK.

Label button

5   Add a label control above the new list box, and change its caption to **Page**.

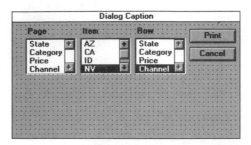

When you create a control, the control gets a name—something like *List Box 8* or *Label 9*. You can see the name of the control in the Reference area to the left of the formula bar. Give the list boxes more meaningful names that you can use when you refer to them from a procedure.

6   Select the Page list box, click the Reference area, type **dlgPageList**, and press ENTER. Select the Item list box, click the Reference area, type **dlgItemList**, and press ENTER. Then select the Row list box, click the Reference area, type **dlgRowList**, and press ENTER.

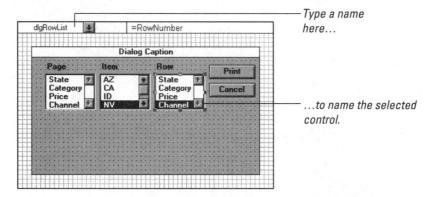

Type a name here...

...to name the selected control.

With the list boxes named, you can now add a macro to the Page list box so that whenever you change an entry, the Item list box will point to a new list.

Edit Code button

7   Select the Page list box, and click the Edit Code button in the Forms toolbar.

A new procedure appears on the DialogModule sheet, ready for you to enter code into. The new macro has the name *dlgPageList_Change*, which is obviously derived from the name of the list box.

Note In some versions of Visual Basic, you can't change the name of a procedure that is linked to a control on a form. In Visual Basic for Applications, you can change the name of the procedure, but then you have to manually link the new procedure to the control. You link a procedure to a list box or some other dialog control the same as you link a procedure to a button on a worksheet: Use the right mouse button to click the control, and choose the Assign To Macro command.

8   Enter these two statements as the body of the dlgPageList_Change procedure:

```
ActiveDialog.ListBoxes("dlgItemList").ListFillRange = _
        Worksheets("Control").Range("PageField") & "List"
ActiveDialog.ListBoxes("dlgItemList").Value = 1
```

The first statement assigns the name of the appropriate range to the ListFillRange property of the dlgItemList list box:

The word *ActiveDialog* is a globally known property of the Application object; it returns the currently displayed dialog box. The ReportDialog dialog box is showing on the screen when the dlgPageList_Change procedure runs, so you can use the word *ActiveDialog* to point at it.

The word *ListBoxes* is a method of a dialog box; it returns a ListBoxes object (a collection of ListBox objects). You want the item named dlgItemList from the collection.

The word *ListFillRange* is a property of a ListBox object; it determines the source for the list box's list of entries. If you select Category in the Page list box, you want to change the source for the Item list box to CategoryList.

The expression *Worksheets("Control").Range("PageField") & "List"* retrieves the value from the cell named PageField on the sheet named Control and then appends the text string *List* to the end of it.

The second statement changes the Item list to select the first entry whenever the list changes.

9   Press CTRL+SHIFT+D to run the dialog box, and select various entries in the Page list box.

The entries in the Item list box change depending on which field name you select in the Page list box.

10   Select Price as the page field, select Mid as the item, and click Cancel.

Make the worksheet formula change lists

The macro changes the source list for the Item list box dynamically. You can now easily choose which page field and which page item to use. On the Control worksheet, however, the formula in the PageItem cell still returns an entry from the list of states. You need to change the PageItem formula to retrieve the item from the correct list.

1   Activate the Control worksheet, and select the cell named PageItem.

Even though the list on the dialog box displays the names of Price ranges, the PageItem cell still shows the name of a state.

The INDEX function in the cell is returning a value from the StateList range. You want to calculate the name of the range for INDEX to use.

2   In the formula *=INDEX(StateList,ItemNumber)*, replace the word *StateList* with the expression **INDIRECT(PageField&"List")**. The final formula should be

=INDEX(INDIRECT(PageField& "List"),ItemNumber). When you press ENTER, the value in the cell changes to *Mid.*

The INDIRECT function allows you to calculate a range. You append the suffix *List* to the current page field name and the INDIRECT function turns that text string into a range. You can watch the INDIRECT function at work.

3   With cell B12 selected, select the expression *PageField& "List"* in the formula bar and press F9.

The text string *"PriceList"* appears in the place of the expression because *Price* is the current value of the PageField cell.

4   In the formula bar, select the expression *INDIRECT("PriceList")* and press F9.

The list *{"High";"Low";"Mid";" (All)" }* appears in the place of the expression. (The braces mean that this list is an array inside the formula.) The INDEX function retrieves a value from this list.

5   Press ESC to restore the formula.

6   Save the workbook.

7   Press CTRL+SHIFT+D to run the dialog box. Select different entries in the Page and Item lists and watch the cells change on the Control worksheet. Click Cancel when you are finished.

Now the dialog box and the Control worksheet display the correct values.

Make the dialog box prevent errors

When you use list boxes in a dialog box, you reduce the possibility of errors. With your dialog box, you *cannot* select an invalid page field or select a category when you should have selected a state. This dialog box does allow one error, however, that you must still prevent: If you use State as the page field and then also use State as the row field, the pivot table will produce an error. The entry in the Page list box and the entry in the Row list box must never be the same.

The Print button dismisses the dialog box and allows the PrintReport procedure to run. You can make the Print button refuse to dismiss the dialog box if the selected entry in the Page list box is the same as the selected entry in the Row list box.

In Lesson 2 you learned how to mark the position for recording.

Note If you have closed and reopened the LESSON14.XLS workbook since you last used the Edit Code button, the Edit Code button will create a new module sheet for the new procedure. You can persuade the Edit Code button to put new procedures where you want them.

You mark the position for the Edit Code button to create a new procedure in the same way that you mark the position for the macro recorder to create a new procedure: Activate the DialogModule sheet, and scroll to the bottom. From the Tools menu, choose the Record Macro, Mark Position For Recording command.

1   Activate the ReportDialog sheet, select the Print button, and give it the name **dlgPrintButton**. (Type the name in the Reference area.)

Edit Code button

2   With the Print button selected, click the Edit Code button in the Forms toolbar.

The DialogModule sheet appears with a new procedure: *dlgPrintButton_Click.* This procedure will now run whenever you click the Print button.

3   Enter this code as the body of the dlgPrintButton_Click procedure:

```
If ActiveDialog.ListBoxes("dlgPageList").Value _
        = ActiveDialog.ListBoxes("dlgRowList").Value Then
    MsgBox "Page field should not match Row field"
    ActiveDialog.Buttons("dlgPrintButton").DismissButton = False
Else
    ActiveDialog.Buttons("dlgPrintButton").DismissButton = True
End If
```

The first statement compares the selected value in the Page list with the selected value in the Row list. If the two values are the same, it displays an alert message.

The word *DismissButton* is a property of a Button object. If the DismissButton property for the button is True, the dialog box goes away. If the DismissButton property for the button is False, the dialog box stays. If you attach a procedure to the button, you can change the setting of the DismissButton property.

4   Run the dialog box. Select the same field in both the Page and the Row list boxes, and click Print.

The message box containing your message appears.

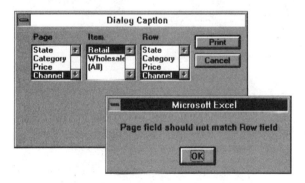

5   Click OK to dismiss the message box. Select a different field in the Row list. Then click Print to create the report.

6   Press ESC to close print preview.

The dialog box now allows you to enter control settings for the page field, page item, and row field, without any possibility for entering an invalid selection.

Clean up the dialog box

When you put controls onto a dialog box, you don't have to worry too much about their exact position and size because you can easily go back and adjust their size and position later. Take a moment to get your current dialog box looking its best.

1 Activate the ReportDialog sheet, drag through the caption (*Dialog Caption*) at the top of the dialog box, and replace it with **Order Status Selection**.

2 Select the Page list box, and change its height so that it shows only four list entries at a time. Repeat this step for the Item and Row list boxes. Adjust the widths of the boxes as needed to make them look good.

Group Box button

3 Click the Group Box button, and drag a rectangle around the Page and Item list boxes (and their labels). Then type **Select by** as the caption for the group box.

The group box does not change the function of the list boxes, but it clarifies the fact that these two list boxes are closely related.

4 Align the controls on the dialog box to get a result similar to this one:

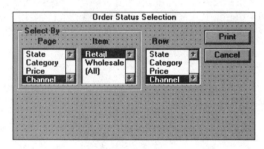

5 Save the workbook.

Adding Options to the Dialog Box

The macros on the ReportModule sheet can switch between portrait and landscape orientations, and they can send the report to Microsoft Word for Windows. You can add those capabilities to the dialog box as well.

Add a print orientation option

1 Drag the bottom of the dialog box frame down to allow about twice the space used by the existing controls.

Option Button button

2 Double click the Option Button button in the Forms toolbar, and create two option buttons below the Row list box. Label them **Portrait** and **Landscape**, and name them **dlgPortraitOption** and **dlgLandscapeOption**.

3   Create a group box around the option buttons, and change its caption to **Orientation**. Make sure that the left sides of the option button boxes do not extend beyond the border of the group box.

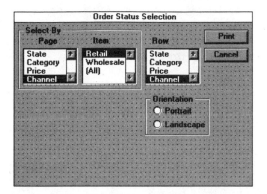

These option buttons allow you to specify portrait or landscape orientation for the report. Put the result of the choice into the Orientation cell on the Control worksheet so that the other macros can use the value when you produce the report.

4   Activate the Control worksheet, enter **OrientationNumber** into cell A21, and use that label to name cell B21.

5   Activate the ReportDialog sheet, and select the Portrait option button. Double click the border of the Portrait option button, type **OrientationNumber** in the Cell Link box, and click OK.

6   Activate the Control worksheet, and press CTRL+SHIFT+D to run the dialog box and try out the option button.

As you click the option buttons, the number in the OrientationNumber cell changes. When you click the Portrait option, the Landscape option is cleared, and vice versa. When you put a group box around multiple option buttons, Excel recognizes them as a group and will only allow one button to be selected at a time. Option buttons that are outside of a group box form their own group.

You didn't have to link the Landscape option button to the OrientationNumber cell because all option buttons in a group are automatically linked to the same worksheet cell as the first option button in the group.

7   Select the Landscape option, and click Cancel to close the dialog box.

The OrientationNumber cell has the value 2 because Landscape is the second option in the option group. You need to enter a formula into the Orientation cell to calculate the correct word based on the value in the OrientationNumber cell.

8 In the Orientation cell (B14), enter the formula **=CHOOSE(OrientationNumber,"Portrait","Landscape")**.

The word *Landscape* appears in the cell. The word *CHOOSE* is an Excel worksheet function that uses the value of the first argument to count through the remaining arguments to find the value to return.

Show the print orientation graphically

Sometimes the words *portrait* and *landscape* do not adequately convey the idea of vertical and horizontal. If you add a picture to the dialog box, you can make the effect of the option choice obvious.

1 On the Control worksheet, scroll down to row 30.

The Control worksheet contains two simple pictures you can use to show the effects of choosing the portrait and landscape options. These pictures were created in Windows Paintbrush and pasted onto the Excel worksheet as bitmaps.

2 Click one of the pictures, hold down the SHIFT key and click the other picture to select them both, and then copy the selection.

3 Activate the ReportDialog sheet, and paste the pictures.

4 Click the dialog box background to deselect the pictures, and then click the portrait picture. Drag it to the left of the Orientation group box, and give the picture the name **dlgPortraitPicture.**

5 Click the landscape picture, drag it on top of the portrait picture, and give it the name **dlgLandscapePicture**.

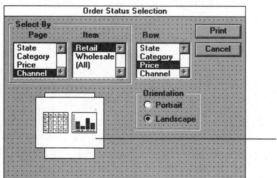

—————Position both pictures like this.

You want the dialog box to display the portrait picture when the Portrait option is selected, and the landscape picture when the Landscape option is selected. You can attach code to the option buttons in the same way you attached code to the Page list box.

Edit Code button

6   Select the Portrait option button, and click the Edit Code button.

Excel creates a new procedure, named *dlgPortraitOption_Click*, on the DialogModule sheet. (If you closed and reopened the workbook since the last time you used Edit Code, use the Macros, Mark Position For Recording command in the Tools menu to control where the new procedure is created.)

Note   If the Edit Code button does not create the macro you want, delete the macro and remove the macro assignment from the control. To remove a macro assignment from a control, click the control with the right mouse button, choose Assign Macro, clear the Macro Name box, and click OK.

7   Insert these two statements as the body of the dlgPortraitOption_Click procedure:

```
ActiveDialog.Pictures("dlgLandscapePicture").Visible = False
ActiveDialog.Pictures("dlgPortraitPicture").Visible = True
```

The first statement makes the landscape picture invisible, and the second makes the portrait picture visible.

8   Activate the ReportDialog sheet, select the dlgLandscapeOption button, click the Edit Code button, and insert these two statements as the body of the new dlgLandscapeOption_Click procedure:

```
ActiveDialog.Pictures("dlgPortraitPicture ").Visible = False
ActiveDialog.Pictures("dlgLandscapePicture ").Visible = True
```

These statements do the opposite of the ones in the dlgPortraitOption_Click procedure: They hide the portrait picture and show the landscape picture.

9   Save the workbook, run the Order Status Selection dialog box, and try out the option buttons. Click Cancel when you are finished.

When you click the Landscape option button, the picture changes to the landscape picture. When you click the Portrait option button, the picture changes to the portrait picture.

Switching the picture on the dialog box makes the dialog box easy to use and understand.

Note   When you hide a drawing object on a dialog box (like the landscape or portrait picture, or even a list box), the object stays hidden even in the design mode of the dialog box. When an object is hidden in design mode, you can't select it or unhide it. To display all the hidden objects on a dialog box at once, activate the module sheet and display the Debug window. In the Immediate pane, type **Sheets("ReportDialog") .DrawingObjects.Visible = True** and press ENTER.

Add output location options

Sometimes you want to send the report directly to the printer. Sometimes you want to send the report to Word for Windows. Sometimes you want to send the report to both the printer and to Word. The Control worksheet already has cells named SendToPrint and SendToWord. You can add check boxes to the dialog box to select these options.

Check Box button

1   Activate the ReportDialog sheet, double click the Check Box button, and create two check box controls under the Orientation group box. Change the caption of the first check box to **Send to Print** and the caption of the second check box to **Send to Word**.

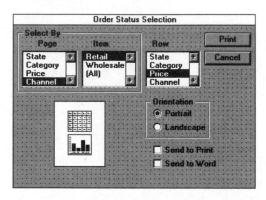

2   Select the first check box and name it **dlgPrintCheck**. Then double click its border, and enter **SendToPrint** as its cell link.

3   Select the second check box and name it **dlgWordCheck**. Then double click its border, and enter **SendToWord** as its cell link.

You don't need to attach code procedures to these check box controls because they link directly back to the cells, putting True into the cell if the check box is selected and False into the cell if the check box is cleared.

Note If you send a report to Word, activate Word and close it. Close Word each time you send a report. Later in this lesson you will change the macro to close Word for you.

Check the output location options

You need to make sure that at least one of the check boxes is selected. You can have the Print button make that check.

Edit Code button

1   Activate the ReportDialog sheet, select the Print button on the dialog box, and click the Edit Code button in the Forms toolbar.

The dlgPrintButton_Click subroutine you created earlier appears. You can add another check to this macro. Enter these new statements above the Else statement:

```
ElseIf ActiveDialog.CheckBoxes("dlgPrintCheck") = xlOff _
        And ActiveDialog.CheckBoxes("dlgWordCheck") = xlOff Then
    MsgBox "Please select at least one output location"
    ActiveDialog.Buttons("dlgPrintButton").DismissButton = False
```

2   Save the workbook, run the dialog box, and try out the check boxes.

If the PrintReport macro starts running, press CTRL+BREAK and click End to stop the macro.

If you click Print while both check boxes are cleared, the alert message appears.

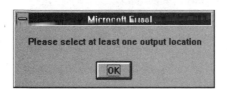

3   Click OK, and then click the Cancel button to dismiss the dialog box.

Make the options optional

The dialog box now contains all the options you will ever need. But it always displays all the options. Most of the time, when using your Print Order Status application, you will want to use the list boxes and print the report. You don't want controls that you use only occasionally to distract you when you don't need them, but you do want the controls available when you do need them. You can make the dialog box display the optional controls only when you need them.

1   Drag the bottom of the dialog box frame up to just below the list boxes.

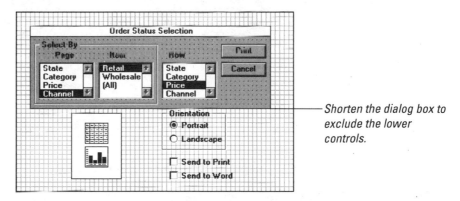

Shorten the dialog box to exclude the lower controls.

The new options are now below the bottom of the dialog box frame, and they will not appear when you display the dialog box.

Edit Code button

*Five points equals
one grid box on the
dialog sheet.*

2 Add a new button below the Print and Cancel buttons. Give the new button the caption **Options**, and give it the name **dlgOptionButton**.

You will assign a procedure to this button that will extend the dialog box frame to include the additional options.

3 With the Options button selected, click the Edit Code button in the Forms toolbar.

4 Insert this statement into the new dlgOptionButton_Click procedure that appears:

```
ActiveDialog.DialogFrame.Height = 190
```

5 Press CTRL+SHIFT+D to run the dialog box, and click the Options button.

The height of the dialog box frame extends to 190 points. You may need to adjust the actual height for your dialog box.

6 Click the Options button again. Nothing happens. Click Cancel to dismiss the dialog box.

Every time you click the Options button, the procedure sets the height of the dialog box frame to 190 points. If only the Options button could *toggle* the height of the dialog box frame...

7 Change the body of the dlgOptionButton_Click procedure to this:

```
With ActiveDialog.DialogFrame
    If .Height < 170 Then
        .Height = 190
    Else
        .Height = 95
    End If
End With
```

Note When you set the height of the dialog box frame to 190, the actual height of the frame may end up as 189.5 or some other slightly different number. If you always test using rounded values and either the greater than operator (>) or the less than operator (<), the test will give you the result you want.

8 Save the workbook, run the Order Status Selection dialog box, and click the Options button.

The shortened version of the dialog box appears.

Set initial values for the dialog box

The Options button toggles the height setting of the dialog box frame, but if you close the dialog box while the options are displayed, the next time you show the dialog box, the options will still be displayed. You can attach a procedure to the dialog box that runs each time the dialog box is displayed. This procedure will set the dialog box frame to the default height.

1   Activate the ReportDialog sheet, select the dialog box frame, and give the frame the name **dlgFrame**. (Enter the name in the Reference area, the same as naming a control.)

Edit Code button

2   Click the Edit Code button to create a new procedure named dlgFrame_Show.

3   As the body of the dlgFrame_Show procedure, enter the statement

```
ActiveDialog.DialogFrame.Height = 95
```

4   Save the workbook, press CTRL+SHIFT+D to display the dialog box, show and hide the options, and click Close when you are finished.

The dialog box will now always start up without displaying the optional options.

Taking Control of Microsoft Excel

Microsoft Excel is a free-form program. Anyone who uses it can add worksheets, create charts, change formulas, and just about anything else. The fact that Excel can be used in so many ways is what makes it a very effective spreadsheet program. When you write an application designed for a specific task, however, you may not want the person using it to create charts, add worksheets, or change formulas, You may want to keep your application on track.

Excel provides various mechanisms for restricting access. You can protect a worksheet or a workbook to keep others from making changes. You can also assign a password to keep others from turning off the protection. You can change the menu bar, removing commands you don't want anyone to use.

The single most effective way to keep your application in control of Excel is to never let the person using the application out of a dialog box. When a dialog box is active on the screen, you can't select cells, scroll, or use any menu commands.

If you open your dialog box as soon as anyone opens your application workbook and then close the workbook as soon as the dialog box closes, you can make your specialized application foolproof.

Keep the dialog box active

When you press CTRL+SHIFT+D to run the dialog box, you can click Print if you want to print the report or Cancel if you don't. In either case, the dialog box goes away, and you must press CTRL+SHIFT+D again to get it back. You can change the dialog box so that every time you click the Print button, the dialog box redisplays after printing the report.

1   Activate the DialogModule sheet, and change the body of the Sub RunDialog()
     procedure to this:

```
Do While DialogSheets("ReportDialog").Show = True
    PrintReport
Loop
```

The Do While statement displays the dialog box and, if the return value from the
Show method is True, prints the report. The Loop statement makes the procedure
go back to the Do While statement to continue.

2   Press CTRL+SHIFT+D to run the dialog box. Click the Options button, select the
     Send To Print check box, clear the Send To Word check box, and click Print to
     see the report in print preview mode.

3   Click Close to exit print preview and redisplay the dialog box.

4   Click the Cancel button to dismiss the dialog box.

Now that the dialog box redisplays after you print a report, the label *Cancel* is not
appropriate.

5   Activate the ReportDialog sheet, and change the caption of the Cancel button to
     Close.

6   Save the workbook.

Hide the application workbook

When you run the application and the dialog box appears, you can still see the
workbook in the background. The application, in fact, will work only if
LESSON14.XLS is the active workbook. See what happens when you try to run the
application with the workbook hidden.

1   Activate the DialogModule sheet and insert this statement immediately after *Sub
     RunDialog()*:

```
ActiveWindow.Visible = False
```

2   Press CTRL+SHIFT+D to run the application.

The workbook disappears, but then an error message informs you that an object
variable is not set.

3   Click the Goto button.

The workbook reappears, displaying the statement with the error. It is the
statement *DialogSheets("ReportDialog").Show*. The DialogSheets method is a
globally known method of the Application object. If you do not give the
DialogSheets method an explicit Workbook object, it assumes the active
workbook. As long as LESSON14.XLS is the active workbook, the procedure
works. If LESSON14.XLS is not active, the DialogSheet method fails. Excel
provides a tool expressly for situations like this.

4   After the statement *ActiveWindow.Visible = False*, insert the statement
ThisWorkbook.Activate.

The word *ThisWorkbook* is a globally known property of the Application object. It
works just like the ActiveWorkbook property, except that it points to the
workbook containing the currently running procedure, even if that workbook is
not the active workbook.

In this case, you can simply activate the application workbook, even though it is
hidden. Then everything else in the application will work as expected using the
active workbook. In some situations you may not be able to activate the
application workbook. In those cases, insert the ThisWorkbook property before
each global method that assumes the active workbook. (In Excel 5 you can print
or print preview only worksheets in the active workbook.)

5   Save LESSON14.XLS, press CTRL+SHIFT+D, and try out the application.

6   Click Close to dismiss the dialog box when you are finished.

The application runs with the workbook hidden, which gives it a much more packaged
look. You can now complete the process of packaging the application.

Initialize the application

On the Control worksheet are three buttons: one to create a single report, one to
initialize the data, and one to close the report (which closes Word for Windows if you
opened it). During any one session of creating reports, you would typically initialize
the data, then produce several reports, then close the report. You can make the macro
run InitializeData when it starts and CloseReport when it finishes. While you're at it,
impress your associates by changing the Microsoft Excel caption at the top of the
application to Print Order Status.

1   Unhide the LESSON14.XLS workbook window. (If the Window menu is not
visible, choose the Unhide command from the File menu, select LESSON14.XLS,
and click OK.)

2   Activate the DialogModule sheet, and after the statement *ThisWorkbook.Activate*
at the beginning of the RunDialog procedure insert these statements:

```
Application.Caption = "Print Order Status"
InitializeData
```

3   At end of the procedure, before the End Sub statement, insert these statements:

```
Application.Caption = "Microsoft Excel"
CloseReport
```

4   Save the workbook, and press CTRL+SHIFT+D to run the application.

The macro changes the application caption from Microsoft Excel to Print Order
Status, reloads the data from the database, and displays the dialog box.

5   Click Close to close Word (if necessary) and to restore Microsoft Excel as the
application caption.

Run the dialog box when the workbook opens

If you display the dialog box as soon as the workbook opens and close the workbook as soon as the dialog box closes, you will have complete control of Excel as long as the workbook is open.

Name a procedure Auto_Close to run it when the workbook closes.

1   Unhide the LESSON14.XLS workbook, activate the DialogModule sheet, and change the name of the RunDialog procedure to **Auto_Open**.

The name *Auto_Open* has special meaning in Excel. When you open a workbook, Excel runs any procedure that has the name *Auto_Open*.

2   Save and close the LESSON14.XLS workbook.

3   Open the LESSON14.XLS workbook.

The dialog box appears; the Auto_Open procedure ran automatically.

Note If you hold down the SHIFT key while you open a workbook, the Auto_Open procedure will not run. Holding down the SHIFT key allows you to test and modify the application while others use it. If you need to distribute an application that is impossible to modify, you can make an add-in from your workbook. For more information about making an add-in, search Microsoft Excel Help for the phrase *making add-ins*. Add-ins in Excel 5 are more secure than add-ins in Excel 4.

---

4   Click the Close button.

The dialog box closes. You want the workbook to close as soon as you click the Close button.

5   Unhide the LESSON14.XLS workbook, activate the DialogModule sheet and insert the statement **ThisWorkbook.Close SaveChanges:=False** after the Loop statement in the Auto_Open procedure.

The revised procedure should look like this:

```
Sub Auto_Open()
    ActiveWindow.Visible = False
    ThisWorkbook.Activate
    Application.Caption = "Print Order Status"
    InitializeData
    Do While DialogSheets("ReportDialog").Show = True
        PrintReport
    Loop
    ThisWorkbook.Close SaveChanges:=False
    Application.Caption = "Microsoft Excel"
    CloseReport
End Sub
```

6   Save the workbook and close it.

7   Open the workbook, print one report, and then click Close.

The dialog box disappears and the workbook closes. It's not just hidden; it's gone.

Prevent error messages

Even though your dialog box prevents a user of the application from making incorrect choices, errors may still occur. For example, external resources such as the database, the printer, or Word for Windows may not be available. These are run-time errors, as discussed in Lesson 11. In case of a run-time error, Excel displays a message and halts the application without closing the workbook. You want to display your own message and close the workbook.

1   While holding down the SHIFT key, open LESSON14.XLS. Then activate the DialogModule sheet.

2   Immediately after the Sub Auto_Open() statement, enter the statements **On Error Goto HandleError** and **Application.EnableCancelKey = xlErrorHandler**.

For more information about controlling the cancel key, search Help for the word EnableCancelKey.

The EnableCancelKey property controls what happens when the user presses CTRL+BREAK while the macro is running. Setting EnableCancelKey to xlErrorHandler will cause a run-time error when you press CTRL+BREAK.

3   Immediately before the End Sub statement at the end of the Auto_Open procedure, enter these statements:

```
Exit Sub
HandleError:
    Dim myMsg
    Let myMsg = "Sorry, an error has occurred: " & Err
    Let myMsg = myMsg & " - " & Error()
    MsgBox Prompt:=myMsg
    CloseReport
    Application.Caption = "Microsoft Excel"
    ThisWorkbook.Close SaveChanges:=False
```

This error handler code is very similar to the error handler from Lesson 11. Instead of simply halting the macro, however, this error handler also closes the workbook. Simulate an error by pressing CTRL+BREAK while the report runs.

4   Save the workbook, and press CTRL+SHIFT+D to run the application. Click the Options button and change the orientation. (Changing the orientation slows the report enough for you to press CTRL+BREAK.) Send a report to the printer, and while the *Calculating Pivot Table* message is in the status bar, press CTRL+BREAK.

The warning message appears, displaying the message *Sorry, an error has occurred: 18 - User interrupt occurred*, and then the application closes.

Note   Once you know the number of an error, you may choose to have the error handler respond to that specific error by executing the Resume statement to return control to the main program.

Now, your LESSON14.XLS workbook is a complete application. When you open the workbook, the dialog box appears, limiting access to Microsoft Excel's features. When you close the dialog box, the workbook closes with it. The application also handles any run-time errors that may occur. It is ready to give to your boss.

Lesson Summary

To	Do this
Create a new dialog box	From the Insert menu, choose Macro, Dialog.
Add a control to a dialog box	Click a control button in the Forms toolbar and drag a place for the control on the dialog box.
Run a dialog sheet named *ThisDialog*	Use the statement *DialogSheets("ThisDialog").Show*.
Interpret the value of a list box	Use the INDEX worksheet function.
Interpret the value of option buttons	Use the CHOOSE worksheet function.
Prevent a button from closing a dialog box	Set the button's DismissButton property to False.
Extend a dialog box to display optional controls	Change the Height or Width property of the dialog box frame.
Run a procedure when a workbook opens	Give the procedure the name *Auto_Open*.
Point at objects in the application workbook	Use the ThisWorkbook property.

For more information on	See
Using dialog boxes	Chapter 11, "Controls and Dialog Boxes," in the *Microsoft Excel Visual Basic User's Guide*.
Running procedures automatically	Chapter 13, "Creating Automatic Procedures and Add-in Applications," in the *Microsoft Excel Visual Basic User's Guide*.

Preview of the Future

Congratulations! You have now completed all the lessons in this book. You have created simple macros for everyday tasks using the macro recorder. You have made macros easy to run using controls on a worksheet. You have explored the wealth of objects available in Microsoft Excel. You have learned how to use Visual Basic commands and statements to control an application. And you have built a complete application using Visual Basic in Microsoft Excel.

Microsoft Excel and Visual Basic are both very powerful and complex tools. You can continue learning new skills with both Excel and Visual Basic for a long time. The concepts and skills you have learned in this book will enable you to write useful and powerful applications now, and they will also serve as a good foundation as you continue to learn.

Index

Special Characters

A

B

Build Your Spreadsheet Expertise

Microsoft® Excel Worksheet Function Reference
Covers version 5 for Windows™ and the Apple® Macintosh®
Microsoft Corporation

Tap into the number-crunching power of Microsoft Excel by using worksheet functions! By using worksheet functions in your spreadsheets, you can solve nearly any type of numerical problem—on the job or at home. And with worksheet functions, you don't have to be a genius at mathematics, statistics, or finance. Simply enter the right worksheet function with the required data, and Microsoft Excel does the rest. This reference provides complete information about each of the more than 300 worksheet functions built into Microsoft Excel 5 and is the hard-copy documentation for the Microsoft Excel 5 worksheet function online Help.

336 pages $12.95 ($16.95 Canada)   ISBN 1-55615-637-5

Microsoft® Excel Visual Basic® for Applications Reference
Microsoft Corporation

Now programmers have even greater flexibility and power to create custom applications using Microsoft Excel 5's new macro language—Visual Basic for Applications. This complete A–Z Visual Basic for Applications reference lists all the objects, properties, methods, functions, and statements, and provides functional descriptions, syntax, and code examples. If you're an Excel power user, a programmer who customizes Microsoft Excel applications, or if you write applications that interact with Microsoft Excel, you need this reference.

900 pages $24.95 ($33.95 Canada)   ISBN 1-55615-624-3

Field Guide to Microsoft® Excel 5 for Windows™
Steven L. Nelson

If you're new to Microsoft Excel for Windows and you want quick answers about Microsoft Excel commands, this is the guide for you. This handy guide is arranged by task and is organized in easy-to-use, easy-to-remember sections with rich cross-referencing for instant lookup. Look for the friendly guy in the pith helmet—he'll guide you from start to finish.

208 pages $9.95 ($12.95 Canada)   ISBN 1-55615-579-4

*Microsoft*Press

Train Yourself
With *Step by Step* books from Microsoft Press

The *Step by Step* books are the perfect self-paced training solution for the busy businessperson. Whether you are a new user or you're upgrading from a previous version of the software, the *Step by Step* books can teach you exactly what you need to know to get the most from your new software. Each lesson is modular, example-rich, and fully integrated with a timesaving practice file on the disk. If you're too busy to attend a class or if classroom training doesn't make sense for you or your office, you can build the computer skills you need with the *Step by Step* books from Microsoft Press.

Microsoft® Excel 5 for Windows™
Step by Step
Catapult, Inc.
368 pages, softcover with one 3.5-inch disk
$29.95 ($39.95 Canada)   ISBN 1-55615-587-5

Microsoft® Word 6 for Windows™
Step by Step
Catapult, Inc.
336 pages, softcover with one 3.5-inch disk
$29.95 ($39.95 Canada)   ISBN 1-55615-576-X

Microsoft® Windows NT™
Step by Step
Catapult, Inc.
360 pages, softcover with one 3.5-inch disk
$29.95 ($39.95 Canada)   ISBN 1-55615-573-5

Microsoft® Windows™ 3.1
Step by Step
Catapult, Inc.
296 pages, softcover with one 3.5-inch disk
$29.95 ($39.95 Canada)   ISBN 1-55615-501-8

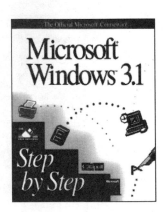

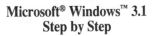

Microsoft Press® books are available wherever quality books are sold and through CompuServe's Electronic Mall—GO MSP.
Call 1-800-MSPRESS for direct ordering information or for placing credit card orders.*
Please refer to BBK when placing your order. Prices subject to change.
*In Canada, contact Macmillan Canada, Attn: Microsoft Press Dept., 164 Commander Blvd., Agincourt, Ontario, Canada M1S 3C7, or call (416) 293-8464, ext. 340.
Outside the U.S. and Canada, write to International Sales, Microsoft Press, One Microsoft Way, Redmond, WA 98052-6399.

IMPORTANT — READ CAREFULLY BEFORE OPENING SOFTWARE PACKET(S).
By opening the sealed packet(s) containing the software, you indicate your acceptance
of the following Microsoft® License Agreement.

Microsoft License Agreement

MICROSOFT LICENSE AGREEMENT
(Microsoft Press® *Step by Step* Series)

This is a legal agreement between you (either an individual or an entity) and Microsoft Corporation. By opening the sealed software packet(s) you are agreeing to be bound by the terms of this agreement. If you do not agree to the terms of this agreement, promptly return the book, including the unopened software packet(s), to the place you obtained it for a full refund.

MICROSOFT SOFTWARE LICENSE

1. GRANT OF LICENSE. Microsoft grants to you the right to use one copy of the Microsoft software program included with this book (the "SOFTWARE") on a single terminal connected to a single computer. The SOFTWARE is in "use" on a computer when it is loaded into temporary memory (i.e., RAM) or installed into permanent memory (e.g., hard disk, CD-ROM, or other storage device) of that computer. You may not network the SOFTWARE or otherwise use it on more than one computer or computer terminal at the same time.

2. COPYRIGHT. The SOFTWARE is owned by Microsoft or its suppliers and is protected by United States copyright laws and international treaty provisions. Therefore, you must treat the SOFTWARE like any other copyrighted material (e.g., a book or musical recording) except that you may either (a) make one copy of the SOFTWARE solely for backup or archival purposes, or (b) transfer the SOFTWARE to a single hard disk provided you keep the original solely for backup or archival purposes. You may not copy the written materials accompanying the SOFTWARE.

3. OTHER RESTRICTIONS. You may not rent or lease the SOFTWARE, but you may transfer the SOFTWARE and accompanying written materials on a permanent basis provided you retain no copies and the recipient agrees to the terms of this Agreement. You may not reverse engineer, decompile, or disassemble the SOFTWARE. If the SOFTWARE is an update or has been updated, any transfer must include the most recent update and all prior versions.

4. DUAL MEDIA SOFTWARE. If the SOFTWARE package contains both 3.5" and 5.25" disks, then you may use only the disks appropriate for your single-user computer. You may not use the other disks on another computer or loan, rent, lease, or transfer them to another user except as part of the permanent transfer (as provided above) of all SOFTWARE and written materials.

5. LANGUAGE SOFTWARE. If the SOFTWARE is a Microsoft language product, then you have a royalty-free right to reproduce and distribute executable files created using the SOFTWARE. If the language product is a Basic or COBOL product, then Microsoft grants you a royalty-free right to reproduce and distribute the run-time modules of the SOFTWARE provided that you: (a) distribute the run-time modules only in conjunction with and as a part of your software product; (b) do not use Microsoft's name, logo, or trademarks to market your software product; (c) include a valid copyright notice on your software product; and (d) agree to indemnify, hold harmless, and defend Microsoft and its suppliers from and against any claims or lawsuits, including attorneys' fees, that arise or result from the use or distribution of your software product. The "run-time modules" are those files in the SOFTWARE that are identified in the accompanying written materials as required during execution of your software program. The run-time modules are limited to run-time files, install files, and ISAM and REBUILD files. If required in the SOFTWARE documentation, you agree to display the designated patent notices on the packaging and in the README file of your software product.

LIMITED WARRANTY

LIMITED WARRANTY. Microsoft warrants that (a) the SOFTWARE will perform substantially in accordance with the accompanying written materials for a period of ninety (90) days from the date of receipt, and (b) any hardware accompanying the SOFTWARE will be free from defects in materials and workmanship under normal use and service for a period of one (1) year from the date of receipt. Any implied warranties on the SOFTWARE and hardware are limited to ninety (90) days and one (1) year, respectively. Some states/countries do not allow limitations on duration of an implied warranty, so the above limitation may not apply to you.

CUSTOMER REMEDIES. Microsoft's and its suppliers' entire liability and your exclusive remedy shall be, at Microsoft's option, either (a) return of the price paid, or (b) repair or replacement of the SOFTWARE or hardware that does not meet Microsoft's Limited Warranty and which is returned to Microsoft with a copy of your receipt. This Limited Warranty is void if failure of the SOFTWARE or hardware has resulted from accident, abuse, or misapplication. Any replacement SOFTWARE or hardware will be warranted for the remainder of the original warranty period or thirty (30) days, whichever is longer. Outside the United States, these remedies are not available without proof of purchase from an authorized non-U.S. source.

NO OTHER WARRANTIES. Microsoft and its suppliers disclaim all other warranties, either express or implied, including, but not limited to implied warranties of merchantability and fitness for a particular purpose, with regard to the SOFTWARE, the accompanying written materials, and any accompanying hardware. This limited warranty gives you specific legal rights. You may have others which vary from state/country to state/country.

NO LIABILITY FOR CONSEQUENTIAL DAMAGES. In no event shall Microsoft or its suppliers be liable for any damages whatsoever (including without limitation, damages for loss of business profits, business interruption, loss of business information, or any other pecuniary loss) arising out of the use of or inability to use this Microsoft product, even if Microsoft has been advised of the possibility of such damages. Because some states/countries do not allow the exclusion or limitation of liability for consequential or incidental damages, the above limitation may not apply to you.

U.S. GOVERNMENT RESTRICTED RIGHTS

The SOFTWARE and documentation are provided with RESTRICTED RIGHTS. Use, duplication, or disclosure by the Government is subject to restrictions as set forth in subparagraph (c)(1)(ii) of The Rights in Technical Data and Computer Software clause at DFARS 252.227-7013 or subparagraphs (c)(1) and (2) of the Commercial Computer Software — Restricted Rights 48 CFR 52.227-19, as applicable. Manufacturer is Microsoft Corporation, One Microsoft Way, Redmond, WA 98052-6399.

This Agreement is governed by the laws of the State of Washington.

Should you have any questions concerning this Agreement, or if you desire to contact Microsoft for any reason, please write: Microsoft Sales and Service, One Microsoft Way, Redmond, WA 98052-6399.

CORPORATE ORDERS

If you're placing a large-volume corporate order for additional copies of this *Step by Step* title, or for any other Microsoft Press title, you may be eligible for our corporate discount.

Call **1-800-888-3303, ext. 63460** for details.

Replacement Disks Available

If you have a damaged or defective disk, replacements are available. To order, request item number **097-0001028**. Send your name, address (no P.O. boxes, please), and daytime phone number to: Microsoft Press, Attn: Excel VB SBS disk, P.O. Box 3011, Bothell, WA 98041-3011. Allow 2–3 weeks for delivery. Offer valid in the U.S. only.

097-000-681

The Step by Step Companion Disk

The enclosed 3.5-inch disk contains timesaving, ready-to-use practice files that complement each lesson in this book. To use the practice files, you'll need the Microsoft® Windows™ operating system version 3.1 or later and Microsoft Excel version 5 for Windows.

Each *Step by Step* lesson is closely integrated with the practice files on the disk. Before you begin the *Step by Step* lessons, we highly recommend that you read the "Getting Ready" section of the book and install the practice files on your hard disk. Remember, as you work through each lesson, be sure to follow the instructions for renaming the practice files so that you can go through a lesson more than once if you need to.

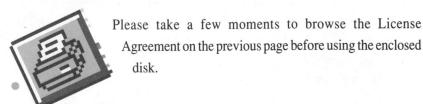 Please take a few moments to browse the License Agreement on the previous page before using the enclosed disk.